MISCHLINGE

MISCHLINGE

The untold true story of the Holocaust, Hitler and my family

SHARON RING

HarperElement
An imprint of HarperCollins*Publishers*
1 London Bridge Street
London SE1 9GF

www.harpercollins.co.uk

HarperCollins*Publishers*
Macken House, 39/40 Mayor Street Upper
Dublin 1, D01 C9W8, Ireland

First published by HarperElement 2026

1 3 5 7 9 10 8 6 4 2

© Sharon Ring 2026

Sharon Ring asserts the moral right to
be identified as the author of this work

All photographs courtesy of the author

A catalogue record of this book is
available from the British Library

HB ISBN 978-0-00-880277-6
PB ISBN 978-0-00-880278-3

Printed and bound in the UK using 100%
renewable electricity at CPI Group (UK) Ltd

All rights reserved. No part of this publication may be reproduced, stored in a retrieval system, or transmitted, in any form or by any means, electronic, mechanical, photocopying, recording or otherwise, without the prior written permission of the publishers.

Without limiting the exclusive rights of any author, contributor or the publisher of this publication, any unauthorised use of this publication to train generative artificial intelligence (AI) technologies is expressly prohibited. HarperCollins also exercise their rights under Article 4(3) of the Digital Single Market Directive 2019/790 and expressly reserve this publication from the text and data mining exception.

To my remarkable darling mother – Edie –
who never, ever let her past determine her future.

And my dear Uncle Heini, who kept finding
himself caught up in the historical events of the
last century – but always on the wrong side.

Contents

	Introduction	1
1	Berlin, 1935: The Knock	7
2	Schooldays and the Olympics	27
3	Exclusion	39
4	War, Arrest and Disappearance	49
5	The Final Solution	67
6	Imprisonment	85
7	Torture and Kindness	111
8	Survival and Sadism	131

9	Defiance and Punishment	151
10	Liberation	165
11	Soviets and Returners	181
12	Reunions and Beginnings	203
13	Refugees and Promised Lands	229
14	Old Habits and New Starts	249
15	The Berlin Wall	275
16	The Last Chapter	305
	Acknowledgements	321

Mischling (plural: Mischlinge)

A German word meaning 'mongrel', 'half-breed', 'mutt'. Used in Nazi Germany to legally define not dogs but people of mixed Jewish and Aryan ancestry.

A *Mischling* of the first degree (*Mischling ersten Grades*), or half-Jew, was a person with two Jewish grandparents who did not belong to the Jewish religion or who was not married to a Jew. A *Mischling* of the second degree (*Mischling zweiten Grades*) was someone with one Jewish grandparent or an Aryan married to a Jew.

In 1939, 72,000 first-degree *Mischlinge* and 39,000 second-degree *Mischlinge* were still living in Germany.

The *Mischlinge* issue was very important to Adolf Hitler. The policy in Germany was to assimilate second-degree *Mischlinge* into the Aryan nation while first-degree *Mischlinge* were to be considered like Jews.

Adapted from the Holocaust Resource Center: www.yadvashem.org

Introduction

First, a confession. Despite spending a lifetime as a journalist on several national newspapers and then editing magazines like *OK!*, I'd no idea of the incredible story hidden within my own family. My mum and uncle's dramatic and deeply moving story was almost never told – and I certainly never heard it – because they found their past too full of horror and pain to talk about.

That was until the day I discovered my uncle's memoir, a yellowing manuscript hidden away in a box in my mum's home in Norfolk, where it had lain unopened and unread for decades. What I discovered was one of the great untold stories of the Holocaust. The story of an innocent brother and sister is also the story of many *Mischlinge*, a word I'd never even heard of.

The Nazis took the word *Mischlinge* to legally define persons with both Jewish and Aryan ancestry. In a new decree, part of the Nuremberg Race Laws that came into effect in 1935, it was applied to thousands of men, women

MISCHLINGE

and children across Europe. As my mum Edie and Uncle Heini were to find out, being labelled a *Mischling* led to exclusion, persecution, hard labour and the threat of death.

Mischlinge are the Holocaust victims you and I have never heard of, condemned not for their religious beliefs but for the religion of their grandparents.

The revelations began one rainy day when my mum, then in her final years, showed me where she kept her will in the safe box she'd stashed away with other important documents in the back of her wardrobe. When we found the locked black metal box, I opened it and found a fat brown envelope on the top, well sealed with the letter 'H' scrawled on the front.

'What's this?' I asked.

'That's your Uncle Heini's memoir,' she replied, casually. 'I've never read it because I know it will be painful. I know it because I was there too.'

'May I look?' I asked Mum, and when she nodded, I opened the envelope and read the first page, headed 'Quite an Adventure'. It began:

> I have often rejected the idea of telling the story of a part of my life which thanks to the insane political ideas of the time took an unusual course ...

As I scanned the manuscript, even with my limited German, it was clear that here was a searing eyewitness account of a working-class family who lived under Hitler's nose in Berlin, some of them for the duration of the Second World War.

I was overwhelmed with curiosity and desperate to know more. Mum had told me when I was a child that she'd been born in Berlin and that my dad, a British soldier she met there

INTRODUCTION

soon after VE Day, had 'rescued her', marrying her and bringing her back to his home in London. But she'd never given me, or indeed anyone else, much detail about her first 18 years in Berlin, although when I was a little older she'd explained simply, 'My life really began when I met your dad, and I decided long ago that all our happiness depended on looking forward not back.'

I asked Mum if I might have her brother's memoir translated, as my German was not good enough to really understand it all. I was very proud of her response.

'Yes,' she said, 'it deserves to be read. I think it cost him a lot to write it. And perhaps the time has come for me to tell you all that I witnessed too. I think it's a story that should be told.'

While Heini's lengthy memoir was sent off for translation, Mum and I sat down in front of the fire in her cosy bungalow on the Norfolk coast, and over many mugs of tea I gently questioned her about the experiences she'd buried in her mind and not revisited for 50 years.

My mum Edie and her brother Heinz – or Heini, as she called him – were born in central Berlin, innocent children of just five and nine years old when Hitler came to power in 1933. They were raised as Christians but condemned as Jews – branded as *Mischlinge* for the 'crime' of having two Jewish grandparents.

Incredibly, my mum survived in the capital of the Third Reich throughout the whole of the Second World War while others in her family were imprisoned, tortured and murdered, with many simply disappearing off the face of the earth. What follows is their true story.

MISCHLINGE

I recognised it was a brave decision of mum to sit down with me and reveal for the first time what I felt sure were the terrible things that she'd witnessed and might have happened to her. I had no doubt that to reawaken these memories and speak of them now, even to me, her daughter, would come at great cost to her. But she'd agreed to it and I wanted to hear her account before I read Uncle Heini's.

When the translated memoir arrived, it was nothing short of a revelation. And the fact it arrived in instalments added to its thriller-like quality. Would my uncle survive the cruelty and the disasters that befell him, I wondered? I could hardly wait for each chapter to arrive at my doorstep. Heini confided at the start that even writing about what had happened was painful – he'd previously never shared the story with anyone. As I read his words, what struck me most was that he reported what he'd seen and experienced without an ounce of self-pity. It was riveting.

From childhood to manhood, here was an eyewitness accounts of events, from singing at the Berlin Olympics, to his arrest by the Gestapo, detention in labour and concentration camps, torture and escape attempts, alongside the unexpected kindnesses he'd received. How would it end? I was gripped.

Like a tragic, poignant version of *Forrest Gump*, Heini, my mum and the whole Bernstein family seemed to be involved in some of the major events of the century, before, during and after the Second World War, in Berlin, London and across the world. Some survived – and some were not so lucky.

What unfolded was the everyday life of working-class Berliners, a mixed family of Jews and Christians, who, without the money or contacts to leave, were forced to remain in

INTRODUCTION

the city of their birth, even when it removed the rights as citizens of many of them, condemned them to death and was the epicentre of the greatest war the world had seen.

Heini and Edie are pretty young things throughout much of the action: my mum a shy, naive teenager, my uncle a resourceful young lad with Hollywood good looks, determined to look after her. It's a real-life story that moves out of Berlin across Europe to London and beyond, through the horrors of the Holocaust, with light and shade, death and romance. There's also a touch of mystery, as some events and outcomes remain unknown, thanks to the Nazis' destruction of records at the end of the war in a bid to avoid prosecution as war criminals.

Neither Heini nor Edie are alive to see their stories combined on the page, but both very much wanted them to be known. Their story opens with the day the secret police knocked on the door of their family home and Edie – my mum – learnt the meaning of the word *Mischling* for the very first time.

1
BERLIN, 1935: THE KNOCK

The first sign of trouble appeared one early autumn evening in 1935 when antisemitism came knocking on the door of the Bernstein family's tenement flat in central Berlin. Erna, a petite woman and mother to three youngsters, was up to her elbows in flour as she made dumplings for supper, so she called out to her youngest daughter Edie to answer the door.

'Tell them we have a couple of extra eggs to swap,' she called out.

Neighbours were always popping in and out of the flats, sharing hard-earned food or exchanging clothes their own children had outgrown. Theirs was a poor neighbourhood in Berlin-Mitte near Alexanderplatz, where Heini and Edie had grown up playing ball and marbles in the cobbled backyard with other kids from the same block.

Edie reached up and opened the flat's front door to find two men in uniform.

'Go get your mother!' one of them shouted.

MISCHLINGE

Eight-year-old Edie had no idea who they were, but she knew these men weren't any of their neighbours, so she did what they said.

'Stay here,' Erna told Edie, who had heard the gruff command. 'Start making the dumplings.'

As Erna came out of the kitchen, wiping her hands on her apron, her expression did not betray the pounding of her heart when she recognised them as Gestapo officers.

'How can I help you, officers?' she smiled, looking up at the unsmiling pair.

'We're here to help you,' said the taller of the two. 'Just tell us that you will divorce your husband and we will take him away right now. Your divorce will be issued in a matter of days, and your life and those of your two *Mischlinge* children will be considerably better.'

The word *Mischlinge* cut through Erna like a knife. She'd only recently learnt of the cruel name invented by the Nazis to brand those with Jewish as well as Aryan blood, comparing them to animals – mongrels, half-breeds. And now they were using that word to describe her children.

Erna might have been small in stature at five foot three, but she was by no means lacking in courage and conviction.

'Thank you,' she said, with as much politeness as she could muster to the man towering over her. 'But I don't want to divorce my husband.'

'Madam,' said the other Gestapo officer. 'You are a *Christian*. Why would you want to live with a filthy Jew? We will give you a few days to reconsider, and then we will be back.' And with that they turned and left.

Erna had heard rumours of these Gestapo visits and that some Christian wives and husbands had actually given up

BERLIN, 1935: THE KNOCK

their Jewish spouses for divorce Nazi-style, simply allowing them to be taken away to make life easier for themselves. She, however, had no intention of doing that. Her husband Sigi could be trying at times, but she loved him despite his faults. She closed the door and leant against it for a minute until she heard their footsteps fading away down the central stair block as they left the building. Composing herself, she went back into the kitchen.

Edie, who had heard every word, saw just how shaken her mother was. Even at the tender age of eight, she knew that being Jewish put you in danger and meant restrictions and even threats to your life, but hearing herself and her brother called *Mischlinge*, as if they were dogs, really hurt.

The whole family had seen and heard the Nazi celebration of Hitler's election victory in the same year that Edie had started at her local primary school. A noisy torchlit procession of brown-shirted stormtroopers brandishing their red, white and black swastika flags, banging drums and singing martial songs, had marched through the cobbled streets below their flat. Some of their friends and neighbours had joined in from the sidelines, waving the same flags as the procession marched close to their building. It was when the chants of '*Deutschland erwacht, kommen die Juden*' (Germany awakens, the Jews are coming) started up that her father had slammed the windows shut.

Since that night, Erna had become increasingly aware of antisemitism. Hitler lost no time in acting on the threats he'd set out a decade earlier in his book *Mein Kampf*. It seemed that he blamed all Jews for Germany's economic downturn, even though they accounted for less than 1 per cent of the population of the whole of Germany at the time. Just weeks

MISCHLINGE

after being voted in, the new government began passing the first of almost 2,000 laws depriving Jews of citizenship and access to many professions, and banning them from public places.

Hitler wanted all Jews expelled from the country, and by imposing a compulsory national census, with every family member obliged to reveal their religion, alongside their full address, the Nazis soon knew who and where to target. This is how the Gestapo had known exactly who was living in Erna's little flat. And since that knock on the door, not only did she need to worry about Sigi being targeted as a Jew, but also that their children, who had been branded as *Mischlinge*, were now also in danger. When the Gestapo men had spat out the words *Jude* and *Mischlinge*, the insults marked her husband and her children as different to herself, something she'd never previously felt, filling her with fear and foreboding.

Erna was a mother first and foremost. Warm and gentle in temperament, she liked nothing more than cooking and pottering around at home, fussing over her playful son and pretty daughter, who were only four years different in age. Heini, the older of the two, had his father's olive skin and deep brown eyes, and a warm engaging manner. He was the more outgoing, made friends easily and was always on the look-out for adventure, somehow always charming himself out of the scrapes he got himself into. Resourceful and caring, he was keen to play a part in providing for a few little extras for him and his sister in what was an impoverished household. Edie loved to watch her brother's clever tricks bear fruit – like the bent spoon he attached to a long piece of firewood and then used as a fishing tool to scoop out small coins that had slipped through the grills over street drains. He used all

BERLIN, 1935: THE KNOCK

the pfennig and groschen coins he recovered to buy treats like chocolate, liquorice and jelly snakes, which they ate together.

Little Edie was a shyer character. She adored and looked up to her handsome brother and enjoyed their jolly outings around the city together, but was more often found curled up inside reading a book or head down working on her homework, which she enjoyed.

Their father Sigi, a rather slight figure who could never be described as handsome, had a pensive, austere manner and was something of an introvert. Even with his family he was cool and undemonstrative, leaving the kids mostly to his wife, whom he relied upon for everything. His small pleasures when he had the funds were watching his football team Hertha Berlin and smoking the occasional cigar while reading the newspaper in his chair.

Edie didn't know quite what to make of her family 'being Jewish' and her label as a *Mischling*. She wasn't really clear what either of those words meant. She definitely didn't feel different to her mother – her family were all the same to her. Somebody had said Bernstein was a Jewish name, but she'd never seen or heard anything about Jewish beliefs at home, or any other religion for that matter. The most Christian thing the Bernsteins did was to put up a Christmas tree each year, a much-loved annual ritual, but none of them ever set foot in either a church or synagogue.

Later, when Edie asked Heini what it all meant, her brother explained that new laws had made mixed marriages between Aryans and Jews an act of racial shame, and told her all about being a *Mischling ersten Grades* or a *Mischling zweiten Grades*. Being a *Mischling* meant you weren't equal to other Germans. It meant you only partly belonged to the German race and nation, you couldn't go to certain schools, universities, even go to parks and cinemas or enter certain professions – many places and activities were off-limits.

Erna's listing of Heini and Edie as 'no religion' on the census had proved to offer no protection. The Nazi regime's twisted ideology cared only what religion your ancestors were. Now these two children, having never been brought up as Jews, knowing nothing about the religion, were deemed Jewish and denied the rights of other Germans even though they had been born in the capital.

For the Bernsteins to be persecuted as Jews was somewhat ironic, since Erna not being Jewish had already caused Sigi's Jewish family to cut them off completely. When the 22-year-old Sigi had fallen in love with Erna and told them he planned to marry the petite Berliner, who worked as a seamstress, his father immediately opposed the match because she was from a Christian family, and, despite all of Sigi's pleading, he couldn't be persuaded otherwise. While Erna's widowed mother, Emma, accepted her daughter's choice, she was not best pleased her 19-year-old daughter was pregnant.

Robert Bernstein, Sigi's father, was an Orthodox Jew, deeply religious and observant, who lived according to the many strict laws of the Talmud, one of which stated that Jews had to marry other Jews. Robert would make no exception for his youngest son and told him that if he married Erna, neither he nor Sigi's mother, brother or sister would come to the wedding, and according to traditional Jewish custom, Sigi would be 'shunned' – never again welcome in the family home or spoken to by any of his family. Sigi tried his best to change his father's mind, even delaying the wedding until Erna was very heavily pregnant, but to no avail.

BERLIN, 1935: THE KNOCK

Young Erna and her dog Flocky.

So Sigi and Erna's wedding at the local register office was tinged with sadness, attended by none of his family, just Erna's mother Emma, her brother Max and a few friends. The wedding feast was no more than a toast at the pub on the corner before returning to Erna's mother's flat, where the couple would begin their married life in her spare room. True to his word, Robert and the rest of the family turned their back on Sigi. From the day of his wedding, they never spoke to Sigi and he never again set foot in the family home where he'd grown up. Sigi's family even 'sat shiva' for him, the Jewish ceremony invoked by 'shunning', usually reserved for mourning the dead.

MISCHLINGE

So it was that Heini and Edie were now branded as *Mischlinge* and condemned by the Nazis because of their Jewish grandparents, even though the children had never even met them – because Sigi had married a Christian. When the Bernsteins declared themselves as 'no religion' on the census form, it was true.

When Erna gave birth just a few weeks after her marriage to Sigi, they named their daughter Eva. She had her mother's pale skin, blue eyes and fair hair, more Aryan than Ashkenazi Jew, as was Sigi's heritage, and for the first few months of her life she seemed healthy. But, as she grew, Erna noticed various deficiencies in her development that she believed she'd either been born with or which may have been caused by an accidental fall while having her nappy changed. Fortunately, help was on hand as Erna's mum Emma was a supportive grandmother, providing extra care and showing Eva tender love and affection.

By the time Heini was born a year after Eva in 1923, Sigi was established as a skilled upholsterer with a good job working at Opel, the car manufacturer, and they could afford to move into a little flat, with a shared indoor toilet, right next door to her mother. Four years later when Edie was born, times had become much tougher, with hyperinflation causing food prices to soar and antisemitic rhetoric dramatically increasing.

Sigi had once been so lauded for his upholstery skills that Opel offered him a better-paid job in America that he now wished he'd accepted, but he hadn't been willing to leave Berlin, his mates and his local pub.

But then came the US economic crash of 1929 that saw American bankers recall their loans, bringing the German

BERLIN, 1935: THE KNOCK

economy down with it. As the Great Depression swept across Europe, unemployment soared – and so did antisemitism. Even though only 4 per cent of Berliners were Jewish and most didn't know anyone Jewish, it was no barrier to their scapegoating. Many Germans who had never practised Judaism soon found themselves caught up at the centre of the Nazi whirlwind of terror. Sigi's surname – Bernstein – cost him his job and proved a major handicap to him finding another.

Heini remembers his father often coming home hauling his tool bag, his head hung low after having lost another job. With two children to feed, no savings or family to call upon for support, the children saw their father fall into dark moods when he was out of work, which their mother struggled to contain. Heini and Edie just saw a grumpy dad and a mum under pressure.

Erna had nearly died giving birth to Edie, her third child by caesarean delivery, and her scars and health were slow to recover. The woman doctor who delivered Edie was so concerned she offered to adopt the baby, as she was childless herself and beguiled by Edie's unusual dark eyes and skin.

Erna would have none of it, but she did accept more and more help from her mother to care for Eva, whose special needs were now evident and, with two other children to look after, increasingly challenging. When Sigi couldn't land another job, Erna found work in her old trade as a seamstress and was mightily relieved when her mother Emma suggested Eva move in permanently with her grandmother next door. The old lady was happy for the company.

The Gestapo's knock, the following year, was a wake-up call for Erna. It was not just Heini and Edie that were under

MISCHLINGE

threat as *Mischlinge*; Hitler had declared the physically and mentally ill unfit to live. Did they know about Eva? When they had completed the census in 1933, Eva was registered as living next door with her Christian grandmother, and her increasingly obvious disability had gone unnoticed and undeclared. Now there were reports of the compulsory sterilisation of disabled young women, so Eva too was at risk. Erna was shocked when she heard of one *Mischling* mother who had been ordered to take her disabled daughter for compulsory sterilisation. The woman told the Gestapo officer that her daughter was baptised and should be exempt, only to be told, 'When you pour water over a dog, it's still a dog,' and the sterilisation went ahead.

Erna had also heard stories of many Christian wives who had agreed to the Gestapo's request to remove their husbands and seen them taken away there and then when the Gestapo visited. A Jewish husband's unemployment was grounds enough to divorce him, the Gestapo had told Erna that night, but she could scarcely believe it when she heard of more spouses being taken who knew where. Hearing these stories brought her to tears every time.

Erna's anxiety since the day of the knock had grown to such an extent that she decided she'd capitalise on the Christian side of the family's lineage and have Heini and Edie baptised. She wasn't sure how much it might help them, but what else could she do? The whole country was being Nazified, with 50,000 Berliners joining the party the month after Hitler came to power. Many professions insisted on Nazi Party membership if you wanted to keep your job.

In the first six years after Hitler came to power, Jews deeply felt the effects of more than 400 new laws affecting their

BERLIN, 1935: THE KNOCK

work, play, sickness and health. The more influential and well-connected Jewish families left Germany, among them Albert Einstein and over a dozen future Nobel Prize winners. It was Nazi policy to encourage Jews to leave, but their laws also made it impossible for them to take much of their money or assets with them. Few countries would accept Jews as residents, and those that did stipulated that they needed a wealthy sponsor to be allowed in.

The Bernsteins weren't leaders in any fields, they weren't famous or well connected, they didn't know anyone in another country and couldn't afford the fare to get to one, nor, as a rather ordinary, working-class family, were they well informed of the growing threat facing Jews and *Mischlinge*.

It even proved impossible for children to escape the hatred and exclusion the regime fostered. Heini saw some of his well-off Jewish schoolfriends and their families leave Germany, but as the teachers at his school joined the Nazi Party and sported the sinister hooked cross on their lapels, that was not an option for him or his sister.

On the way home from their different schools, Heini had often taken Edie to play around the magical Märchenbrunnen Fairy Tale Fountain, a major attraction in the heart of Berlin, featuring the Brothers Grimm characters of Cinderella and Little Red Riding Hood among others. Now Heini made sure he and his little sister avoided their favourite place, as well as the swimming pool, because of the scary signs saying 'Jews can't sit here' or 'Jews not wanted' that had sprung up all over the place. Now they had to take a longer, roundabout way home.

But a treat for the children emerged from an unexpected direction. Sigi's father Robert wrote out of the blue to invite his grandchildren to join him for the traditional Jewish family celebration of Friday-night supper. While he made it clear he hadn't changed his mind about Sigi and his marriage to a Christian woman, he wrote that he wanted to get to know his grandchildren. Not one to hold grudges, instead of turning her back on her hostile in-laws, Erna welcomed the invitation. With money tight at home and food limited, she was grateful that her children would now be eating at least one proper supper each week. She saw them off in their best clothes and told them, 'Don't be greedy, but do eat as much as you can.'

Edie recalls, 'Dad took us across town to an imposing street called Schönhauser Allee, in a much smarter part of the city where our grandparents lived. The street was grand and the entrance imposing, so I was a little scared. When grandfather Robert opened the door, his round face lit up with pleasure – he was short, and he hugged me and kissed me on the nose. He ushered Heini and me in, and we were so wide-eyed and entranced at this grander place as we stepped inside, we hardly noticed that grandfather simply said "*Guten Tag*" and shut the front door in our father's face.'

The celebratory Friday-night supper soon became a weekly treat for the children. Robert, a charismatic and loving man, always squeezed Edie and kissed her on the nose, then bear-hugged his grandson, making the children feel welcome and accepted. And there was more family for them to get to know: Sigi's stepmother Tinchen; Lottie, his unmarried sister; and Georg, his elder brother, his wife Susi and their daughter Anita, who was close to Edie in age. The two families lived in a large corner property in spacious apartments side by side with the tailoring businesses they ran, where they employed

BERLIN, 1935: THE KNOCK

around 20 people making coats, skirts, suits and blouses for women.

At first on those visits, Edie was so shy she barely spoke, but both children were immediately fascinated by the unusual clothes, rituals and traditions of the Friday-night Sabbath meal in this strict Orthodox Jewish household. They had never seen any of these things before: from the little tube on the doorway they touched as they entered, to the blessings said over the bread and wine, and the little cap that the men wore on their heads, while their grandfather took his seat at the head of the table and sat with a shawl around his shoulders.

But, of course, it was the food that Edie and Heini focused on the most. Edie savoured every mouthful. Delicious light chicken soup with little dumplings they called *Lokshen* and *Kneidlach*; roast chicken, roast potatoes, vegetables and gravy; and then a sweet dumpling with sugar and raisins, all eaten with an ornate candelabra on the table. It was a feast all right. 'I was fascinated by my grandfather's funny little cap,' Edie recalls, 'because he was bald and I wondered how he kept it on. And I noticed his wife wore a wig but never knowing anything about being Jewish I didn't understand the significance of any of these. I just felt their kindness and warmth towards me.'

And for Edie, the added bonus of a girl to play with – a cousin her own age – came with a mixture of delight and awe. She never forgot that first meeting. 'Anita was really friendly, pretty and had beautiful clothes. We played in her bedroom, which was decked out with the sort of girly things that I'd never seen before. That first-time visit almost took my breath away when I saw that next to Anita's bedroom she had an adjoining playroom – a whole extra room of her own fitted out like a little shop. It had a big dresser full of jars with all sorts of real sweets, as well as scales to weigh some of the goodies before we ate them. We had such fun.'

For both Edie and Heini it was the highlight of their week. It was certainly their biggest meal, but much more than that they enjoyed the loving attention and taste of luxury their grandparents and wider family lavished on them. Theirs were innocent pleasures and they were completely unaware of the difficulties their grandfather was facing in bringing food to the table.

Despite the Friday-night feast and the comfortable surroundings, life had become increasingly tough for this family of easily identifiable Orthodox Jews. By now the Nazi regime was urging the public to boycott Jewish businesses, actively pursuing their downfall and ruin. Uniformed stormtroopers stood outside Robert's and other Jewish businesses urging Berliners not to buy from Jews. Their visits were terrifying for the family who lived in the same building as the commercial premises, but even when the stormtroopers left, Robert worried that his suppliers would hear of their visit, turn their backs on him, and then customers would stop coming and he wouldn't be able to pay his staff or support his family or that of his older son Georg, who ran the blouses part of the business.

Erna's mother Emma was also affected by the growing wave of antisemitism in Berlin. The newspapers reported trials of relatives who had been seized because they had Jews or *Mischlinge* in the family. Frightened for herself and her granddaughter, Emma was gradually distancing herself and Eva from her daughter and the Bernsteins, worried

BERLIN, 1935: THE KNOCK

she'd be singled out. She no longer welcomed Erna popping in to visit them both, and asked her to visit less often and after dark.

Being Christian was no barrier against hardship. The Depression hit everyone, with unemployment spiralling and the cost of food and rent going through the roof, affecting millions. One of those was Max Kosse, Erna's brother, who lived in the same block with his wife Anne and their two sons Günther and Joachim, youngsters who were occasional playmates of Edie and Heini. Max had been laid off work and, despite months of searching and a willingness to do anything, he just couldn't find a job. He ran out of money completely and – unable to feed his family – became so depressed and desperate that something in him snapped. In a moment of madness he got involved in one of the riots that broke out on Berlin's streets and, as windows were smashed and the looting began, he ran into the Leiser shoe shop and tried to steal some cash. Spotted by a policeman, he was shot dead on the spot. He was 27 years old.

Erna was shocked, devastated at the death of her brother and racked with guilt that her own meagre income had meant she was unable to help him and his family. The children were fond of their uncle and were shaken by what had happened. But things went from bad to worse at home when, paying the price of her surname and marriage to a Jew, Erna too lost her job.

Edie remembers, 'The only work Mum could find was poorly paid piece work that meant collecting heavy coats from the manufacturer, lugging them up the stairs to our flat, then spending the day and evening hand-sewing linings in and returning them finished the next day. Mum was still

MISCHLINGE

frail and struggled to carry the heavy coats, and although Heini would help her carry them if he was home from school in time, the work didn't pay much for the time she spent.'

On top of this, Sigi was losing jobs almost as soon as he secured them, due to the progressively harsher labour laws against Jews. Living as they did in the historic centre of Berlin Mitte, a stone's throw from the Reichstag, Brandenburg Gate and Unter den Linden, they were right at the epicentre of Nazi hatred. Sigi stuck to the quiet backstreets as much as he could for fear of encountering gangs of young stormtroopers, many of whom were no more than thugs now roaming the streets looking for Jews to attack, incited by the inflammatory speeches of Joseph Goebbels, mayor of Berlin and Hitler's master of propaganda.

Sigi felt increasingly sad, humiliated and lost. He loved his wife Erna very much, but by marrying her he'd lost his whole family, his home and all he held dear, and he felt it now more than ever. At just 22, the 'shunning' by his family had – in one fell swoop – denied him any contact with his father, mother, brother and sister. Every Friday night he took his children to see their grandparents at his old home address, but never being welcomed inside was hard. On the walk home after he returned to collect them following their meal, he'd ask Heini about his father, but his son would mostly enthuse about the food and Edie would chatter about Anita's playroom, the pathos of the situation completely passing the two youngsters by.

It was hard for Sigi to cope with the pressures he was under without the support of his family, as well as the friends and places that gave him a sense of belonging. Now he was Jewish

BERLIN, 1935: THE KNOCK

in name only, condemned twice over – first by his family, then by his country and countrymen. No wonder he was becoming more withdrawn and silent than usual. So maybe it wasn't surprising that, when he did find a job and earn some money, he was more often than not found in his local *Eckkneipe* – the corner pub – taking comfort in drink. The pub was close to their flat, served Berlin's own Schultheiss beer and became a refuge where Sigi now counted the landlord as one of his few friends. But Erna found Sigi's liking for his local pub and the publican hard, particularly when payday came round. She feared he'd be buying drinks and not bringing the much-needed money home.

Edie was horrified when her father returned from the pub one evening in a foul mood. 'Mum had cooked a white bean stew with bacon and when she put it on the table, Dad burnt his mouth and threw the plate across the floor. He shouted, "I've been out to work and all I've got to eat is beans and they're too hot. Couldn't you have cooled them down?" And then he slapped her across the face. Heini was so upset and leapt to her defence, pulling Dad off her. But he was only about 12, so what could he do?'

This incident was the beginning of the rift between Heini and his father. And while Erna had empathy for her husband because she knew the scale of his isolation and persecution, Heini was less sympathetic.

Despite his behaviour at times, Sigi was not an absent or irresponsible man. Swallowing his wounded pride and shame at not being able to feed his family, he went along to the Berlin branch of Jewish Aid, a national charity supporting those who were struggling under Nazi persecution and finding themselves unemployable. Sometimes, when he queued

MISCHLINGE

for food handouts, Edie would keep her father company and enjoy a free hot chocolate in an enamel mug, but as more violence erupted on the streets it was thought safer to have parcels discreetly dropped off at their flat. To Erna's delight they also contained various second-hand clothes she could adapt for them all. These aid parcels were very gratefully received and quickly became essential, keeping the family fed and warm during this increasingly desperate period.

Being reliant on Jewish charity was an irony not lost on any of the family. And no time was trickier than when Erna put up their Christmas tree, a tradition that Heini and Edie loved, helping their mother decorate it with white candles they clipped to its branches and twists of silver foil. Observing the German tradition of serving a dish of *Bunte Teller* on 6 December, the children would enjoy the cakes and sweets and then wait eagerly to see if there would be any presents for them beneath the Christmas tree. As resourceful as her son, Erna always found a little something to put under the tree. And on those special days at Christmas, unwrapping their presents, Heini and Edie felt as if they didn't have a care in the world, deeply appreciative of Erna's love for them.

But by celebrating Christmas, the family risked their Jewish Aid parcels being withdrawn. Observant Jewish families were not allowed to celebrate Christmas, so Erna came up with a solution. The little fir tree had to be put somewhere where they could all enjoy it in the evenings, but out of sight of passers-by and in a place from which it could be quickly whisked away if anyone knocked on the door. Heini volunteered for the job of moving the tree and Erna told the children they must deny its existence if anyone asked. When the Jewish charity delivered their next package, the family

BERLIN, 1935: THE KNOCK

held their breath as Heini leapt up and put the tree out of sight. They practised getting this manoeuvre down to under a minute, and a small Jewish symbolic candelabra – the Menorah – was found and placed on the kitchen table, so it looked as though they had been celebrating Hanukkah, the Jewish Festival of Light, which fell around the same time as Christmas. These were life-sustaining compromises.

This moving of the Christmas tree in and out of view would continue for many years, as the family's constant need to hide one identity or another was not just a tragicomic symbol of their plight but also vitally important to their daily survival. The children were neither Jews nor Christians and, while they had a foot in each camp, they had recently discovered they were not entirely welcome in either.

2
SCHOOLDAYS AND THE OLYMPICS

Heini wrote in his memoir, 'In my 13th year I was being regularly bullied at school because of my Jewish surname, with the silent approval of some of my teachers. I'd grown to be head and shoulders taller than many in my class and I was also the leanest, and that brought me considerable success at several sports. Sport was my passion and, selected to represent the school in a competition, it was a sweet victory when our team won first place. I worked out that it was essential to keep fit and strong to resist the attacks of my classmates, and maybe the only way I would ever win against some of them. Once my sports teacher cheered me by whispering, "You should turn round to see the Germans lagging behind you." His comment was encouraging, but the physical attacks continued, and although I fought back as best I could, I wasn't always successful.'

It was baffling to many that Hitler was still permitted to stage the Olympic Games in Berlin in 1936, as he'd already brought in all manner of new laws against Jews since coming

MISCHLINGE

to power three years earlier and even opened detention camps that were known about in Britain, Europe and the US. There was a threatened boycott in Europe and the US, with the Americans proposing that the Games be moved to Rome, but the sophisticated Nazi propaganda machine skilfully duped diplomatic visitors to Berlin, hiding the full extent of Hitler's persecution of the Jews.

For Heini and many ordinary Berliners it was a time of huge excitement and anticipation that the Olympics was coming. Heini could hardly believe it when he was told his school choir would be performing on the steps of the new stadium at the grand opening ceremony. He and his friends were distracted by the Olympic preparations being made right on their doorstep, and they sneaked down after school choir rehearsals to watch the large-scale building work that was going on nearby. Hitler began by demolishing the city's Jewish market, which had thrived on the same site for many years. The Scheunenviertel market – based in tightly packed wooden sheds – traded all kinds of goods and was run by Orthodox Jews in their traditional headgear and long black coats. Now the sheds were being demolished to make way for the Olympic Stadium, a two-pronged attack by the authorities – both a strike at the Jews and the building of a huge Nazi showcase for Hitler's speeches.

The Olympic site, near Alexanderplatz, was a prohibited area, entirely fenced off and with only those allocated a special identity card allowed in. It was regularly patrolled by uniformed military police units known as 'chained dogs', on account of a gorget hung around their necks and the fact they roamed the whole site looking for intruders. But these 'dogs' did not deter the teenage Heini, who found a hole in the fence

SCHOOLDAYS AND THE OLYMPICS

that he and his friends could wiggle through. Heini and his friends felt united in this daring escapade – their secret peek at all that was new and exciting in their city, each boy imagining himself alongside the international athletes, sprinting to victory on the track. They cheered each other on as they collected their imaginary medals. Heini made sure they didn't get carried away and that they all left the prohibited area before the next 'chained dogs' patrol. So the young Berliners saw close up the building of the iconic stadium, as money was poured in to the impressive 100,000-capacity arena, while Berlin's townhall, the Rotes Rathaus, was given a facelift and lit up with red spotlights in readiness for visitors from around the world.

As the summer opening approached, a jubilant Hitler prepared to host international athletic teams and businesses, and planned what was to be the first global televised broadcasts of the Games. He called a complete halt to his purge on the Jews in a bid to charm foreign investors and visitors, who would bring substantial revenue to the city and help promote his 'new Germany'. To fool the new visitors all antisemitic campaigns were paused, while posters and signs forbidding Jews to be in public places were removed. It was an unexpected and welcome respite for Jewish Berliners.

Heini enjoyed every second of the rehearsals at the stadium as the builders finished their work. On 1 August 1936 the Opening Ceremony was said by all who saw it, including Heini, to be spellbinding. Heini couldn't believe he was there, on the steps of the Olympic Stadium, standing next to school friends and foes singing his heart out for a country that was against his whole family. Richard Strauss conducted the Berlin Philharmonic and a 1,000-strong choir dressed in white sang for Germany. For Heini the highlight of the mesmerising spectacle was not the sight of the great and the famous onlookers in the stands, but the carefully rehearsed display by a vast number of girls in matching outfits performing gymnastics on the Mayfield that looked, he described 'like undulating waves on a cornfield – that no one who saw it could ever forget'.

The atmosphere in the city was heady as the Games proved a success at home and abroad. Many of the diplomats, politicians, writers and athletes who came to Berlin that summer saw none of its dark side. Not everything could be hidden, though, and not everyone's antisemitism could be controlled. One US athlete recorded that, moments after the Games finished, he saw signs around the city of 'Juden verboten', while the *London Evening Post* reported a chant doing the rounds in Berlin: 'When the Olympic Games are done, then with the Jews we'll have some fun'.

For the Bernstein family, the summer of 1936 was the best of times before the worst of times. It was as if the family had some sort of premonition that this time was precious. While the sun was out and the summer days felt more carefree, Heini would perch Edie on their father's bike and take her scrumping in the orchards at Buchholz, while Erna prepared picnics for excursions to Krumme Lanke, a forest beauty spot with a lake where they could swim. There was plenty to carry: homemade potato salad put into jars for the journey, blueberries and strawberries in evaporated milk for dessert, and drinks that were too pricey to buy there. The underground tickets from Alexanderplatz to the last stop at the end of the line were expensive enough but, as the family picnicked by the lake, it felt like an idyllic escape from all their troubles.

SCHOOLDAYS AND THE OLYMPICS

They were joined by friends and someone even took a photograph to capture the happy occasion.

The Olympic respite was not to last long. As the summer sun tanned her children's skin from olive to an even deeper brown, Erna became increasingly anxious. Both her son and daughter were looking less Aryan by the day. As their father found out when he took them for a peaceful day out to watch his local football team, Hertha Berlin, and another supporter pointed at Edie and said, 'Look at her with those big brown eyes. Definitely not a German.'

In a bid to protect her children further, Erna decided to do what she'd heard others in danger had done – she'd have

Swimming at Krumme Lanke, Berlin, 1936 – Edie (centre front) and Heini (back right) are visibly darker skinned than the others. Heini towers over his petite mother Erna (far right).

Heini confirmed in church. She didn't know if it would work, as it hadn't for the poor girl who'd reportedly still been sterilised after her christening, but she needed to do all she could to try to protect her children. Heini was maturing fast and growing in self-confidence, with an easy charm that, together with his developing good looks, was winning him friends and admirers. When Erna suggested the idea to Heini he was ambivalent but willing, especially when she told him she'd saved some money to buy him his first brand new suit for the ceremony. Heini had never had a suit before and Erna noticed her son was developing a love for clothes, possibly because he'd rarely owned any new ones in his life. He thanked his mum enthusiastically and, on confirmation day, Erna and Sigi were proud of their son and the way he looked in his dark blue suit, new shirt, bow tie and polished shoes.

The whole family embraced the occasion and the small celebration afterwards, at which even their Christian grandmother Emma and sister Eva joined the rare treat, although any hope it might act as protection was not voiced by anyone. Heini was so full of pride after his confirmation that he decided to visit his Jewish grandparents to show off his very first suit.

To his great surprise his Jewish grandparents were pleased to hear about his confirmation – perhaps they understood the motivation behind it – and they even gave him some money to mark the occasion. Heini always felt loved and cherished at his grandparents' home and took pride in being their only grandson. He never fully understood why his grandparents accepted him and his sister Edie while rejecting their father and never wanting to meet their mother. But as he admitted to himself later, he didn't give it much thought when he was a teenager.

SCHOOLDAYS AND THE OLYMPICS

That summer Heini made a new friend, Gerhard Cranzow. The two soon became inseparable, going crab fishing at the local lake and spending most of their free time at Gerhard's house.

They made an unlikely pair, Heini being tall, athletic and calm by nature, earning him the nickname 'the Bear', while Gerhard was smaller, slighter and much livelier in temperament, and always known as 'the Mouse'. Not only did the pair become firm friends, but Gerhard's family welcomed him with open arms. They knew his status as a *Mischling* with a Jewish surname, but it didn't seem to matter to them. Gerhard's mother always invited him to stay and join them at mealtimes and his father, a warm, humorous character, told stories round the table, while his younger sisters were always ready for a game of cards afterwards. As Heini confided to Edie, he was now increasingly clashing with his father, sometimes escalating to big teenage rows, so being able to take refuge at Gerhard's came as a welcome relief.

With life in the city reverting back after the Olympics, the signs banning Jews from many public places reappeared and the atmosphere changed now that Berlin was no longer full of foreign dignitaries or featuring on international newsreels.

For many ordinary Germans who weren't Jews or *Mischlinge*, life was improving under the Nazis as Hitler's hugely increased military spending opened up numerous jobs in the burgeoning armament industry. Ironically, this massive spending on armaments was in part funded by the Nazis' confiscation of Jewish wealth, largely from the middle classes.

In Schönhauser Allee, where Robert Bernstein and his extended family both lived and worked, they'd now felt under siege for years from Nazi laws, propaganda, boycotts and an increasing campaign of harassment against them. In what has been called 'the greatest theft in history', the Nazi government steadily and stealthily 'aryanised' Jewish businesses, dismissing a company's Jewish managers and workers, while arranging for non-Jewish Germans to buy them at bargain prices, fixed by government or party officials, often for as little as 20 per cent of their real market value.

Uniformed Nazis turned up regularly at Robert and his son Georg's and tried to frighten them into packing up shop. They hassled and harangued customers, and even longstanding business colleagues of the Bernsteins now felt the pressure not to supply them. Some of Robert's friends had no choice but to sell their businesses to non-Jews for a fraction of their worth, while others simply saw their businesses fold.

Robert and Georg were in an impossible position, to which there was no solution – the might of the state was ranged against them. They endured many sleepless nights racking their brains about how to keep the two tailoring businesses going, as well as worrying about feeding not just their own families but also the 20 or so employees' families who depended on them. They woke every day to the sinking feeling that their livelihoods – and their very lives – were under serious threat.

By 1937, four years after Hitler came to power, around two-thirds of German Jews had left the country, taking little with them. Many of those who could not emigrate were driven to despair, and, tragically, many Jewish businessowners and others took their own lives. At first the authorities were open about Jewish suicides, but as the numbers increased, they stopped publishing the statistics.

SCHOOLDAYS AND THE OLYMPICS

Erna and Sigi heard of an increasing number of violent attacks on Jews, communists, homosexuals and others by the young stormtroopers, brownshirts and Hitler Youth who operated around their district. Erna decided it was unsafe to let her children cross the city to visit their grandparents on Friday nights anymore. Sigi dare not take them and she was unwilling to let them go alone. Erna hated telling them that these visits were to stop, so she did it as gently as she could. Of course, Heini wasn't ready to accept the new reality and resolved to sneak over to visit his grandparents when the streets seemed quiet.

For his part, Robert Bernstein had gone one step further, as his home was so central and close to the government buildings that were the beating heart of the Third Reich. He simply forbade any of his family to leave home without very good reason. With their reduced income, the family's comfortable lifestyle had long gone, while the fear of being attacked had left a lingering sense of dread in all of them, so the whole family confined themselves to their home and just hoped that trouble wouldn't come knocking on their door.

Across the city, Edie was loving her junior school and proving a keen student, focused on learning. Her mother had taught her to read before she even started school and she was already hungry for more challenges. Her form teacher praised Edie, and she excelled at maths and science. Her mother was delighted at her progress and the fact that she'd made friends with the girls in her class and had settled in well, but after that first year at school things began to change.

'I was horrified when I discovered I was the only *Mischling* in my class. Everyone else was Christian. Most of my teachers and classmates treated me just like the other children, but some dropped me – and it hurt,' Edie remembers clearly. 'It was the older girls mostly who referred to me as "the *Mischling*", and all I could do was keep my distance from them.'

A new law had made it an offence *not* to perform the Heil Hitler salute as a greeting, and this had immediately singled out Jews and *Mischlinge*, as they were forbidden to make the salute. Special courts punished those who did not salute with fines or imprisonment, so almost everyone saluted wherever they met others.

School was no refuge for Heini, as many of his teachers were among the Nazi Party's most ardent supporters. A staggering 97 per cent of Germany's teachers were members of the National Socialist Teachers' League and many attended the league's week-long courses in army-style camps where they had to wear uniforms, march and sing Nazi songs.

Heini recorded, 'I was particularly terrified of one of my schoolteachers, a man who taunted me about my name, encouraging my classmates to jeer at me. I was fit and able to fight back in the playground, but powerless against the teacher's cane. My regular beatings were humiliating as well as painful.'

When the Berlin authorities announced public schools were not to admit Jewish children, 14-year-old Heini decided to leave before he was excluded. He was fed up with the bullying, felt he was learning little and decided to see if he could find work, perhaps as a plumber. With his customary enterprise he soon found an employer who seemed unperturbed by his surname; 'As long as you work hard there is a job for you here,' the man told Heini, and offered him a plumbing apprenticeship. Heini gave some of his earnings to Erna to help put food on the table, which made him feel he was doing some good, while also learning a practical trade that might help him realise his ambition to buy himself his own bicycle. He knuckled down to the training and found he enjoyed learning the plumbing trade.

Despite this apparent normality, life was slowly unravelling for the whole family. When her sister-in-law Annie knocked on the door one afternoon, Erna was shocked to see her nephews dressed from head to toe in the full Hitler Youth uniform. Annie laughed off Erna's reaction, telling her that all the kids at school had joined the Hitler Youth, so why wouldn't they? Their teachers had encouraged them to join, she said, and some in their school had been refused their school leaving certificate if they didn't become members. Still, Erna was relieved that neither Sigi nor Heini were at home when her sister-in-law called. Their response would have been less measured.

3
EXCLUSION

Many Germans believed Hitler's claim that he simply wanted to recreate the first German *Reich* (empire) that ended over a century earlier and peacefully reunite with German-speaking countries like Austria, and both Germans and Austrians seemed to approve of the idea. So when German soldiers marched into Austria in March 1938 in the so-called *Anschluss* (joining), it went mostly unchallenged at home and abroad.

But Austria's large Jewish population was immediately attacked, and around 80,000 Jews were forced to leave their homeland. In response to this mass exodus and obvious persecution, Britain, the US and 30 other countries gathered for a refugee conference in Evian, France, to discuss offering a home to some of these Jewish refugees. The week-long conference could not reach agreement on accepting any Austrian or German Jews, or even agree a statement condemning their persecution by the Nazis. Many historians now argue that the world's silence in the face of Hitler's

MISCHLINGE

conquest of Austria and his expulsion of its Jews gave him the confidence to increase his measures against them.

In Berlin, Sigi was horrified at the imposition of yet another new law, this time compelling every Jewish man over 18 to report to his local police station and obtain an identity card stamped with a large J for Jew and the name Israel that he must carry at all times and show on demand.

Erna could think of nothing to console him when he returned home with the awful card that would make him an easy target for abuse on the street. They both knew the vigilante brownshirts took it upon themselves to stop Jews, and any non-Jews with them, and invite onlookers to deride or spit on them – or worse. Erna had seen a non-Jew with a sign saying '*Rassenschade*' (racial shame) hung around their neck just streets away from their home. Sigi, who had always felt pride in his country, confided to his wife that he felt as if the state hated him personally and that it was ramping up excessive hysteria, robbing his whole family of any semblance of normality.

Devastated by this new derogatory name change to 'Sigismund Israel Bernstein', Sigi avoided entering any public buildings where he'd have to show his identity card with the big J marked on it for all to see. It made him feel vulnerable and isolated as he faced danger on the street every time he went to look – mostly unsuccessfully – for work. He'd complained to Erna that if even Jewish doctors and lawyers were banned from working, what chance did he, a mere upholsterer, have? Rather than talk about it with his wife or his friends, however, Sigi would sit in silence, bottling up his thoughts, and his brooding presence at home made life tense and often uncomfortable for the rest of the family.

EXCLUSION

With less work and an ever-reducing income, Sigi and Erna were forced to move home and find somewhere smaller and cheaper. Packing up and leaving her home to go to a strange neighbourhood was hardest of all for Erna. She wasn't seeing much of her mother or daughter Eva anyway – at her mother's request – but now they were moving further away it would be virtually impossible to meet up with them at all, given the danger of moving about on the streets, and she knew the emotional distance between them would grow even deeper.

Erna and Sigi consoled themselves that a new start elsewhere, where no one knew them, might keep them safer. But with antisemitism becoming more widespread, it was harder to know whom to trust, especially as Erna had heard stories of betrayals between neighbours and even within families by those wanting to ingratiate themselves with local Nazi officials.

Although sad to be leaving the area she knew, Edie was excited about starting in an all-girls secondary school, near the family's new home in Koppenstrasse in Berlin's Friedrichshain district. She couldn't wait to get to school every morning, and told her mother she loved every minute of her time there. She was now 11 years old and had ambitions to be a doctor, something her teachers and her mum encouraged. Her aptitude for maths and interest in science made one teacher in particular think that medicine was an achievable goal for her, especially because, although shy, she was a compassionate and kind girl who made friends easily and liked to look after them.

Heini was the least fearful of the family and, with all the confidence of youth, headed out of the city every weekend

MISCHLINGE

with his friend Gerhard. Using the savings from his apprenticeship he'd bought a rickety old bike, and when the pair weren't racing each other they were polishing and fine-tuning their bikes together at Gerhard's house. But these joyrides weren't to last long.

On the night of 9 November 1938 the simmering hatred against the Jews that had been so carefully orchestrated by the Nazis burst into the open on what became known as 'Kristallnacht' – the night of shattered glass. In a spree of violence lasting two days and nights, 7,500 Jewish businesses across Germany were targeted and destroyed, 1,000 synagogues burnt, around 100 Jews murdered and countless more attacked and humiliated, while 30,000 were rounded up, with many taken to the concentration camps that had been set up in Buchenwald and Dachau.

By some lucky chance the Bernstein family were at home in their new flat on that fateful night. 'We were scared but felt safe,' recalls Edie, 'because we were in a first-floor flat and few people knew us. But we could hear the screams from the streets and next morning I could hear my parents talking in whispers about what had been happening. Dad was so terrified he made us all stay in for 24 hours. But Heini, of course, defied him as usual and left to go to work at his plumbing apprenticeship. But when he returned that night he told me how many tailor shops and other shop fronts he'd seen smashed to bits, and I could tell he was scared too.'

The nearest Jewish-owned shop to the Bernsteins' flat had been wrecked, all its contents smashed, and there was water gushing everywhere as the stormtroopers had deliberately broken the waterpipes. A neighbour had told Erna that the elderly man who ran the tobacconist had been dragged out

EXCLUSION

and beaten, and he was now wandering around bruised and battered trying to find anything worth saving from the chaos of destruction.

Sigi told Erna he couldn't bear to hear any more about it and retreated to the pub as soon as he could. But there, he overheard the shocking account of how stormtroopers had entered a synagogue in the city and desecrated the Holy Scriptures with excrement. The man telling the story at least shook his head in empathy, and Sigi did not repeat it to anyone when he returned home.

Three days after Kristallnacht, an all-encompassing anti-Jewish law dealt a hammer blow to Sigi. The Decree on the Elimination of Jews from Economic Life banned Jews from carrying on any trade and selling any goods or services, in a stroke closing all Jewish-run shops and businesses.

One month later another new law, the Decree on the Utilisation of Jewish Property, forced Jews to sell all their assets – property, businesses, anything of value they owned – to non-Jews for a fraction of their worth. What had already been happening for years was now incontrovertible official government policy.

Sigi thought about his father Robert and his brother Georg, whom he'd had no contact with for some time now, and wondered how they were coping. Surely their business on Schönhauser Allee would have been taken over by the Nazis and sold for a pittance to a non-Jew, while Robert's family would struggle to pay the rent and put food on the table. Their fate and that of those he knew were loyal, long-standing employees dominated his thoughts. But what could they – or anyone – do? Jews had no citizens' rights at all, no court of appeal, no escape, with the dehumanisation process now carved into law. Since Kristallnacht it was plainer than ever that hatred for the Jews was official policy, out in the open, and no one, not even children, was immune from it. By the end of 1938, it was estimated that only 16 per cent of Jewish breadwinners were now in work and able to support their families.

At school, Edie got a new teacher. 'His name was Herr Eisenblatt, who one day appeared in our classroom wearing the swastika badge on his lapel. I didn't think much of it, but over time he became bossy and short with me. I began to notice that he treated me differently from the other kids, shouting and saying cruel things. One wintry morning, as I was finishing breakfast with Mum and getting my schoolbag ready, the postman knocked. We rarely received post, so I was excited as to what it might be. But as Mum read it I could see her body become tense and her face flush with anger. She turned to me and said, "You're not going to school today – please just stay in the flat. I've got to go and do something, but I'll be back soon." Still holding the letter in her hand, she grabbed her coat and dashed out of the door.

'About an hour later, she returned looking pale and drawn. She sat me down and told me what the letter said: "Do not send your daughter Edie to school anymore. We don't want her to mix with the Aryan race." Then she explained she had gone straight to my school and told Herr Eisenblatt in no uncertain terms that she herself wasn't Jewish and her daughter wasn't either, but he wouldn't change his mind. He just told her, "Your daughter is a *Mischling* and cannot return to school."

'Mum could not have done more to protect me or Heini. I'd seen that every time we moved home, she had to register

EXCLUSION

the family with the police – everyone did, it was a police state – and Mum always wrote "No religion" on the forms, but I suppose our surname gave us away.

'I was so shocked and upset that I would never go through the doors of my school again. When I read that letter from the school, it made me realise that being *Mischling ersten Grades* was excluding me from so much – it was a real moment of reckoning. Until then I never really felt different from anyone in my class. And I don't think that many people at school even knew I was half-Jewish, or even cared. I heard later I was the only girl to be thrown out of her class, the only one with some Jewish blood.'

Now there was no escaping it. In the current climate, no one would – or could – fight for Edie except for her mother. At the tender age of 11, Edie's education had been terminated not long after it had started. It marked the end of not just school but playing with her classmates and any kind of normal childhood.

After Kristallnacht, more and more reports reached the Bernsteins of menace and terror on Berlin's increasingly unruly streets. Neighbours spoke of young and old Jews and *Mischlinge* being taunted and attacked, of humiliating scenes where Jews were forced to lick pavements, were spat at and beaten. There were sightings of men and women separated from their families and taken away, no one knew where. Some said that men were being rounded up on street corners and used as forced labour in factories. Perhaps worst of all were the sounds that came at night. Sometimes, after the children had gone to bed, Sigi and Erna heard shouts and screams drifting up from below; at other times, what seemed like gunshots echoing in the woods that surrounded the city.

MISCHLINGE

And so Erna decided the safest place for her daughter was at home in their flat, where she would try and keep her busy and continue her education. Erna begged and borrowed books for Edie to read from the neighbours and friends she could rely on, as well as any old discarded schoolbooks. There weren't many to be had from among her similarly impoverished neighbours, but they were better than nothing and Edie had a voracious appetite to learn. Erna had her hands full trying to keep Edie busy and occupied while trying to soothe Sigi's black moods now he was also at home so much.

Confined to the flat, Edie was only too happy to sit and read for most of the day, and for variety her mum would also set her sums, which she would check and mark every evening. Erna was now the only one of the family that could freely move about the city without fear of being challenged – or worse – but she kept her outings to a minimum, only venturing out to and from work and when shopping for food, to minimise the risk of getting tangled up in any violence on the streets.

But the long, dark days within four walls got tougher for Edie as they dragged into weeks, with no end in sight, and she felt like a prisoner within her own home. She missed her friends and all the little delights of daily life at school – the games in the playground, the lessons, some of the teachers. The highlight of her day was her adored brother's return from work, when Heini would do his best to cheer her up. The two would sit together in a corner playing simple card games, with Heini teaching his sister new ones and Edie reluctant at ever having to stop for bedtime.

As the dark nights drew in and Berlin's bitter winter temperatures began to bite, Erna had another pressing worry:

EXCLUSION

how to heat their little flat and put food on the table now Sigi's earnings were not coming in to pay for wood or food. She took on more night-time piecework whenever she could and Edie started to help her mum with the sewing, relishing spending time with her, having been alone for most of the day. The whole family looked forward to the Jewish Aid parcels they still received, but Erna worried how much longer these would continue.

To be hungry and cold was a depressing prospect. Unable to find paid work, Sigi searched for any way he could to at least heat their little flat. Having heard of a tough way to find wood to burn, he bought a wood licence from a forest warden that entitled him to dig up tree stumps. Sigi asked Heini to join him at weekends, and the pair shared the back-breaking work of digging long and deep to uproot the old, gnarly stumps. Then they had to tie them to Sigi's bicycle to transport them, which proved awkward and tricky and took two hours despite the short distance. Once back home, they had to saw and split the stumps before they could make a fire. But the challenge and success of their joint efforts brought father and son a little closer. And later in the evening, when the fire was crackling in the hearth and Erna and Edie were basking happily in its glow, both warm for once, Heini felt proud of their efforts and even sensed some semblance of peace with his father.

Heini was enjoying his plumbing apprenticeship and felt pleased with his progress, but not everyone at work was so happy. 'Gradually I became aware that some of the other apprentices were annoyed that I had a contract,' he recalled. 'There had been difficulties with some of them ever since I started there, the same kind of difficulties I had with some teachers at school, but they just grew. It seemed my surname simply didn't fit with those in charge.

'I turned up for work as usual one morning and the boss told me with a shrug, "I'm afraid I've got to tear up your apprenticeship contract. It's nothing you've done. It's just the way things are."

'I was upset and angry. I'd enjoyed the job for two years and relished learning a useful trade, but now I was out on the street again halfway through the training and with no certificate to show for it. I'd left school with no qualifications and now this was a second blow, but I was determined not to be demoralised. I had the handicap of a Jewish surname and no real contacts to call on – I knew I had to rely on my wits and my determination, and that I'd continue to search for any job I could turn my hand to.'

At 15 years old Heini had the usual dreams of a teenager – smart clothes he'd seen in the shops, bike trips to the mountains with the Mouse and going to dances with girls – but he needed money to make them real. And without a job he couldn't even afford to buy little treats for himself, his sister or his mum. He refused to lose hope and resolved to find a way to make money. It was just a question of how.

4
WAR, ARREST AND DISAPPEARANCE

The Bernsteins were both surprised and fearful at the start of September 1939 when their radio brought news that Germany was now at war. They and their children had been born and raised in Berlin, had always felt German and never set foot outside the country, but they could summon no enthusiasm for a war they felt certain would only make life worse for them.

When German troops invaded Czechoslovakia that spring, Sigi and his friend Otto, who ran the local pub, speculated that their ambitious leader wouldn't stop there. And when Hitler made a pact with Stalin and ordered German troops to invade Poland, the men talked of the prospect of war over a beer in the pub's cellar where Sigi felt safe to relax, away from prying eyes. They guessed Hitler would ignore the British and French ultimatum to withdraw, but they were downcast when both countries jointly declared war on Germany and the Second World War began.

War brought a further rise of nationalism and public displays of patriotism. Now there were even more patrolling

MISCHLINGE

brownshirts, and with their shouts of *Führer, Volk und Vaterland* they invited all those they met to make the Heil Hitler salute. Heini was ever more cautious as he ventured out in the day looking for work … and in the evening looking for fun.

Sigi's fears were realised as stricter restrictions were imposed on Jews than on others in the country. A curfew was imposed on Jews from 9 p.m. to 5 a.m. in summer and 8 p.m. to 6 a.m. in winter, which Sigi and Erna stuck by rigidly, telling their children to do the same. Edie had long been confined to home anyway, reading and studying, but Heini, who hadn't had much truck with his parents' earlier attempts at a curfew, wouldn't obey a rule he felt didn't apply to him. Not only did he not identify as Jewish but also, like many other teenagers, he hadn't yet felt the effects of war that deeply. His focus was on having fun. Despite the Nazi government's best efforts, Heini wouldn't allow either religion or now war to dominate or impinge upon his zest for life.

Heini was a gregarious teenager, and he headed out at night, dressed smartly, in the hope of finding girls to talk to and friends to have fun with, just like any other 16-year-old. He and Gerhard – Bear and Mouse – spent as much time at Gerhard's house as they could, which meant that Heini could avoid his grumpy father. They found all sorts of ways of evading the curfew. If Heini wanted to go to a dance after work and needed his smart confirmation suit, he would get Edie to lower his clothes from a rope out of the first-floor window, then slip into his new gear and send his work clothes back upstairs the same way. Edie was only too happy to help her beloved big brother.

WAR, ARREST AND DISAPPEARANCE

It didn't take long for Erna and Sigi to work out what was going on and his father gave him quite a telling-off. But Heini wasn't easily deterred, and he still managed to sneak out regularly. Lack of money didn't put him off either, and he thought up a crafty ruse to reduce the cost of dances held in the cafés on Friedrichstrasse and the Kurfürstendamm so he'd have enough left to buy a drink. He would stand on the dance floor or in the aisles and wait for the music to begin and then ask a girl to dance. Being with people his own age, just hanging around together and teasing and flirting with girls was great fun, providing a little light relief from the serious challenges life now presented.

War meant that rationing was imposed on all Germans, but the rules around Jewish food rations were much harsher than for German citizens. Jews could only buy rations from certain stores at a specific time at the end of the day when there wasn't much left to choose from. Erna immediately recognised that these were barely subsistence rations, so the weekly food shop was such a crucial event that she treated it like an expedition. She'd spotted the effect that being alone in their small flat all day long was having on her daughter and suggested Edie accompanied her, under strict conditions.

Edie relished the release. 'I never told my mum how I felt, but it was lonely and as time went on I felt increasingly anxious. Mum must have noticed the change in me, so she said I could come out to do the weekly shop with her, as long as I realised it was dangerous out there and I must stay close, keep my head down and not draw attention to us in any way. I agreed and we set off together to queue for our ration books, which were stamped JUDE in large letters across them. Mum tucked them away and hurried along to our local

MISCHLINGE

butcher and the grocer, carefully avoiding any uniformed men we spotted loitering on street corners.

'Our rations were very meagre – half what other Germans got – and as we were only allowed to shop late in the day, the counters were quite bare by the time we got there. Mum had to make every pfennig of our much-reduced income count, so she shopped carefully, eking everything out. She knew a couple of places she could find potato peelings, and she'd make soup from them later. We found very little meat at the butchers, meaning that we ate a lot of bread and whatever veg was left on the shelves.'

Erna tried her best to cook nourishing meals, but she could hardly afford the basics, and try as she might all four of the Bernsteins often left the table hungry after dinner. Even essentials like soap, shoes and clothes were rationed now, and, while the family had rarely bought new clothes before rationing, now even soap was treated as precious.

The family income dwindled further as Sigi could no longer dig up tree stumps for wood with the licence he'd bought. A new wartime law forbade Jews to own a bicycle and demanded they be handed in to the authorities, which not only meant that he couldn't bring home the precious fuel, but made finding work even harder as Jews were not allowed to ride on buses unless they lived more than four miles from their place of work. Any less than that and they were expected to walk, and being on foot would expose Sigi to greater risk of abuse or attack.

That first wartime winter was bleak for Berliners, for although there wouldn't be any direct bombing of the city for some time, its location in the east of the country meant it was extremely cold. Strict blackout regulations forbade any lighting at all on side streets, and with the subdued lights on main roads, and masked street and traffic lights, the whole city descended into a depressing frozen gloom from mid-afternoon onwards.

Blinds, sheets and special sheets of dark paper were given to all households to black out windows and hefty fines were imposed if families did not comply. Outside, there were few cars on the streets as most workers who weren't Jews used bicycles. Kerbstones, bus stops, entrances and lampposts were painted with glowing paint to help people negotiate the dark, but many still fell or bumped into things on their way to and from work in the dark.

The combined effect of these dangers and restrictions on the Bernsteins was to keep them indoors all the more, even though they could afford little heating.

An entirely unexpected new threat to the family now emerged, this time to Eva Bernstein, Heini and Edie's elder sister. Eva had been living with her grandmother Emma for 12 years now, entirely separately from her parents and siblings. The old lady, long widowed, had enjoyed caring for her granddaughter and taking the pressure off her own daughter after Edie was born.

At first Erna had seen a lot of Eva, but as antisemitism grew it was Emma – as a Christian – who feared persecution by association and insisted on minimal contact with her Jewish son-in-law, her two *Mischlinge* grandchildren and even her daughter, to protect herself and Eva from drawing attention to themselves.

Eva had come to think of her grandmother more like her mother. Erna was hurt as she came to realise this, but she told herself that it was inevitable given the time Eva had lived with her grandmother and the fact that both seemed happy with the arrangement. Eva had grown into a gentle, quiet teenager of simple habits and needs. Eva and her grandmother fared well together, happy and secure in each other's company, helping each other in their enclosed world. Erna was relieved that at least one of her three children was safe. This was soon to change.

As a young child Eva's mental disability was hardly noticeable, but as the years passed it became clearer that Eva was not developing as a 'normal' child should, which placed her in great danger when the Nazis came to power. Hitler had long declared his belief in euthanasia for the mentally and physically disabled, so neither mother nor grandmother had dared take Eva to a doctor or psychiatric unit for a proper diagnosis, let alone consider treatment. Both had simply done their best to care for Eva in the privacy of their homes.

Edie remembers, 'We saw very little of Eva growing up, but when we did – even as children – Heini and I could see that she didn't really mature but looked and behaved like a child half her age. And to be honest, neither of us ever thought of her as a sister; she was a stranger to us. She'd never lived with us, and then years passed without us seeing her, so we just didn't know her. She was pale and wan, a shadowy figure, I suppose, hard to get to know, but gentle and quiet.'

Now that Eva was 17, with an obvious mental disability, she too was threatened by Nazi ideology. Using war as his excuse, Hitler declared that 'those unworthy of life' should not live when the healthy were dying in battle. He asked his health secretary to widen the 'euthanasia' scheme so that

WAR, ARREST AND DISAPPEARANCE

mentally and physically disabled adults and children were systematically killed.

As such, Eva was very much at risk, living in the centre of Berlin close to the authorised murder squad headquarters at Tiergartenstrasse 4, from where the policy – known as *Aktion T4* – was rolled out across Germany. It would have taken only one report from the increasing number of informants wanting to ingratiate themselves with the Nazis for the authorities to classify her as mentally ill and have her legally put to death. Doctors were appointed to decide who would die, based not just on medical grounds but on who was capable of doing useful work, with the murders being carried out at six gassing centres and in mobile vans rolled out across Berlin, as well as by lethal injection and even starvation.

Her adoption by her grandmother and subsequent isolation had served to protect Eva, and it was clear this had to continue to keep her safe. She was to be kept indoors and hidden for her own safety – just like Edie in the next-door neighbourhood. But men, women and children with a range of mental and physical disabilities from slight to severe in Germany, Austria and later Poland were not as lucky as Eva, and were murdered in their thousands.

Heini had been pounding the streets looking for work without any specific talents to offer, but after weeks of rejections his perseverance paid off and he found a job as a worker for the furniture firm Metropol, in Berlin's Warschauer Strasse.

He soon showed what a keen and quick learner he was, his easy charm winning over his older and more experienced colleagues. They showed him how to work with wood, teaching him the skilled arts of veneer cutting and furniture-making.

'I got on so well with my workmates,' he recorded in his memoir, 'and so enjoyed their tutelage that I took it as welcome proof that not everyone in Berlin was antisemitic. I felt more relaxed and at ease there than I had for a long time. I took to furniture-making so naturally that I asked the boss if I could stay behind after working hours to make something for myself. A few weeks later, I felt especially pleased to have completed a small wardrobe. When I hauled my handiwork home my mother beamed from ear to ear and even my father congratulated me on the finished piece.'

That winter, Berlin experienced its coldest temperatures for more than a hundred years, with the thermometer falling to around −40°C, driving up the demand for coal and leading to an acute fuel shortage. To save supplies, people were only allowed warm water twice per week, but the Bernsteins struggled to afford even that.

One moonless night, with the blackout making it extra dark, Erna spotted a small store of coal at the bottom of an embankment near their home. She returned home and fetched some bags to fill up, posting Edie as a look-out. Glancing round to check the coast was clear, Erna hitched up her dress and climbed down the embankment to steal the coal. Edie was both frightened for and proud of her, later telling Heini that it had been a steep scramble down and an awkward climb up for their petite mum. Erna made a couple of sorties to retrieve the precious fuel, with Edie still keeping a watchful eye out and helping her take it home, and when they could both carry no more, they hurried back under the cover of darkness, delighted at the thought of warm nights ahead.

In the first year of the war there was no doubt Hitler was winning the conflict he'd started. Having launched his

WAR, ARREST AND DISAPPEARANCE

Blitzkrieg campaign across western Europe, in just six weeks his armies had attacked and overrun Denmark, Norway and – a few weeks later – Belgium, the Netherlands, Luxembourg and much of France, to add to his earlier conquest of Czechoslovakia and Poland.

In the summer of 1940, a few days before Edie's 13th birthday, Berliners were given a public holiday to celebrate Hitler's victorious return to the capital for a grand ceremonial to celebrate his conquering of eight previously sovereign countries. A seething mass of Berliners – men in uniform, families, children and local bands – turned out in their thousands to watch the pomp and ceremony planned to greet Hitler at the railway station during his progress to the Reich Chancellery. The Bernsteins could hear the music, the shouts and exclamations of 'Heil Hitler' from the parade even from a distance, and, once again, Sigi shut the windows to block out the noise.

The only work Heini could find by now was as part of the nationwide compulsory war effort, first as a transport worker at a ball-bearing factory on Ritterstrasse and then at a weapons factory. At both workplaces, with the heightened sense of nationalism that swept the country in the wake of the seemingly effortless German victories against all and sundry, workers were finding it easier and easier to call the teenager all sorts of names with relish and without qualms.

Edie too was in a bad place physically and emotionally, having been kept for her own protection as a virtual prisoner in the Bernsteins' small flat for more than two years. The lack of natural daylight and her very poor diet over such a long period had given her the painful and disfiguring bone-warping disease of rickets. The teenager now had pronounced

MISCHLINGE

bowed legs from knee to ankle and her spirits as well as her body were suffering from the effects of such extended confinement. Aside from the weekly outing of an hour or so to collect food rations with her mum, her parents forbade her to leave the flat and never to answer the door if anyone knocked.

But in among all the gloom there was some good news, as Edie recalls. 'Mum came back from work one evening, laughing and smiling and hardly able to get through the door before telling me she'd found me a job. I'd spent the day re-reading the Brothers Grimm fairy stories again as there was nothing new to read and rushed to hug her and hear her news. Mum said she'd heard from one of the women she sewed with that with so many men away at war, there was an opening at a local printing business nearby. I wouldn't have to go far and she felt it was safe enough as it was so close.

'Mum took me there the next day and I discovered it was a small family printing and bookbinding company called Moritz und Kummer, on Königin-Elisabeth-Strasse. The job was to be an *Anlegerin* (feeder), an easy role that involved putting paper in the big machine, pulling a press down to print and then taking it off, then checking it later on and processing whatever stationery was ordered. I was to join a small group of girls doing the job and if all went well it would be an apprenticeship where I would be trained in other roles and my wages would increase.

'I practically ran out of the flat every morning and really enjoyed the job working alongside girls of a similar age to me, something I hadn't done since I was barred from school. It turned out that I was the youngest, but to my relief it soon became obvious that we'd all get on. As well as the sense of freedom that I now felt, it was good to hand Mum my earn-

WAR, ARREST AND DISAPPEARANCE

ings every week, although she always let me keep some to spend on our rationing trips.'

Just under a year since the war started, Berlin was bombed for the first time. On the night of 25 August 1940, British aircraft targeted Templehof airport and the Siemensstadt industrial district. German anti-aircraft guns lit up the sky just after midnight, and although the bombs themselves did only slight damage, the raid came as a shock to Berliners and the German military. Reichsmarschall Hermann Goering – the head of the Luftwaffe and chief minister of Prussia and Berlin – had boasted that no enemy planes could ever penetrate German airspace, and many believed him. 'You can call me "Meyer" if that happens,' he's said to have joked.

That night all the Bernsteins took cover from the raid in the cellar of a local house. Many Berlin homes had them, and the family just followed locals in, without any recriminations. But to her horror, when Erna enquired the following day about the location of the nearest air-raid shelter, she learnt that Jews and *Mischlinge* were forbidden from taking cover in them during bombings. She thought it depraved but this was just another of the 101 brand-new antisemitic measures made law, just another of the endless repressive rulings. Goering had decreed that Jews should build their own air-raid shelters, which of course the Bernsteins in an upstairs flat in a tenement block had neither the place nor the means to do.

Heini arrived at Gerhard's one evening after work to learn that his friends, Gerhard the Mouse among them, had received their conscription papers and a date when they had to meet up with their unit. He joined Gerhard and his whole family in a poignant evening farewell supper, during which

MISCHLINGE

they all tried to put on brave faces and wish him luck. As the weeks passed, he learnt that an ever-increasing number of young men in his district had been called up. Now there were fewer mates to go out with, leaving Heini to wonder whether he would be next or if his *Mischling* status would mean that serving at the front was impossible.

Then some official papers arrived in the post, although he wasn't sure what they meant. They looked like call-up papers and were accompanied by an army identity card with the entry Kv1, z.b.V., but they contained no date or place to report to, as Gerhard and others had received.

Heini certainly wasn't going to ask anyone. He was developing a policy of secrecy to keep himself safe, and he certainly didn't want to fight for the country that was persecuting him and his family, one that had taken away many of his rights. But discreet enquiries later revealed that Kv1, z.b.V. meant he was deemed capable of special service in the war, although in what precise capacity he never discovered. Did it mean he would fight alongside Germans? He couldn't believe that. But, as ever, there was no one he could safely question. Staying away from all authority and state organisations was best, he felt sure. All he could do was wait to discover what was expected of him.

As the war escalated, Germany launched their invasion of the Soviet Union, the long-planned and massive Operation Barbarossa, which commenced in June 1941 and would have direct consequences for the Bernsteins. Now that Hitler had abandoned his pact with Stalin, the Eastern Front became the focus of some of the largest battles, worst atrocities and greatest numbers of casualties of the war.

WAR, ARREST AND DISAPPEARANCE

Returning home one evening Heini found his mother in the kitchen crying, with Edie – looking strained and scared – trying to comfort her. 'I pressed them to calm down and sit down,' Heini recalled, 'and when they told me the Gestapo had just taken Dad with some other men, I became frightened too. The three of us just sat there for a while in a complete state of shock and disbelief. Mum said that the Gestapo had given no explanation as to why Sigi had been taken. I could only think I had seen it so often that year already – men rounded up to be deported – and what could be done?

'After trying to calm my mum and little sister, with a heavy heart I gathered myself to head out again to see what I could find out. I wandered gingerly around our district and as I approached our local school clearly something big was happening. There were Gestapo and SS men everywhere, shouting at locals and forcing them inside the school building. As I got nearer and saw these henchmen close up, I felt like I was entering a den of lions. I had to summon up all my courage to enter the school grounds.

'A guard barked at me, "Show me your papers and tell me what you're doing here." All I could think of was to show him my recently received army identity card marked Kv1, z.b.V., and say I was looking for my father.

'I could see my father out of the corner of my eye in front of me in the schoolyard, and I pointed at him. To my amazement the guard I was talking to signalled to another to let my father go free, even apologising and saying that they had made a mistake. I had to resist every instinct to run, and the two of us just walked calmly out of the gates and headed for home. I let myself take a quick glance back when we'd got some distance away, but no one was following us. Mum and

MISCHLINGE

Edie's faces when we walked through the door were a picture I'll never forget. We were all well aware of what might have happened and it was one of our happiest evenings.'

Sigi's reprieve was, however, only short-lived. On 1 September 1941 another new Nazi decree obliged all German Jews over the age of six to wear a cloth badge on their outer clothing, a yellow Star of David with the word 'JUDE' inscribed on it, which obviously made him a highly visible target the second he stepped out of his home. It was to be worn outside at all times. For Sigi, this badge was the final dishonour and disgrace.

With fear in her fingers, Erna sewed the yellow star onto her husband's jacket, following the authorities' instructions that it must be so tightly attached a finger could not fit behind it if tested on the streets. These humiliating yellow badges were made by a Berlin textile company that ironically had been founded and owned by Jews – but three years earlier a forced auction had taken place, with the proceeds being pocketed by the Reich, who now benefited from their production.

The government also announced that all Jews would soon be assigned an unskilled manual job and paid a minimal wage, with no rights or time off work. Sigi's orders arrived soon enough. He was to be an 'essential' war worker – effectively a slave labourer – on the German railways at Wriezener Station, a goods station not far from Schlesischer Station in Berlin. The pay given to a Jew – who, in the eyes of the Reich, possessed a life with no value – was the bare minimum that afforded little food or comfort.

Sigi tried to remember that he was more fortunate than some. Erna's refusal to divorce him and give him up to the Gestapo was what was keeping him safe, and he was earning

WAR, ARREST AND DISAPPEARANCE

a little money to put food on the table. Erna's support was what protected him and their *Mischlinge* children from being deported. As Hitler's armies conquered Europe they heard reports of how Jews, *Mischlinge*, Slavs, homosexuals, Roma, and the mentally and physically ill were being rounded up and sent to the ever-expanding network of concentration camps within the new 'Greater Germany'.

Berlin was being bombed more heavily and more frequently now, as both the British and the Soviets were targeting the capital from the air. Although Erna was allowed to take cover in an air-raid shelter, she couldn't possibly think of leaving her daughter, husband or son outside, so they all headed for those nearby cellars they had learnt were willing to let them shelter when the sirens sounded. As Erna occasionally reminded her husband and children, there were still good Berliners who didn't care what religion their neighbours were.

Across the countries that Hitler had conquered, his twin obsessions of hating Jews and expanding the German empire were much in evidence. Erna Bernstein was ever mindful of the many dangers her children might face so, as she'd done with Heini, she arranged for Edie to be confirmed. In March 1941 Edith Emma Erna Bernstein was confirmed at St Markus Church in Berlin, wearing a new dress she was proud to have paid for herself from her Moritz und Kummer wages. She was given a little paper certificate as evidence, which she hid away in the house for safekeeping. It was a happy day for all the family as they celebrated together, albeit with little food on the table.

As Heini's 18th birthday approached, he too was feeling happy as he'd been swept off his feet by pretty Margot Kunze,

MISCHLINGE

a young woman he'd met while out partying with Gerhard and who seemed just as taken with him. Heini had matured into a handsome young man, tall and lean, with an easy smile and a confident manner. Heini had courted a couple of girls, but after quite a short time he felt sure Margot was 'the one' and that he was falling in love with her. She had short, shiny hair and a raucous laugh, and they laughed a lot together. Margot liked clothes as much as Heini, and she always looked elegant. It was a bonus that, although her family were Christians, neither she nor any of them were in the slightest bit bothered about his *Mischling* status.

Heini was wondering about asking her to marry him after he came of age. Both events felt like milestones and made him think of family, of visiting his grandparents. He knew he'd

Heini Bernstein was turning into a handsome teenager.

WAR, ARREST AND DISAPPEARANCE

neglected them, but his parents had banned him and his sisters from undertaking Friday-night visits across the city for their own safety. Armed with his good news, he decided to take the risk.

Arriving at their home and business address in Schönhauser Allee, Heini rang the doorbell. The building felt eerily quiet, so when nobody answered he peered in as far as he could and discovered, to his horror, that their apartment had been sealed. Too frightened to enquire further – there was no one he knew to ask without potentially placing himself in danger or putting others at risk – he quickly turned on his heels.

Heini knew the scene only too well – the entire family had been taken away by the Nazis, their property sealed so party officials could loot it later and take any valuables. As Heini and Edie hadn't been to Friday-night dinner for some time, no one even knew where they lived to tell them, had anyone even wanted to.

Shaken and scared, Heini rushed home and broke the terrible news to his parents. Erna couldn't stop crying, while Sigi just stared ahead, empty and uncomprehending. Edie could barely take it in, desperate to know where Anita was and whether she and all her beautiful possessions were safe.

Sigi had not seen or spoken to any of his family since his marriage, but he'd always hoped reconciliation might be possible one day. Awful as it was to have been shunned by them, he'd always taken comfort from the fact that his children had been welcomed and indeed spoilt on their regular visits to his old family home for Friday-night dinner. Now there was no escaping the terrible reality – his family had been taken away to who knew where, by men who wanted them dead ...

5
THE FINAL SOLUTION

Edie hadn't long turned 14 when she was compelled to wear the yellow star. She sewed it on herself onto her warmest jacket and her mum checked it was tight. But as soon as Edie reached work at the printing press she'd take her jacket off and stuff it into her bag before entering the building. It was another humiliation to endure – there were now so many that all she could do was try to put them out of her mind.

Edie offered to sew her brother's star on his jacket but Heini was having none of it, refusing to wear one at all. At 18, and fuelled by first-time love, he was becoming more audacious, with romance and his enterprising spirit as a black-market wheeler-dealer keeping him on his toes. Nevertheless, it was a dangerous act of defiance.

The whole Bernstein family were now suffering under immense mental strain. Of course they thought of their family who had disappeared. Heini remembered, 'When I was very young our neighbours neither knew nor cared what your religion was. But now – whipped into hysteria by Goebbels and

MISCHLINGE

other Nazis, and blamed for all the problems in the world – the threats that under which Jews and *Mischlinge* like us lived seemed to increase by the day. The fact we had so little income made everything worse.

'So I focused on how I might raise funds. At 18 I'd received my cigarette coupons and, as I hated smoking, I decided to either exchange them for all kinds of hard-to-come-by goods, like food, alcohol and clothes, or just sell them. The authorities called this buying and selling "black marketeering", but to me it was survival. I got to know an incredible number of people also willing to buy or sell this or that and it meant I could give some money to my mum to help feed us all, and had some to spend on Margot and me.'

Heini's black-marketeering – which his father disapproved of, despite the benefit to the family – was conducted discreetly at night, and by day he was still working in the weapons factory. Unlike his fellow workers, he was not swept up by the tide of nationalism sweeping the country now Hitler's armies were winning victory after victory across Europe. After the tough times of the Depression, Berliners were in a jubilant and celebratory mood all around the city, but Heini's feelings were more complicated – how could they not be when he'd been stripped of his schooling, apprenticeship and any normal life at every turn? He loved much about his country and his city, but his focus now was on seizing every opportunity to earn money and stay safe.

Sigi was now one of around 28,000 Jewish forced labourers in Berlin. He was only paid a pittance for his manual labour and he felt both humiliated and resentful, returning home every night both exhausted and bad-tempered.

Heini found the arguments with his father draining and,

hoping to avoid them altogether, he went from being rarely at home in the evenings to leaving home altogether. He and Margot had got closer over the months, dancing, meeting up with friends or just being together at her family home, where he always felt welcome. So Heini didn't hesitate when Margot told him to stop grumbling about his father and move in with her and the family. He brought his handmade wardrobe and his best confirmation suit with him.

Life was more relaxing living with Margot's family. Her parents never once mentioned his Jewish heritage and being under the same roof made him even more smitten with Margot. She wasn't just pretty; she was full of fun and sparkle, and really took Heini out of himself. Most important of all, she'd shown by her affection and commitment to him that she was a strong personality too – she loved him for himself. After a few months Heini proposed, and after asking her father's permission, the two exchanged rings to mark their engagement.

Heini returned home at least once a month to collect his food ration coupons, to the delight of his little sister Edie. 'I missed him in those absences, as at home Heini had always been such a source of laughter and fun. He seemed to brighten a room when he was in it, turning up unexpectedly with something delicious for me to eat, hidden under his jacket. He would hug me close and then tell me tales of his adventures, enlivening those long, blacked-out evenings with his skill at all kinds of board and card games and his patience teaching me new ones.'

The family's only escape from reality now was their forbidden radio set – as well as the imposition of yellow stars, 1941 had seen the banning of radios for Jews – and they

MISCHLINGE

were meant to have handed theirs in to the authorities. But as they were also forbidden to buy newspapers and magazines, and couldn't afford them anyway, Sigi was prepared to take the risk of keeping it, as it was their only source of information.

Like their clandestine Christmas tree, Sigi hid the radio in the daytime, only taking it out after supper when the three of them huddled around the set, keeping the volume as low as they could. They couldn't risk it being heard by their closest neighbours; walls had ears, and in those increasingly fraught times, they never knew who might be willing to betray them for some perk or other.

That year also saw the Nazis ramp up their persecution of Jews, with increasing focus and organisation. The Bernsteins' anxiety grew as reports of more late-night disappearances reached their ears. The regime did not hide the new concentration camps they had built across Europe, although many Germans believed the Nazi line that these were simply prisons where criminals, undesirables and Jews worked cheerfully towards the war effort, enjoying sports in their leisure time. The foreign press were reporting the grim truth that these were brutal hard-labour camps, and some well-informed Germans knew the reality, but the Bernsteins only knew what the German radio stations told them. Over the airwaves on their hidden radio, the war was *always* going well for Germany.

One night there was a knock at the door. Erna went to answer it with some trepidation, quite prepared to defy the Gestapo once again if they were back to 'suggest' she divorce her husband, but she was mightily relieved to see it was her brother-in-law Georg. He was alone and agitated, looking

THE FINAL SOLUTION

around fearfully before he stepped through the door. She welcomed him in, tears in her eyes, as the brothers, who had not seen each other for almost 20 years, put their arms around each other. She felt a deep sadness that she'd been the cause of her husband losing all his family, the reason for his shunning. Poor Sigi had lost every member of his family when he chose her, and to see his brother on her doorstep was wonderful.

In the light Erna could see how ashen Georg looked and she quickly guided him to a chair as he looked like he might collapse. He said he had some awful news, and Erna took that as her cue to leave the brothers in the kitchen to talk; this was not a conversation for her daughter's ears. She grabbed Edie and hurried her next door, with the excuse that they must get on with their sewing. Edie could hardly concentrate as she thought of her cousin Anita and their special time in her playroom, but neither of them spoke as they could hear both men arguing.

After a spell of raised voices and shouting, followed by a slammed door, Sigi called out for Erna. She found her husband alone in the kitchen, his head in his hands, wailing. 'My father is dead,' he told her, 'and nobody knows how or why. Georg says he was found in the street just outside the flat, and no one seems to have seen or heard anything. Papa could have been the victim of a violent attack or suffered a heart attack – we will never know. He was apparently worried sick about the growing threat of his business collapsing, and his family being made both destitute and homeless.

'And this didn't just happen, it wasn't recently – it was a long time ago – but Georg wanted to respect our father's wishes to shun me. He has only come now because our stepmother, Tinchen, has been taken away and their flat sealed – as Heini discovered.'

Erna did her best to console her shocked husband, but he continued: 'She was really the only mother I ever knew, because my birth mother Amalie died when I was eight years old, and Tinchen was the one who cared for me throughout my childhood and adolescence. I hadn't seen her for so long, but now I have lost her too.'

'Where is Georg?' Erna asked, 'and why were you arguing?'

'Because I said I couldn't hide him and the family here,' Sigi sobbed, and Erna saw her husband break down and cry for the very first time.

'He came to ask me to hide him and his family. He said they were all terrified to stay in their flat next to our father's, now that Tinchen had been taken. Would they return soon and take him and his family? They'd been living like mice, he said, hiding in the shadows but every day feeling more and more frightened and unsafe. Then he asked me directly if I would hide him, along with his wife Susi and their daughter Anita.'

Sigi turned to Erna and said, 'How could I? In this tiny place? It would only endanger us all. We rowed, we raged, but I had to tell him, I was very, very sorry, but I could not hide him and his family and put my own family in even more jeopardy than it was already in.'

He fell into a prolonged silence, but Erna could clearly see his torment. He hadn't seen Georg since their father told him he couldn't, but he was still his brother – they had grown up together, and he wanted to help him, his wife and his child. Yet what could he do? Their home was only a small flat and he had his wife, Edie and Heini to think of. If he hid his

THE FINAL SOLUTION

brother and family in his home, how would they manage for food rations? Coupons were linked to an address and even Heini wouldn't be able to secure enough for all of them. Three new people would surely be noticed by someone in their block or street, and if they were reported to the authorities they could *all* be taken away. It would be to risk *all* their lives.

The fallout for both families was wretched. Georg had returned to Susi and Anita that night with the awful news that offered no hope; and Sigi was plunged into a deep black mood, wracked with guilt at having turned away his own brother, much as Robert had done in shunning him. The awful decision he'd been forced to make tormented him for months, often revisiting him in the early hours of the morning, when he'd wake in a cold sweat. For a few moments after he knocked on the door, Sigi had hoped his big brother had called on him to heal the family rift, perhaps spurred on by the war. But the truth was so much worse. And what a cruel parallel fate had now served up, Sigi having to refuse his own brother entry to his family home, just as he'd been turned away from his family home almost two decades earlier.

Erna was deeply upset too. She was grateful her husband had put their family's safety first, but at what price? She was appalled she couldn't offer her brother-in-law's family a safe refuge, and she also felt haunted by the events of that night. All she could do was keep what had happened from Edie and Heini; Edie hadn't taken much in that evening, and she wanted it to stay that way.

In the months that followed there was no news of Georg and his family, and Sigi and Erna could only keep their

MISCHLINGE

anxieties to themselves, as every evening their radio brought darker news. Hitler had now authorised that all Jews be deported from Germany and their property automatically confiscated at the Reich border. The Bernsteins were hearing of more people they knew being taken off the streets, and more alarming were the rumours of what might have happened to them. The realisation that they were utterly powerless, unable to fight against what was happening, brought on a sense of utter desperation. The feeling of helpless submission tormented Sigi, who knew that if he'd had money or contacts, he might have got his family out of the country, just as more than half the Jews of Germany had done by the time war broke out. Now it was certain there was no way out of Berlin.

It didn't take long for the Berlin police to discover that Heini was not living with his parents at the address officially registered as his home, which was completely illegal. Returning from work at the weapons factory one evening, he was met by a policeman at Margot's family home asking questions about where he was living. It was no good asking the policeman how the authorities knew he was living with Margot. In this Nazi-run state, *Mischlinge* and Jews could be reported by anyone at any time for infringing the harsh rules they were compelled to live by – and they'd never know who had reported them. Heini was learning fast that figuring out who to trust was essential.

As a *Mischling,* Heini was in no position to put in an official request to move in to Margot's home, and as much as he'd tried to bluff the policeman that he just spent a lot of time there, he knew it would endanger Margot and her family if he were to stay put. So reluctantly he moved back to his parents' flat, still spending almost every evening with Margot but returning home every night to sleep.

It wasn't all doom and gloom, however. Heini's self-motivated bartering and wheeling and dealing were going well, so well in fact that he was able to save a little money and buy himself a much-coveted leather jacket. He loved the jacket and valued it as his most prized possession. He'd recently met a man who was selling alcohol on the black market and Heini had extended his business by doing a deal with him, selling bottles from a suitcase in a discreet spot on the street. There was no shortage of takers, alcohol being a last vestige of pleasure for many.

The nightly bombings of Berlin increased in 1941, and the Bernsteins were often woken by sirens and twice a night had to pull more clothes on and rush out in the dark to the nearest cellar. Any glimmer of pride that the Bernsteins might have felt that their country was winning the war – having invaded both Yugoslavia and Greece by April – was offset by the constant and demoralising propaganda that Jews were criminals and subhumans who'd caused Germany's decline after the First World War. In December that year the Bernsteins learnt from their radio that the US had entered the war against Germany. It added to their feeling they were under siege. It was hard to know what to feel about the war when every day felt like their own personal battle for survival.

Heini was concerned for his great friend Gerhard the Mouse, who was serving with the army somewhere and went to visit his parents to see if they had news of him. He was relieved to hear that they'd received a letter from him – so he was still alive – but restrictions meant he could not disclose

MISCHLINGE

where he was. Heini could still make no sense of his own rating as 'fit for service', and wondered if he'd soon be called up.

In January 1942, at a villa on Lake Wannsee, a beautiful rural idyll on the outskirts of Berlin, where the Bernsteins had often enjoyed summer picnics – Reinhard Heydrich, Adolf Eichmann and other senior Nazi officials planned in detail the mass murder of millions of Jewish men, women and children from all across Europe. This secret plan was codenamed the 'Final Solution'. Existing labour and concentration camps, they decreed, would now become extermination camps, and new death camps would be built to facilitate human slaughter on a never-before-seen industrial scale. These Nazis were highly educated men – eight held doctoral degrees – yet they all enthusiastically sat around over lavish meals and cigars to work out the best ways to eliminate a target of 11 million men, women and children.

Although the Bernsteins were ignorant of these horrific plans being drawn up just a short distance from their home, a new wave of anti-Jewish laws soon had an immediate impact on their lives. In September that same year, rations assigned to Jews were drastically reduced to starvation level, and Jews were no longer to be given coupons to buy meat, milk or eggs. Along with the rigorous enforcement of these new laws came a decree that breaking them could mean a spell of detention at a forced-labour camp, or worse.

As the war continued, Jews and *Mischlinge ersten Grades*, who were treated as Jews, saw their rations reduced further, as were the time periods in which they could shop and the stores they could use. If a ration book had 'J' for 'Jude' stamped on the front, the shopper had a very poor choice.

THE FINAL SOLUTION

Erna and sometimes Edie queued at the town hall once a month to collect all the family's rations, and when Erna presented these between four and five o'clock in the afternoon there wasn't much remaining in the shops, and what was left was often not very appetising.

Thankfully, as Heini observed, there were many Berliners who couldn't care less what your religion or surname was, and so when Erna walked into the butcher and the greengrocer she was welcomed as a regular, well-liked customer, not a pariah. Knowing of her situation, the butcher and the greengrocer would often keep a little something for her under the counter. This small act of kindness could have ended violently for the shopkeeper and mother and daughter.

Erna and Edie would have to wait quietly out of the way until there was no one else in the shop and then they'd slip her what they'd saved. These shopkeepers placed themselves at great risk in doing so, as breaking the law no longer meant a fine or imprisonment – if witnessed by one of the more violent patrols, they risked being beaten or even shot for this petty crime. But their humanity and decency somehow transcended their fears, and such kindness and everyday bravery warmed Erna and Edie's hearts, as well as filling the family's empty tummies. No wonder the two women were on edge most of the time when out and about, wondering if people were watching them and were going to tell tales.

It was early January 1943 when Heini fell ill with a bug. He got a sick note from his doctor to excuse him from work and let him recover at home, and a couple of days later he felt well enough to meet his friend Hans in a billiard room above a café to do a little wheeling and dealing with a man they knew. Two envelopes – one with money, the other with food coupons – changed hands. Flushed with some cash, the pair of them went out for the rest of the evening and Heini didn't return home until the early hours.

'It was 3 a.m.,' he recalled, 'and I hadn't been long in bed when there was a loud commotion at the door. I heard mum go to answer it, and my first thought was that they had come for my father again. Three Gestapo men then stormed into my bedroom, shouting, "Get up, get dressed and hurry up. You're coming with us."

'My dear mum was protesting that there must have been a dreadful mistake because her son had done nothing wrong, while Edie just looked on, speechless and terrified. But they didn't bother to reply.'

Left alone, Erna, Edie and Sigi were all reeling from what had just occurred, and there was no thought of returning to bed despite the hour and the perishing cold. They sat around the kitchen table, Erna comforting Edie as best she could. When the shock started to subside, Sigi and Erna speculated about where their son might have been taken. Erna told her husband that she was the only one who could go and find out, because as a Jew he was banned from all public buildings. She would go first thing in the morning. So they retreated to bed, but not much sleep was had that night.

'I was extremely scared,' Heini remembered, 'as I was marched at pace through the dark streets to the local station, where with several others I was ordered to face the wall. We were searched from head to foot, then told to turn around and hand over our identity cards. I also handed over my call-up papers.

'In the early hours of 9 January 1943 I was taken at great speed to the local police station on Magazinstrasse where I had to hand over my service book and identity card, and then about 14 of us were taken to the police headquarters on Alexanderplatz. Amid a lot of shouting, we were all divided up and thrown into large cells with several other men already in them. I was utterly bewildered and confused, and I didn't have the slightest idea why I had been arrested. I knew in a heartbeat that I was in terrible trouble – I knew my identity papers, service card and medical records were in order, and I'd had a legitimate sick note for being off work. Of course, anyone might have reported me for the black-market activity that night, but then why wasn't I arrested there and then? I could only sit there, plagued by the uncertainty.'

There were lots of noises and movements inside and outside Heini's cell, and as the days ticked by Heini became aware of several other people in the same position as him, sitting in the holding cells. He could only listen as names were called out for interrogation, doors slammed shut and orders shouted that people were to come and go or take their food. He was astute enough to observe that none of his fellow prisoners confided in each other while in police custody. People spoke only briefly, and then only when it was absolutely necessary. After four days waiting and wondering why he'd been arrested, it was his turn to be interrogated.

A policeman led him through a metal gate, which was sharply slammed shut behind him, into a special department inside the headquarters used by the Gestapo. A man in civilian clothes sat behind a desk in a completely bare room. He told Heini to empty his pockets and then sit down opposite him.

'Why didn't you go to work?' he barked, and when Heini handed him his illness certificate, he took it, gave it a brief glance, then tore it into pieces. 'You won't be needing that anymore,' he said. 'Now, what type of Jew are you?'

'I'm a *Mischling*,' replied Heini. 'I'm Protestant and I've got a fit-for-service record.'

'So, you're a Jew then, after all', the man said, and went on to insult and abuse Heini, ranting and raving about 'the inferior Jew'.

Heini kept his hands on the table as he'd been instructed, summoning all the courage he had to remain calm. 'All of a sudden, the interrogator grabbed my hand and thrust it hard backwards so that my engagement ring stabbed me in the eye'.

'Why do you have an engagement ring?' he shouted.

Starting to get angry now, Heini told him the truth – that he was engaged to a local girl. The interrogator demanded Margot's address and wrote it down, then a vitriolic outburst about Jews and non-Jews being together spewed from his mouth, before he repeatedly struck Heini across the face with his ruler. He ordered him to take off his engagement ring and put it on the table along with his watch, his wallet with various precious photos in it and the key to his flat. All of these, he told him, were being confiscated. Then he was taken back to another holding cell.

At this point Heini realised he wasn't going to be released and lost any of the self-confidence he'd had on entering the building. The torn-up illness certificate – his proof – had gone, and it suddenly dawned on him that the company he worked for had most likely had a hand in all of this. Only his employer knew he hadn't been at work. Heini spent a miserable night thinking about Margot and how alarmed his family were going to be at his continued absence. His

THE FINAL SOLUTION

despair grew as he realised he had no way of contacting them.

The following day he was transferred to a collection point in Grosse Hamburger Strasse, previously a Jewish old people's home, and started the process of waiting all over again. He wondered if he'd be put on trial for getting engaged to a non-Jew and be sent to prison. Perhaps his grandparents and others that were taken had been in this same place. Perhaps like him they weren't allowed to write to anyone outside. Gerhard had told him of a Jewish lady in his block who'd been taken away. Later, she'd sent a card from Theresienstadt but then was never heard of again. Depressed and uninterested in the other inmates around him, Heini just ran over things in his head and waited to hear about his trial.

Back at the flat, Erna and Sigi were overcome by an ever-growing sense of dread. Surely things could only get worse? Erna knew there was no way she could keep her husband or her children safe, but she wouldn't stop trying. Once again, she forbade Edie to leave the house except to go to work, and after some discreet but fruitless enquiries about where Heini might have been taken, decided she would be endangering them all if she persisted. She returned home, utterly deflated.

When Heini didn't turn up at Margot's home as he usually did, she went to see his parents and was horrified to hear of his late-night arrest. As the days passed and no news came, their anxiety grew. So when Margot received a letter in the post summoning her to police headquarters, she dashed off to the Bernsteins. Edie said she'd like to go with Margot for moral support, and the pair headed off, filled with dread at entering the place. Margot showed her official summons and was taken straight to another room. Edie had planned just to wait for Margot, but she was immediately questioned and asked *why* exactly she was there. Having explained she was just keeping her friend company, she was escorted to a small room where Margot was sitting opposite an official.

Neither girl had any idea why, but it was clear they were both now going to be interrogated – and they were terrified. The intimidating official immediately subjected Margot to a highly personal and intrusive interrogation, along the same lines as the insulting questions that Heini had been asked. Was she having a sexual relationship with a Jew? Did she know her fiancé was a Jew? Completely overawed and frightened, she said she didn't know that Heini was Jewish, at which point the officer demanded that she take off her engagement ring and declare herself no longer engaged. Margot amazed herself by doing just that, quickly stuffing the ring in her bag, and as she squirmed in her seat just wanting the interview to end, the official turned his attention to Edie.

She was asked about any boyfriends – were they Jewish or Aryan? Edie was shocked but forewarned by what she'd just heard, answering truthfully that she was only 15 and had never had one.

Edie and Margot reached out and clasped each other's hands under the table, as both felt increasingly threatened and scared at what might happen next. When the Gestapo man had finished writing things down, he stood up and told them they could leave. They hadn't yet dared ask about Heini, but could hardly get out of the door quickly enough. When they got back to the Bernsteins, neither could say how long they'd been questioned, so shaken and hurt were they both by their ordeal. They felt vulnerable and very sad that

THE FINAL SOLUTION

they weren't any wiser about Heini's fate, with no idea whether he was in the cells in the same building.

Waiting to hear what had happened to their beloved Heini was torture, but although they longed for news, they also feared the dreaded knock on the front door. So when Sigi, not long afterwards, opened their door and saw it was just a neighbour, he felt sure it must be something innocuous. But the man had come to tell him that he'd seen his brother Georg being led away by the Nazis, along with his wife Susi, their little daughter Anita, Sigi's sister Lotte and her husband Heinz. All five had been bundled into a van outside their home in Schönhauser Allee. No explanation had been given and no one knew where they'd been taken.

Sigi was wrenched apart by guilt. The very worst had happened. His elder brother Georg, just 47 years old, who had appealed to him for help, had now been taken. Erna tried to soothe both him and Edie, who was similarly distraught for Anita. But what hope was there of mercy from such men? All three felt only worry and dread about what might be happening to their much-loved son and brother Heini, and perhaps to them next.

That winter had very short, dark days and long nights for all of them as they waited and waited, with only hope – and each other – to rely on.

6

IMPRISONMENT

A week after being interrogated, assaulted and held without charge by the Gestapo, Heini was put into the custody of the SS and driven out of Berlin in a police van. He had no idea where he was headed, or why.

'I stepped out of the van,' he recalled, 'and immediately saw an austere, bleak labour camp, a place surrounded by a well-lit barbed-wire fence, with armed guards in towers at every corner, and barrack blocks and a drill square in the centre. There wasn't a tree or a blade of grass in sight.'

The sign outside the complex identified it as Wuhlheide, one of the brutal *Arbeitserziehungslager* (AEL or workers' educational camps) that the Nazis had built across Germany and the occupied territories, filling them with prisoners of war, political opponents, resistance agitators, distrusted foreigners and the racial groups they wished to wipe out. These AEL camps were run by the Gestapo with the express purpose of providing cheap labour for the Reich's war effort, and to subjugate, humiliate and punish the incarcerated men. SS and Gestapo chief Ernst Kaltenbrunner, would later describe the camps as 'more severe than concentration camps. This is necessary in order to achieve the intended goal.'

Once he'd entered the camp, Heini was left reeling as he tried to take it all in. 'One of the gun-toting guards barked at us to stand against a wall with a group of newly arrived inmates. The first thing I noticed was that most of us didn't even shave as we were all so young. Some were German, some Polish and one man was Greek.

'"Bernstein," said one of the guards. "Are you a Jew?"

'"No," I replied. I felt sure I had nothing to lose and everything to gain by hiding my *Mischling* classification; perhaps these other young men were political prisoners and would fare better than Jews or *Mischlinge*.'

Heini was hustled into a larger group of men, speaking various languages, into what turned out to be a disinfection room. There they were all stripped of their clothes – Heini had to hand over his beloved leather jacket, which each of the guards were eyeing up and clearly wanted to keep for themselves. Then they were deloused, disinfected and given stiff two-piece grey work suits with a white vertical line on the back of the jacket, as well as underwear, wooden boots and a cap.

The accommodation block did not look welcoming. Nine bunk beds, each with a straw mattress, were to be shared by 18 men. The washing conditions were cramped and unhygienic; the only source of warmth was a small oven, the only source of light, a dim bulb, which gave out just enough light to see when blackout came. Heini got little sleep on his first night at the camp, as sharing a huge room with strangers

IMPRISONMENT

unnerved him; what crimes had landed them there and what would tomorrow hold?

Over the next few days he explored the site to see what the other buildings contained. The administration block near the entrance housed the SS command post, the guards, medical room and sick bay, food and ammunitions store, as well as the 'punishment' room and toilets. In the stone building next to the disinfection room was a laundry and a uniform store.

Heini's start at the Wuhlheide labour camp in January 1943 coincided with the worst of winter. The very next day, an SS officer appeared and sent the youngsters out to work a 12-hour shift in temperatures of $-10°C$, where they were forced to do tough physical work in clothing that offered little warmth or protection. 'We were woken at 6 a.m. that day – and every day apart from Sunday – by the banging of an iron pipe in the block's corridor,' he said. 'After a quick splash of water on my face, we'd be called by whistle to assemble in the drill square for the morning roll call.

'Then an SS officer would sort out the 12 working parties and announce the plans for the day. Divided into working parties of 25, an armed guard escorted us all to the track and then watched over us as we worked in the cold winter temperatures building stretches of the new dual-track S-Bahn line of the German Reich Railway between Mahlsdorf and Strausberg.

'The shifts were long and dull,' he recalled, 'and sometimes we just stood around waiting, freezing in the cold, while at other times we had to work flat out, forced to put our backs into digging even in rain and snow. Cramming the ballast under the sills of the tracks was a horrifically tough job,

MISCHLINGE

which all us detainees absolutely dreaded. Lunch provided little comfort, as a sloppy helping of warmish cabbage, potato or barley soup was hardly nourishing. And the way we had to eat this meagre tasteless meal from a rough bowl and spoon we had to keep tied around our waists made the meal just another act of humiliation and subjugation. At the end of the day, all we could do was flop onto the hard floor of the goods wagon to rest a little before our walk back to the barracks in the half-light, then assemble for evening roll call, standing on the camp's drill square.'

At last, back in their barracks, the inmates all had tasks to complete before they were allowed to eat or sleep. A rota on the wall allocated the daily jobs of fetching water and fuel, and doing the cleaning. Only when these chores were done were they allowed to eat together in the cramped, dimly lit room. The oldest detainee in each room was responsible for maintaining order, receiving the cold rations and distributing them. Each prisoner received 400g of bread, 50g of salami and 20g of margarine in total for their breakfast and evening meal, along with a coffee substitute made of malt and barley. They wolfed it down before falling onto their straw mattress and hauling a sheet over their tired and weakened bodies.

On cold nights everyone slept in their clothes, but if it had been warm enough to take them off, Heini would get up and put yesterday's sweat-laden clothes back on again. Clothing was only collected and washed once a week, the two bedsheets much less often. As the weather warmed up, working outside became a little less unpleasant, but many of the men got lice and Heini's bedding was infested with bedbugs and fleas, making sleep more of a torment than a rest. It was

IMPRISONMENT

a grim existence, and it took all of Heini's reserves to haul himself out of bed each morning.

'The work was like torture to begin with,' remembered Heini, 'and I felt flattened by it. It took a long time to get used to it, and then I felt like a slave in a monotonous routine. I hated the filthy conditions we were forced to live in and the number of us using one latrine made it unspeakable.'

As each day passed, despite Heini realising that the back-breaking work, the appalling food and vile bedding were weakening his body, he was determined not to let them weaken his strength of mind. He began to think how he might improve his situation, to watch out for any opportunity not to let the regime beat him.

Heini was initially reluctant to talk openly to others in his work group because he was the only German. His 24 workmates were either Polish or Soviet, making it hard to talk to them or overhear what they were saying, so it was all but impossible to learn anything about the majority of them and discover why they were in the camp. Not only that – he was also reluctant to trust their stories of what brought them there, as well as being worried about what they might think of him. Surely, as a German not conscripted into the army, they might imagine he was a criminal.

After a few weeks, however, Heini relaxed his caution because of what he saw. As the only German-speaker in his detail he'd been made the go-between for the railway staff bosses and the detainees, and this had meant getting to know them all a little. Over the days and weeks working alongside them, Heini discovered these foreigners were mostly decent men with a sense of fairness and comradeship that he came to admire. And to his surprise they were kind to him. Heini remembered his pal Gerhard the Mouse often teasing him that he was a charmer with people. Perhaps he was right. A bond was certainly forming between the men on his detail, who, despite their different nationalities, all shared the same arduous days and tormented nights.

Day in, day out, Heini and his detail worked on the railways tracks in all weathers. At 19, he was fit and used to working hard, but the job and the long hours were energy-sapping and on a totally different level to anything he'd previously experienced. The lack of respect or care made him feel joyless and broken, and the camp commandant was a law unto himself – there was no court of appeal, so all the inmates could do was obey. After a few months, Heini had to admit to himself, he was becoming strangely accustomed to the exhausting, dreary drudgery of his daily life.

One guard, who went by the name of Sergeant Franke, was charged with watching over Heini and his working party: giving orders, maintaining discipline and monitoring the progress of the work details. He carried a rifle, binoculars and a pea-whistle that he would blow if any of the men strayed too far from where they were meant to be. As Heini spent every day working close to Franke, chatting with him over his cigarette break, he soon formed the view that he seemed half-decent and fair in his dealings. Heini discovered he was also a Berliner and almost twice his age, at 35 years old. After a few more chats about their home city, Heini eventually plucked up the courage to ask him exactly where they were, even daring to enquire if he could tell his parents his current location.

What happened next stunned Heini. The sergeant gave him a stamped postcard and pencil so he could write his parents

IMPRISONMENT

a 'sign of life'. He even suggested sketching his workplace on the card and offered to post it for him. This act of kindness was so unexpected and so different from his previous experiences, that at first he didn't think he'd heard Franke correctly. He paused and took a moment to catch his breath before turning and thanking him.

About a month later, as Heini was working on the stretch of railway track near Mahlsdorf, he heard someone calling his name. He looked up and thought he was hallucinating, but no. There, coming towards him, were his mother and Sergeant Franke. Heini had no idea he'd be allowed a visitor in a labour camp and was so overcome that he had to take a moment to compose himself.

'Mum was standing on a raised platform above where we worked, and Sergeant Franke beckoned me and said I could talk to her for a short time. She'd brought something for me to eat and drink, which I soon polished off as I was so hungry and thirsty. I couldn't properly express how good it was to see her.

'My first question was how were Margot, Edie and my father? I was relieved to hear they were all well, and still in the city. Mum's face looked most forlorn, and she kept asking why I'd lost so much weight. Wasn't I eating? I only gave scant answers to her questions about the camp: the conditions, the food and my feelings. I just didn't want her to worry. So I asked about our street, whether there was any war damage and how she was managing on the meagre rations.

'As Franke signalled the end of our reunion, Mum handed him some cigarettes as a thank you, and he told her she could visit again in a while. I seized the moment and asked her to bring some things from home, chiefly underwear and long,

MISCHLINGE

warm socks that would provide some comfort under my rough and itchy work uniform. Her smile lit up the railway siding as she walked away.

'Mum's visit and the thought that she would come again totally cheered me up. I thanked Sergeant Franke, and for days I could only marvel at my mum's strength and courage to cross the city in wartime and dare to visit me in this fearful place.'

After an emotional goodbye, Erna made her way back home, trying to make sense of Heini's situation. She took some comfort in seeing for herself that her son seemed capable enough to manage the circumstances he found himself in, but she'd not expected him to look so terribly thin.

For her part, Erna hadn't burdened her son with the worsening situation back in the city, where Allied bombing raids and the targeting of Aryan wives and husbands to give up their Jewish partners were ramping up tensions for the Bernsteins. Heini knew nothing of the wider world news or Joseph Goebbels's chilling proclamation calling for Berlin to be made *judenrein* – free of Jews. On 27 February 1943 the Gestapo launched a massive and brutal operation of widespread violence to make that happen. They called it the *Grosse Fabrik-Aktion* (Great Factory Action), during which groups of armed Gestapo were seen jumping out of trucks and literally rounding up anyone with a yellow star where they worked or on the streets. Young and old, men, women and children – around 10,000 in all – were chased, captured, put into trucks and transported out of the capital.

Rumours of atrocities happening to Jews who had been deported were now rife. This violent round-up to make Berlin

IMPRISONMENT

judenrein was so well publicised before it happened that hiding seemed the only option to many, and hundreds of Berliners did precisely that. But hiding, or becoming an '*U-Boot*', as it became known, like submarines disappearing from sight, was fraught with danger. It meant not just leaving family and home behind but your all-important ration card, which meant no food supply. It meant placing yourself entirely at the mercy of those you trusted – to help you, to feed you and bring you essentials, and to keep your secret.

Sigi had become increasingly gloomy in recent weeks and thought it inevitable that he'd be seized by the marauding Gestapo. He wasn't sleeping well, and in the early hours one morning he told Erna he'd made his mind up to hide. He turned to his good friend Otto Stiller, who owned the pub near their home in which Sigi had spent a great deal of time. The building had a sizeable cellar, where Otto – with Sigi's help in earlier days – used to distil the alcoholic spirit called 'schnapps'. To Sigi's huge relief he agreed that his friend could take refuge and hide there. Erna and Sigi waited for Edie to go to bed, and after he'd kissed his daughter goodnight, Sigi packed a very few things in a small bag in preparation for his departure and his future life as an *U-Boot*. When he said goodbye to Erna they agreed they would tell no one of their plan – only they and Otto would know. Erna said she'd tell Edie her father was working away, she could not be put in any danger by knowing the secret.

Arriving at the corner pub under cover of darkness, Sigi had risked being caught out during the blackout curfew. Quickly taking his last breath of fresh air, and with his few clothes and a small food store, he descended into the basement for what was to become a fearful and desperately lonely existence.

Erna tried to see the humour in the fact that she'd so often wished that Sigi didn't go to the pub and instead came straight home to her. Now she could only be grateful to the place, as well as to its owner who had allowed her husband sanctuary there. She would miss him desperately and dreaded being alone, with Edie to protect. But loving him meant wanting to keep him safe. He'd given up so much because he loved her; now it was her turn to give him up for his own safety.

She only allowed herself very occasional visits for fear of giving his presence away, saving any food she could – titbits of this and that – from her rations to give to him. Secrecy was paramount, as the Nazis offered rewards for those willing to betray people's hideaways.

So Sigi remained all on his own, often for months on end. He found the absence of natural light down in the cellar as tough to tolerate as the solitude. Was it day or night? Was it sunny or raining? When he awoke, was it morning or the middle of the night? There was simply no way of knowing. Living in the dark, damp cellar made Sigi cough, and the fear of being heard made him stifle himself with his blanket.

Time hung heavy and Sigi was grateful for his friend Otto's request that he continue to make schnapps. Sigi resolved to stick to routine as much as possible and spent a bit of time keeping his space clean and tidy in a way he'd never done at home. First thing, he tidied his sleeping corner, then washed as best he could before either making some schnapps or moving little barrels and boxes from one place to another in often pointless tasks just to keep sane and moving for a while.

IMPRISONMENT

In the late afternoon – or what he imagined was such – he would reward himself by sitting down with the pack of cards he'd brought with him and a glass of beer or schnapps that hopefully would help him sleep till morning, although he was always careful not to drink too much and lose his wits.

Of course, those vanishingly rare days when either his wife or Otto crept down the stairs were the best. Then Sigi felt less fearful and vulnerable, as he was no longer alone.

Erna planned to visit Heini in Wuhlheide again but not to share his father's secret – the risk of anyone discovering his hiding place was far too great. Without Sigi and Heini's meagre earnings or rations, Erna was finding it harder than ever to feed herself and Edie, let alone trying to bring food to Heini or sneak down to Sigi. The Jewish Aid food parcels that had been such a blessing and saved them from hunger many times had now stopped. Jewish charity organisations had all been disbanded, as most of the staff from the central Reich Association of Jews in Germany had been deported to Theresienstadt, and others, including the local charities who'd long supported their communities, were now closed. Erna had only their two rations, the tiny amount she could earn sewing and Edie's small apprentice's wage to pay for food and heating.

Buoyed by his mother's visit and news of his family, Heini was opening up a little to some of the other inmates, but he remained exceptionally wary, a trait that had served him well so far. One afternoon he bumped into another German detainee, whom he recognised from their arrest. His name was Beck and he told Heini what a tough time he was having in the Soviet barracks, where conditions were worse than elsewhere and they all slept on a bare-wire bed with no mattress and just one thin covering. Heini asked him why he thought he'd been singled out as the only German to be put in the Soviet barracks, and was shocked when he heard Beck's answer. 'I told them I was a *Mischling*,' he said. Heini's by now well-developed sense of caution stopped him telling Beck he was also a *Mischling*. Although part of him wanted to share his secret, he couldn't run the risk of being punished for lying or worse.

When Erna next turned up at Heini's Wuhlheide work detail, Sergeant Franke called her over, thanked her for the cigarettes she'd brought him again and then watched as she gave her son underwear, long socks, a pullover and his old sturdy boots to replace those wooden shoes he was wearing, as well as all the bits and pieces of food she could spare. Once more, she wasn't allowed to stay long and both kept the chat light, but Erna's visit gave her son more than could be counted on a clock. Emboldened by her success, without consulting Heini, Erna asked Franke if she could send someone else next time to visit her son. And just a few weeks later, Heini was thrilled to see Margot arrive at the camp with food from her rations and more of his warm clothes. He was grateful to Franke for keeping his distance so he could steal a kiss and thank her for her visit, and he thanked him after she had left. Her visit meant a great deal to him – she was looking as pretty and full of fun as ever; he just hoped his appearance wasn't too off-putting to her. It was such a distraction to hear news of home, her family and their friends.

But as the weeks turned to months, the sheer strain of daily hard labour was showing on the previously fit, teenage Heini and all the other young men working alongside him. Heini

IMPRISONMENT

had developed painful wounds on both of his hands and had frostbitten feet. One open wound on his hand was deteriorating and swelling so badly that he was allowed to see the camp doctor, a middle-aged Greek man who spoke German and wore some kind of flying uniform rather than a white coat. He diagnosed phlegmon, an infected swelling on and under the skin, and put some cream on it. Ideally, he told Heini, he needed to rest his hand, but camp rules stated that if you could stand you could work, so there was no prospect of not returning to the dismal toil outside on the train tracks. As Heini struggled to protect his hand and keep his wound clean, respite came when dysentery broke out across the camp and the camp commandant was forced to stop all work and impose quarantine. This was a huge relief to all the Wuhlheide inmates as it meant confinement to barracks, giving them a rest from the work and the bitterly cold weather. For Heini it meant time for his hand to heal.

At first Heini and his detail were relieved to avoid the backbreaking work outside on the track, but the dreariness of being confined to their dim, stifling dormitories soon began to cause them emotional, then mental problems. The lack of fresh air, the more frequent air raids overhead and the lack of news from the outside world made them increasingly anxious, for their families, their friends and their homes. Lights were on permanently, only turned off completely when an air raid was in progress. Despite being close to Berlin, they felt entirely cut off from the world. To Heini it was if the world and the war did not exist.

Although Heini and his workmates had found a way to work together on the tracks, their different nationalities, very different backgrounds and lack of a common language meant that they were not a cohesive group. Cooped up together in quarantine, without any way to pass the time or take their minds off the squalor they lived in, exacerbated suspicions and tensions between them and fuelled irritability and mistrust.

Having no privacy or quiet time was the worst of it for Heini. He'd picked up a few words of Russian so that he could communicate at work, but being surrounded by Russian and Polish speakers all day and night and never speaking his own language was starting to get to him. Time and again he asked himself who these men around him were – many were surely prisoners of war, but might some be petty criminals or political opponents of the Nazis? It was most disconcerting to have no idea if any of them posed a threat nor know what their motivations were. It was isolating not to trust and share, but his caution held him back. After two weeks of quarantine, the tortuous claustrophobia made him yearn to get out in the open air again, despite the cold temperatures and the thought of unremittingly harsh physical labour.

But spring was to bring with it some small pleasures. One morning after a nocturnal air raid the men were back working on the embankment when Heini noticed bits of paper scattered around the place. Taking a closer look, he couldn't believe what he saw – cigarette and food ration cards blowing around in the wind. He'd no idea how they had got there – perhaps they'd fallen from a plane or been blown out from a freight train – but he knew they were a heaven-sent gift.

Sergeant Franke had seen them too, and after checking to see they were real, he suggested that Heini collect them and

IMPRISONMENT

then take them all into the nearby village and exchange them for cigarettes.

'Our conversation was quite funny,' Heini recorded. 'Franke said, "I'm bursting with curiosity to know if it would work. I'd really like to go, but then I'd have to leave you my gun – so that wouldn't work. When I come back I might find someone else. So that's no good. You should take off your camp prisoner's jacket, put it over your arm, roll up your sleeves and walk into the village."

'Together with the boots my mum had brought me, I now looked more like one of the railway workers we worked alongside than a labour camp inmate. Franke gave me just five of the cards that had fallen from the skies, a bag and 20 Reichsmarks, and pointed the way to the nearby village of Mahlsdorf, where I was to exchange them for cigarettes.

'Despite our different positions in the camp I'd established some kind of trust with Franke by chatting about our families and our neighbourhoods. We never talked of politics or religion. I'd tried to show myself as decent and Franke showed no signs of being a fervent Nazi.'

Heini had always been quick-witted and daring, and he wasn't going to pass up on this opportunity. With all the nerve in the world, he strolled into Mahlsdorf, exchanged the cards for cigarettes and matches, then daringly returned to the camp.

The Soviet inmates had not initially recognised the German ration coupons that had fallen widely across the site as exchangeable for cigarettes and food. Heini explained to his Russian workmate Boris that Sergeant Franke had agreed that if his countryman helped find more coupons, they'd all share the benefits – but it must be their secret.

MISCHLINGE

They immediately set to it, and when they were done, Heini handed out a cigarette to each of them. He was in his element now, his bartering and easy charm on full display. Friendship was being built between them all by collecting the scattered food and cigarette coupons together, sharing the bounty they brought and scrupulously keeping the secret within their detail.

Flushed with Heini's success, Franke, a heavy smoker, sent him back to Mahlsdorf that very afternoon with food ration cards to get bread, lard and sausage. On his return the friendly guard used his knife to divide up the food and sent Heini to share some of it with the other detainees. Heini hadn't forgotten his natural caution and made sure every workmate on the detail understood that not a single cigarette or piece of food could be taken back to the camp and must be enjoyed where they were, as there were frequent spot checks of pockets and regular body searches.

The 'find' of the coupons brought some relief to the bedraggled labourers. They were really pleased by the bonus and delighted when Franke sanctioned Heini to undertake further bold trips into Mahlsdorf to bring back cigarettes and food. Fearful of discovery, Heini made sure he always visited different tobacconists on his forays. And as their food and cigarette supplies increased, they began using the toolshed at their work site – locked by Franke every night – as the secret hiding place for the cigarettes, tobacco, rolling paper and matches.

Alert and inventive as ever, Heini used one of his trips to post a note to his fiancée Margot. He used a scrap of paper and exchanged some food to buy an envelope and a stamp, asking her to bring with her some of the money he'd left at

IMPRISONMENT

her home on her next visit, now he had somewhere to spend it.

Franke soon suggested Heini changed villages to nearby Kaulsdorf to avoid detection. As they only had a month to use the coupons before they became invalid, Heini suggested he send Margot some to buy tobacco elsewhere, and Franke agreed.

If leaving the camp to exchange illegal ration cards in two outside villages wasn't risky enough, Heini soon found another new line of business: the exchanging of cigarettes for potatoes on the nearby embankment. He'd got to know some locals on his trips into town, and when he found out they grew potatoes, together they hatched a plan to cook them in an old bolt barrel. Heini would organise inmates to help and they'd exchange their contraband cigarettes for cooked potatoes. Heini drafted in inmates who had been off sick to help with the peeling and cooking, and they were only too delighted at the chance to have extra food. And all was accomplished with the inclusion and approval of Sergeant Franke, Boris the Russian and all the others on the work detail. After about six weeks, it all came to an end when tobacco supplies had run out, all having either been bartered or smoked.

Heini had once again shown his entrepreneurship, and, not being a smoker, it meant that he'd got to eat more potatoes than most. His Jewish relatives would undoubtedly have said he showed *chutzpah* (Yiddish for extreme self-confidence or audacity).

Spring brought warmer temperatures, but also a lot of rain. And when it rained all day long, team morale plummeted as their clothes got soaked through. They tried hard in the evening to get them half-dry, but with so little heat from the oven, everything in the barracks remained sodden. The whole dormitory lay in a cloud of mist and even the bedclothes became damp. Their clothes would remain soggy for days on end until better weather dried them out.

Heini did have the jumper that Erna had brought, which proved useful to shield him from the cold. But to help alleviate the dampness, the men used cement sacks and old bolt and pin bags from the building site to act as another layer of insulation. But through all of this nobody in charge, not a single guard, ever showed the slightest bit of concern for any of them. When it rained for days on end the reality of their fate became all too clear, and Heini and all his detail were plunged into misery.

One morning, straight after roll call, Heini was told to report to another block and change into his civilian clothes – he was to leave the camp.

'But no one said where I was being taken, and I was fearful. Was I going to be released? Moved to another camp? Be put on trial ? It was wonderful to take off my awful work clothes, and as I put my own clothes back on again I felt ridiculously happy to see my leather jacket and real joy when I put it on again. But after that moment came a jolt of uncertainty and fear. I was a prisoner who had no idea what his sentence was.'

Heini was right to be cautious. This was no drive to freedom. He recognised the streets of Berlin, and when he reached the city centre he was taken into a Gestapo building on Grosse Hamburger Strasse and put straight into a holding cell with a few strangers. Once again, he spent several days waiting and worrying, and he didn't engage with the others

IMPRISONMENT

held in the same cell. As he didn't know why he'd been arrested in the first place, he wondered if he might get out of the place with just a black eye. In a small part of his heart he retained a little hope.

When his name was finally called, Heini was told they were taking him somewhere else. Again, full of hope, he got into the police car, expecting to be driven to freedom and Alexanderplatz.

'When the car stopped and I got out I could not believe I was right back at Wuhlheide. It seemed incredible that I'd been sent somewhere and kept for days in a cell, only to be returned to this same awful place.

'I was taken to the admin block, given a new work suit and told to report to the same barracks, bed and work detail. I was relieved when Sergeant Franke appeared and said he was happy to see me again, but he could offer no explanation, saying such comings and goings happened regularly and whispered that although no one admitted it, the Reich did make mistakes. But I was too low to be hauled up again. I felt utterly dejected and frustrated by the whole episode.

'Franke tried to console me in his way, urging me not to let my head drop and saying he was pleased to see me back, as he didn't like it when detainees he'd got to know came and went. But his words brought me little comfort and I could only think what a peculiar relationship I had with this guard – a kind of strange friendship that had benefited us both. The work party had become bigger and there were 32 of us now. Franke told me he was obliged to blow his whistle in warning if any one of us tried to escape, and that he would then shoot, as there was a penalty of 100 Reichsmarks that would be subtracted from his wages if anyone escaped.'

MISCHLINGE

A few weeks later, Boris the Russian who worked in his detail asked Heini if he would turn a blind eye to just one of their unit escaping. This was a daring, risky request, but Heini thought highly of Boris, so the two of them discussed the plan. Heini agreed to help, advising that the best time and place would be early in the week at around noon near the wood. That was when Sergeant Franke and the railway official worked out the schedule for the week ahead and would be distracted. Heini told Boris that he would manoeuvre himself to the furthest point he could from where the inmate planned to escape, so that if Franke asked him to chase the fugitive he'd have a head start.

Heini hadn't considered escaping, but the request made him wonder if he should seize the opportunity and escape himself. The unfairness of his situation was beginning to obsess him. He still had no idea why he'd been detained. He thought about his secret *Mischling* status sometimes, and it was confusing to him. He carried some element of being Jewish within himself, but he'd only ever had one foot in that camp because of his grandparents, who in turn had rejected his father.

He did think of his grandparents sometimes and his wider Jewish family – he'd grown to love them and had nothing but respect for them, not to mention concern as to where they all were now. Perhaps they were detained in a place like he was? He'd got to know them at those lovely Friday-night dinners, and often remembered their kindness after his confirmation and their groaning Sabbath supper table. But then again, he'd also had a Christian upbringing, been christened and confirmed, and he'd celebrated Christmas ever since he was born. The memory of hiding the family

IMPRISONMENT

Christmas tree when the Jewish charity delivered their food parcels still made him smile. None of it made sense to him and he certainly had no deep sense of belonging to either religion. He was just himself.

And now his life was exceedingly hard as a prisoner, having to do back-breaking work every day without earning a single pfennig. Yet next to him and his work party, strong young men employed by the railway received a good wage for only an eight-and-a-half-hour day, a half-day on Saturday and all of Sunday off. They were also free to go home to their families and eat as they chose. Heini, on the other hand, was not free, perpetually hungry and treated appallingly. He was tormented by all these unresolved thoughts.

On the Monday of the planned escape, when most of the men were working on the track, some of that same resentment was still bubbling up at the back of Heini's mind as he saw the prospective escapee take up a position farthest away from both him and the sergeant.

Heini was tense as he awaited the arrival of the railway official, the Russian's signal to make a break for it. The man came as usual, and while he and Sergeant Franke were deep in conversation the escapee slipped away. After a while Franke did a head count and noticed they were a man down. Initially he was not suspicious, as none of the men had ever previously tried to escape from their work party. He asked the men to look in between bushes or boulders to see whether the missing detainee had simply collapsed, either from ill health or sheer exhaustion.

But then, from his vantage point on the embankment, Franke looked into the distance with his binoculars, spotted the escapee, and called out to Heini – his trusted ally on account of the shopping trips – and ordered him to run after the escapee and bring him back.

Everything had gone to plan right up to this moment. Heini's leather boots meant he could run much faster than the escapee in his wooden boots. He very quickly got within shouting distance of the Russian in the wood, thankfully well out of sight from Franke on the embankment. He called out that everything was OK and that he should head for his destination quickly. And in a spur of the moment decision Heini decided to escape too.

Heini ran off in a different direction from the Russian and headed to the S-Bahn back to Mahlsdorf. He so wanted to go home and see how his family and fiancée were doing. At the station in Mahlsdorf he swapped a cigarette that his mother had given him from her tobacco ration for a train ticket and got onto the S-Bahn to Alexanderplatz.

Erna was overwhelmed when she opened the door and saw Heini standing there, but her marvellous flood of relief was soon replaced by fear when she realised he was wearing his work clothes and had not been officially released but had escaped. Once she'd stopped hugging him, she hurried to put food in front of his skinny frame, then asked him what his plan was and what the consequences might be.

Heini was painfully aware he had no plan and had just acted on instinct, with no thought of the future. So he did not answer his mum, but carried on eating heartily as she broke the news that his father was hiding in the cellar of Otto Stiller's pub and Edie was out at work at Moritz und Kummer. Heini was very upset not to see his sister – he'd missed her –

IMPRISONMENT

and was shocked to hear about his father, but as soon as he'd cleared his plate he rushed off to see Margot.

He was over the moon to find her at her home, but deeply uncomfortable when she told him about how she and Edie had been interrogated in the Gestapo HQ. It hadn't seemed fair to tell him while he was in that awful camp, but now she felt she must warn him of the danger they'd be in if they were seen together.

Heini's thoughts turned to who in the city might offer him food and a bed. According to Margot, Gerhard was now serving in a tank regiment and his other good friend Hans was at work, so both would be unable to help him. He quickly realised that there was in fact no one he could trust to ask for help. 'I can't feed myself without a ration card,' he said to himself, 'and I would always be dependent on my mother or Margot to help me get by. That would put them in real danger, and I won't do that.'

It was with a heavy heart that Heini decided to go back to Wuhlheide. Margot insisted on going with him, and they tried to make the most of their short time together as they walked to the edge of the deciduous woods that hid the camp. Full of fear and anticipation at what would await him, they said their goodbyes as twilight descended on the wood. Margot wanted to walk with him to the perimeter of the camp, making him feel proud of her loyalty and pluck, but he insisted it was too isolated and dark for her to make her way to the camp and back again. They kissed goodbye and as he watched her disappear back towards the city, he picked his way through the shadowy wood along the dirt track. Heini felt more and more fearful about what explanation he might give the guards when he reached the camp. What reason

MISCHLINGE

could he give for his long absence and failed attempt to catch the escapee?

At about 10 p.m. he saw the lights of the camp, and after he approached the guard on watch, he was marched straight to the camp commandant.

'I didn't find the escaped detainee,' Heini said, trying to look disappointed with himself. 'I hoped to be able to catch up with him and went as far as I could, then I got a lift back with a lorry driver.'

'Don't lie and tell fairy tales,' shouted the commandant. 'We know you visited your fiancée. But don't think that I'd have been in mourning if you hadn't come back. I'd have acquired a nice leather jacket.'

Heini felt sick to his stomach at the commandant's words. Did they really know that he'd visited Margot? He suddenly felt scared stiff to think what the repercussions of his little escapade might be. As the commandant dismissed him, telling him to report back in the morning to hear what his punishment was going to be, his own thoughts of what lay ahead terrified him.

He had so little hope and optimism left. He was worried about everyone who mattered to him – his mother and sister Edie home alone, and his fiancée Margot. Had he put them all at greater risk? And how safe was his father Sigi hiding all on his own in a miserable cellar? There was still no news of the Jewish half of his family, and what of his best friend Gerhard fighting somewhere? All these people faced dangers of different, unknowable kinds.

Heini lay in his uncomfortable bunk that night. Sleep evaded him as he reflected on the life he'd returned to, one where he was always hungry, where he felt degraded and

IMPRISONMENT

treated like a slave, with the toughest level of work expected of him but not a single concession that would make life worth living.

He was already leading a pitiful existence, and now some dreadful punishment would be heaped upon it. Back in the dorm, the others laughed at him for being a failed escapee, and while none of them were real friends, it still hurt. Even Sergeant Franke had teased him, saying 'I did not expect to see you again. I've never had that before – I give a detainee a holiday only for him to come running back voluntarily in the evening.'

Heini felt physically and emotionally exhausted, and in the small hours he doubted himself and his decision both to escape and to return. Most of all he felt deeply humiliated and full of dread at what kind of punishment he'd brought upon himself.

7
TORTURE AND KINDNESS

Heini couldn't believe his luck when he wasn't summoned to see the camp commandant the following morning and wasn't punished for his successful escape and single day of freedom. His excuses and explanation had been pathetic and unbelievable, and the commandant had clearly been angry. For weeks afterwards Heini dreaded being dragged out of his barracks and subjected to humiliating questions and physical punishment. But nothing happened.

We'll never know why Heini was spared, but the hard fact was that by this stage of the war the SS were relying heavily on slave labour inside and outside of the camps, following Germany's massive defeat by the Soviets at Stalingrad and the huge loss of life, with half a million young men dead and around a million more injured. *Zwangsarbeiter* (slave labourers) like Heini were now considered central to the war effort, and these men and women now made up almost a quarter of Germany's workforce.

MISCHLINGE

Heini wondered if Sergeant Franke had put in a word for him. It was something to be thankful for as he continued to face more crushingly hard labour and shrinking food rations, leaving him thinner and weaker. Heini had always been cautious about whom to trust, but as time stretched ahead he kept his head down now more than ever, hoping to avoid any unwanted attention from his captors.

After the bitter cold, rain and perpetual damp of winter and the frostbite wounds Heini had developed, the arrival of summer should have been most welcome. But working outside in the summer was sometimes unbearable, the men facing long days working on the tracks with no shade. Heini and his workmates, thinner and weaker from months of heavy work, with no regular supply of water and a poor diet, suffered from sunstroke on a regular basis, many collapsing and passing out entirely. Some days, those still standing had to carry the others back to the barracks. Dysentery once again felled a large number of inmates, and this time many did not return from the sick room, dying in their droves and being swiftly buried, with no ceremony or anyone to mourn them.

Heini did all he could to stay positive, dreaming of a future in which he was reunited with his family and married to Margot. He wondered if his classification as a *Mischling* and not a German had protected him from being sent to the frontline like his friend Gerhard. Heini had no source of news in the labour camp and could not know that by 1943, after so many victories in the early years of the conflict, the tide of war had turned and Germany was now facing military defeat on most fronts.

The bombing of Berlin intensified. Sigi, hiding in the pub cellar, could only hear the explosions and wonder what was going on at ground level, hoping that he wouldn't be trapped beneath the destruction above his head.

Teenage Edie was shocked by the devastation in the capital. It seemed like hell had come to the family's doorstep. In the centre of the city where they lived, very many of the buildings around them – from historic city landmarks to railway tracks and stations, neighbourhood shops and churches, and many of the streets around them – were flattened in the frequent raids.

As a *Mischling*, Edie was still forbidden from entering bomb shelters. She sometimes relied on her mum to rouse her from her bed, and they'd then rush down into a local cellar together. When they emerged back onto the streets, Erna would walk her daughter swiftly past the walking wounded, the crying families and the smouldering buildings to get back to the safety of their home as quickly as possible. Edie had known real fear for so long now, she had almost got used to it: in the cellar she would sometimes close her eyes and think herself back to those happy days she shared with her brother around the Fairy Fountain. But even those memories now brought pain, as she worried how her beloved brother was and how he was coping with the conditions he was being kept in. She thought about him often and just hoped he was safe. Back alone in their flat, mum and daughter's only comfort was each other.

At Wuhlheide, when the sirens wailed to indicate an air raid, the planes streaming overhead were clearly on the flight path to Berlin, but the alarms weren't always a signal for the inmates to take shelter. Instead, the SS sometimes ordered them to go outside and put out nearby fires.

'One Sunday night the all-clear hadn't yet sounded,' recalled Heini, 'when a guard appeared at our barracks and

MISCHLINGE

ordered a few of us to follow him to the outskirts of the camp, where fallen debris had set the area on fire and it had quickly spread. I was told to bring a large ladder from the store, as the fire had spread through the blazing woodland to some detached houses and allotments, which were now ablaze.

'It was only when I heard the heart-wrenching screams of children coming from one blazing house that was billowing with smoke that I looked up and saw two children standing at an attic window. I propped the ladder against the wall, climbed up, smashed the window and pulled the two children from the room, which was virtually filled with smoke. It was the inmates who stepped into the house and shouted for anyone, but we could see or hear no one. Outside we found a smouldering incendiary bomb, which the guard quickly tackled and extinguished. The warning siren had long stopped but there was no sign of any family, so the guard pinned a note on the garden gate explaining that the children could be found at the camp and took the tearful distressed youngsters back with him, with us inmates following on behind.

'I collapsed exhausted onto my hard bunk, but with my lungs full of smoke, combined with the emotion and exertion of the whole experience, I couldn't sleep a wink. I lay awake all night coughing to clear my throat, and thinking about the children and my loved ones in Berlin under even heavier bombardment. Sergeant Franke told us next morning that the children's parents were alive and that they'd been delayed by the air raid. A cancelled train meant they had a very long walk to get home, but they had just collected their children in the early hours. I was relieved for the family,

TORTURE AND KINDNESS

and wondered whether the other inmates and I might be given some sort of reward in extra rations or cigarettes for rescuing the children. Just for a moment I hoped that, but of course no recognition or thank you was forthcoming from anyone.'

Back in Berlin a new threat hung over Sigi Bernstein, still hiding in his local pub cellar, thanks to the bravery of his friend the publican Otto Stiller, who was risking his life in allowing him to take refuge there. The Nazis' *judenfrei* campaign to rid the city of all its Jewish inhabitants had already seen 10,000 arrested at the armament factories where they had been sent to work, but the Gestapo suspected a few thousand were still surviving underground as *U-Boote*, like Sigi.

They formed a new organisation called the Jewish Investigation Office to capture these *U-Boote*, mounting raids across the capital to find them. Their tactics were various and cruel – every time they captured an *U-Boot*, he or she would be offered money or some other inducement to turn them into 'grabbers' or 'catchers', betraying the hiding place of others like them. If that didn't work, they'd be tortured until they revealed their friend or family members' secret hiding place and led the Gestapo there. It was a successful campaign that saw the capture, imprisonment and more often than not the death of hundreds of Jewish *U-Boote*.

Who – or what – led them to find Sigi we do not know. But one January night in 1944 Erna answered a knock at the door with some trepidation, as no one had called at that late hour since the blackout had been imposed. She was delighted to see a neighbour and friend, but after she invited her in, Erna turned cold when the woman told her, 'I have just seen your Sigi pushed onto a lorry with a number of other men, all being abused by the Gestapo.

'I'm so sorry, Erna, I don't know what to say, but I thought I should come and tell you. I recognised him immediately and he wasn't hurt, just shaking a little.'

Erna was absolutely horrified. This was the moment she'd been dreading every day and every long night since she'd been apart from her husband. Her beloved Sigi – they had been separated for what seemed like an eternity, and she thought that being on his own was keeping him safe, but now this. She felt cold and shivery and sick all at once. She'd tried so hard to shield him when the Gestapo pressed her to divorce him. Had it all been for nothing now?

She bombarded her neighbour with questions: Had they arrested anyone else with Sigi? Anyone she knew? Was he dragged out from a building? Had she heard where they might be taking him? But her friend had no answers. She said she'd only seen Sigi manhandled into a truck full of strangers amid a lot of shouting and kerfuffle, and then she'd hurried away herself and knew no more. Erna of course made no mention of the pub, but she thanked her friend for telling her. After giving Erna a hug, her neighbour couldn't wait to leave. They both knew only too well that these were dangerous times.

Erna felt her life had been shattered. First her son had been taken and now her husband. She felt floored and powerless, with no idea of where to turn for help as she had no one she could ask for advice or information. She didn't know anyone Jewish, let alone in the Jewish underground, and clearly the situation was now so dangerous it would be foolish to go around asking just anyone. She knew she could only focus on

TORTURE AND KINDNESS

Edie, and telling her about her father's capture when she came home from work was just awful. Edie was distraught at the news, full of questions that Erna couldn't answer. Edie simply failed to understand why her family were being persecuted for being Jews when she knew none of them had ever even set foot in a synagogue.

Edie felt more fear than anger. And she couldn't help think how lucky her sister Eva was, untouched by the years of persecution the rest of the family had had to live with, safe at her grandmother's home. Eva had been living a normal life. She'd never had to wear the yellow star or eat starvation rations, but then Edie told herself, Eva had never really been a sister.

The only normality Edie had in her life was her job, her apprenticeship, which for three years now had given her freedom from being confined at home, a little money for food and the companionship of girls her own age. Edie really enjoyed working for Moritz und Kummer, the small family printing firm, and was grateful they were still functioning in wartime and providing her with a paid job.

'The company was run by a middle-aged man and his young son-in-law,' she remembers. 'I noticed the older man was some kind of senior Nazi because he sported their gold pin on his lapel, but we saw little of him. For a long time I just fitted in at the printers, did my job, laughed with the girls and went home to my mum. But then the boss's son-in-law started stopping by my work station to talk to me, smiling and winking and paying me unwanted attention.

'I was only 16 and thought him pretty old. I certainly didn't encourage him, but he persisted in seeking me out on the shopfloor. It was embarrassing. But one day, unbeknown to me, the boss noticed his son-in-law's flirting and things started to unravel for me. As owner of the firm, he obviously looked at my employment record, and he then saw that I was a *Mischling ersten Grades*. This "first-class" label defined me as being *not* German or Aryan, because I had two Jewish grandparents, and I was only useful as a worker for the state.

'As a fervent Nazi, the boss decided to solve his family problem by dismissing me without pay and reporting me to the authorities, which I only found out about when a uniformed member of the Gestapo turned up at the printers. All of us girls looked up and wondered why he was there, and I felt my heart fall into my shoes when he marched straight past everyone else and stopped in front of me. I could barely take it in when he told me, "You no longer have a job here. You're going to be a slave labourer, working at the detention camp at Friedrichshain and sleeping in the barracks there. Come with me now."

'I tried to hold myself upright with my shoulders back as I walked towards the door with the Gestapo man. I just turned my head and mouthed goodbye to the girls who had been such good friends to me.

'The guard told me to report for work at Friedrichshain early the following morning and to bring what I needed as I would be sleeping in a barn until Friday, when I would be allowed home for the weekend only.'

Reeling at this bombshell, Edie was shaken and frightened imagining what might lie ahead. What would the work involve? And surely sleeping in a strange new place might expose her to all kinds of dangers. But as she stepped into their flat, Edie resolved not to let her mum see her fear. As ever, Erna faced the situation stoically too, thinking practi-

TORTURE AND KINDNESS

cally to make sure her daughter had warm clothes, sturdy boots and a little food.

By any standards Edie's first day as a slave labourer was terrifying. When several young men wandered into the large and draughty barn in the middle of a field, she was horrified to find, as she looked round, that she was the only woman there – all the others were youngish men. As she listened, she realised they were from other countries, presumably prisoners of war. An elderly German man explained that he was their supervisor, and their job was to go out onto the streets after a bombing raid and clear away the rubble to allow easy access everywhere.

When Edie looked around the huge barn where she was to sleep every night on a pile of hay in the corner, the danger of it all slowly started to sink in. She saw there was no place to bathe or wash properly, except for some shared toilets with bowls and water jugs. That first night she didn't dare sleep in case one of the men approached her. They were sleeping a little distance away, but she avoided all eye contact and was grateful the elderly German supervisor was close by.

Those first days were physically demanding: clambering over uneven ground, bending over and lifting heavy, sharp bits of collapsed buildings and heaving them onto carts with her cold, bare hands. But the nights in the barn were worse. As the only young woman among so many men, Edie lay awake in fear of being attacked. But she soon realised that the men, who'd all been there a long time, posed no threat whatsoever – they were worked so hard during the day that they returned to the barn weak and exhausted. They showed no interest in her whatsoever, and as they all spoke different languages they couldn't even speak to each other.

MISCHLINGE

In this dire situation Edie found something to be grateful for. 'I think I've always been a lucky person,' she says. 'And I was very lucky that our supervisor, the old German gentleman, was not a Nazi but a kind and fair-minded man who looked out for me. One night when many bombs had fallen and the snow lay thick on the ground, as he walked out with the prisoners to the bomb site he told me I could stay behind in the barn all day as long as I hid, so nobody would know he'd let me off. That was a huge risk and a kindness.'

Allied raids on Berlin were becoming more frequent and damage all over the city was extensive, with old landmarks destroyed, big buildings toppled, railway lines and roads blocked, and homes and sometimes whole streets flattened. Half-starved and skinny Edie and the hard-driven prisoners of war had a huge task every day clearing the debris and keeping the roads clear in the plummeting temperatures of a bitter Berlin winter.

'The worst of it was finding dead and dismembered bodies under the debris to pull out,' she recalls, 'and the smell of burning, smouldering flesh that clung to your clothes is something I'll never forget. They were awful days. We had to leave any body parts we found by the side of the road for collection later, but thankfully that didn't happen every day.'

This was dreadful, abhorrent work for a 16-year-old to endure. Alongside the physically horrifying sights and smells that clung to her clothes long after the day's work was completed, there were the lingering mental images of distraught men and women trawling through the wreckage, hoping to find their loved ones alive and salvage some of their possessions.

TORTURE AND KINDNESS

'I could only try to help as some of them knelt in the rubble, clearing it with their hands alongside me. But I had to concentrate on what I was doing as some of the piles were unstable. I just tried to keep myself together and think about returning home to my mum at the weekend.'

Across the city, Christmas was acknowledged inside the Wuhlheide camp by allowing Heini and all the other inmates a day off from hard labour. But before New Year 1944, Heini was called out at roll call and told he was to have a new job and new name with immediate effect.

He wouldn't be called by the name Heini anymore but *Hofhund* (yard dog), and he was no longer answerable to Sergeant Franke as he was now to be a dogsbody for the SS. His punishment for that escape had finally been delivered. His new job was to carry out all camp and yard duties as instructed by them and report to the duty officer. He realised that being officially reduced to an SS dogsbody wasn't just a punishment but another measure to try to rob him of any last vestige of humanity. It would also mean the end of visits from his mother or Margot – no little moments of freedom, no chats and no information about the outside world. Heini tried to use this attempt to crush him to strengthen his resolve. He wouldn't let these bully boys win, he could cope and endure anything, even this. At least there would be less back-breaking physical labour, he thought.

Sergeant Franke told Heini he wasn't at all pleased about the move and wanted him to know that he'd had no say in it. Somehow that helped, as the fact he'd built relationships, even in this place, added to his sense of self-reliance.

MISCHLINGE

As *Hofhund*, his specific duties were to take note at morning roll call of the numbers in each work party and those in the sickbay, along with the number of spare beds. With that information he was to organise the cold food rations under the sarcastic goading of the SS quartermaster, going back and forth to fetch all the bread, sausages and margarine cubes and divide them into very small amounts for each group. A 1,500g loaf of rye bread had to be cut into seven equally sized pieces, the sausage into 25g slices, the margarine into 10g pieces. Once measured out, he would leave 30 buckets, sorted by group, ready to be handed out when the men returned from their day's labour.

At lunchtime Heini had to dish out a thin and foul-tasting soup to the men who were ill. Those recuperating and prescribed rest by the doctor could stay in the dormitory all day and it would be heated. But when they recovered, even just a little, they had to rake and clean the courtyard, drill square and administration block, and, worst of all, clean and disinfect the latrine with lime. There was little comfort to be found in Wuhlheide, and now that Heini was subject to the humiliation of being whistled for like a dog by his Nazi captors, he vowed never to let his emotions show. It was another level of protection for someone who had always erred on the side of caution.

Heini had always seized any opportunity to improve his position: his 'friendship' with Sergeant Franke, his daring trips to the village with the coupons, the potato business he set up, these had all yielded food and privileges that made him fitter and happier, and won him friends. So he remained alert as to what opportunities this new role might yield. He soon learnt that when the SS quartermaster's back was turned

TORTURE AND KINDNESS

or he was called to the telephone, he could grab some scraps of extra food. He treated these like trophies, extra bits and pieces for those who were ill, as well as himself.

The food storeroom also held much better quality supplies for the SS, a considerable cut above the slop the inmates were given, so he would watch it closely, trying to work out what might not be missed. Mostly it was ground rice or rolled oats, but once he managed to get hold of a tin of potted meat. But then the problem was how to enjoy it without being caught. If he ate it and put the tin into the rubbish bins, it would be clearly visible to the SS guards and get him into serious trouble. Even throwing the tin over the fence would most likely get noticed. In the end, tempted as he was, Heini decided it wasn't worth the risk and decided to bury it while out cleaning the latrine. He hoped to retrieve it later, but never got the chance.

'One winter's day the SS camp commandant whistled for me,' he wrote, 'like you would a dog, and ordered me to fetch the water hose and connect it to the tap on the drill square. I wondered why, when it was not far off being frosty. But I did see one of the more thuggish SS guards run into the accommodation block, force one of the detainees outside with a dog whip, take him to the corner of the drill square next to the fence and make him undress. As I got on with the rations in the storeroom, shouts and screams drew me to the window. The camp doctor joined me and we watched as the SS thug tied the naked man's arms behind his back, dragged him to the flagpole, then tied him to it and turned on the tap, aiming the powerful water jet at the man for about 20 minutes, and leaving him dripping wet in the freezing cold. The torturer then untied his victim and ordered him to get dressed, but he

MISCHLINGE

kept striking him as he hobbled across the courtyard back to his block.'

Heini was outraged at what he saw. It was beyond punishment, just sadism, pure and simple. The poor man had been robbed of the slightest trace of decency, been humiliated, then thoroughly brutalised. The assault affected Heini deeply. He'd never seen such wanton cruelty, and it left its mark deep inside him.

When he took the camp doctor his rations that evening, Heini poured out his feelings of utter revulsion and outrage. The doctor told him that the detainee was a fellow Greek and this was not the first time he'd been attacked in this way by the SS. Sadly, it wasn't the last either. The cold-water torture of the Greek man continued for several weeks until Heini finally received an order to pack the hose away. The doctor confided to Heini that he'd tried to communicate with the guards in German, had mentioned the Geneva Convention and tried to get them to resist the order to torture inmates, but his efforts had been futile.

Heini overheard some of the guards expressing their disapproval at what they too had seen, and then by chance he ran into Beck, his fellow prisoner and *Mischling*, who told him that this was not an isolated incident. He said there was a room set aside for punishment in the admin block called the 'whipping room'. Heini was horrified to hear that being repeatedly late for roll call would be enough to see an inmate be whipped. Beck had seen the same bully boy and another senior SS man bringing the hapless Greek inmate to this room in the past. So when Heini was summoned with a whistle and a yell of '*Hofhund*' to bring a bucket of water to the whipping room, he dreaded what he might find.

TORTURE AND KINDNESS

There was the same Greek prisoner having his trousers removed and being pushed onto a carpenter's bench, then attached to it by straps. He put the bucket of water down as fast as he could, but when he turned to flee, the SS officer ordered him to stay.

'You can cool his arse down,' he said coldly. 'And as he can't count, you can count to 25.'

Heini was then told to dampen a cloth, put it on the man's naked backside and place the bucket between his legs. After five lashes Heini couldn't bear to watch his pain and went to dampen the cloth.

The SS bully stopped him straightaway. 'Your job is to count, not to make decisions. Do you want the same?'

But he was allowed to dampen the cloth again after every ten blows from the whip. Powerless, Heini remained in the claustrophobic room while the two SS barbarians, with their sleeves rolled up, took it in turns to administer the 25 lashes.

'Let him go,' one of them told him, 'and tidy up in here' were the last words Heini heard as they left the room.

Heini immediately released the man from his bindings, helped him to his feet and with simple hand gestures told him to take time to recover himself. The poor man was trying to regain his composure and in considerable pain, but was also in a hurry to escape the awful room. Heini helped him a little way to his barracks, and being unable to exchange a word in each other's languages, he tried to soothe him as best he could with calming sounds and his physical support.

Returning to the whipping room, Heini felt physically sick, not only at what he'd seen but that he'd been forced to be a part of it. These cruel men were not human, he told himself.

MISCHLINGE

He simply couldn't fathom how they could do such a thing. He wondered if he would ever see the man again – perhaps the Greek doctor might translate for him and relay his heartfelt regrets that he could not help him. For days after the incident, haunted by what he'd been forced to witness, he couldn't sleep and a part of him shut down. It had left him feeling powerless, furious and even more vulnerable to the whim of these immoral men.

But one thing he knew for certain: he couldn't complain to any guard and he wouldn't share what he'd seen with any inmate. The only safe thing to do in this place was stay silent and trust no one.

Things went quiet for a few days after that, but when the SS sadists called for the man again, the Greek man paused in the corridor and jumped up through an overhead hatch into the roof space to escape his tormentors.

'*Hofhund*!' the officer yelled out to Heini, 'bring a ladder. The Greek pig is crawling around the roof.'

As he climbed the ladder, shouting at the Greek man to come down, he told Heini to come up behind him and shine a lamp into the attic. To Heini's horror, he drew out his pistol and started shooting randomly. The sound of bullets ricocheting off the walls of the small roof space was terrifying, and the SS officer fired so many rounds he'd had to reload his pistol, his fury now a blinding rage. When the Greek prisoner cried out in pain, he stopped shooting. Crawling out from his hiding place, Heini could see he'd been shot in the mouth, his cheeks were bleeding and he spat out a tooth. The SS officer gave him no respite, pushing him down the ladder and into one of the large toolsheds, where he slammed the door, locked it and strode away.

TORTURE AND KINDNESS

Shocked and shaken, Heini went to get the doctor. Perhaps he might be allowed to treat the Greek man's injury or at least speak to him in his own language. He hoped that doing so wouldn't land him in trouble, but he knew he had to try to help. A guard in the doctor's room asked Heini about the shots he'd just heard, and when Heini told him he got the impression that even the guard disapproved of such behaviour. But the ordinary guards weren't prepared to challenge the SS or open the toolshed door and let the doctor treat him without their permission.

So Heini and the doctor stood at the locked shed door, trying to comfort him, but had no response other than a pitiful whimpering noise as the poor man was obviously almost senseless with pain and had to endure the winter's night alone in the dark shed.

The next morning the doctor asked the commandant if he could urgently treat the prisoner's injuries, and two hours later he ordered Heini to take him by stretcher to the sick bay. The doctor told Heini the man's facial injuries were so extensive that he'd been transferred to the local hospital for an operation. Heini found out from the guard on duty that night that the SS officer had justified firing his pistol in his written report by saying the Greek prisoner had attempted to escape.

Heini kept a watchful eye on this particular SS officer from that time on, knowing him to be an extremely dangerous individual. So when one afternoon in February 1944 he called out '*Hofhund*, you have a visitor,' Heini was too scared to move. When the officer ordered him to the back door of the admin block, he was stunned to see his mother standing next to this sadist. Seeing them together evoked a strange feeling

MISCHLINGE

of the meeting of polar opposites, of hot and cold, of good and evil, accompanied by the sense of impending panic rising within him. As Heini saw it, Erna had a trusting nature, considering anyone who was at all helpful to her to be friendly and nice, and simply trusted them on that evidence. She would expect the SS bully to be like Sergeant Franke, and that would be a big mistake.

Terrified that his mother would mention Sergeant Franke's unsanctioned kindnesses in letting her visit previously, he was horrified to hear the SS officer immediately refuse to let his mum give Heini the food and clothes she'd brought with her. His mum, of course, tried to persuade him, but he snapped back angrily and shouted at her not to push matters. Utterly thrown and in tears, she turned to the officer and said, 'Please let me give my son what I've brought. It's not his fault he's a *Mischling*.'

Heini froze. 'Of all people, my mum had revealed the secret that I'd managed to keep for so long – and to the SS bully I lived in fear of. She'd accidentally revealed what I'd been so careful not to confide to anyone, not even Beck, my fellow *Mischling*. Time and time again when she had visited me, I warned my mother not to say a word about my *Mischling* status – clearly the bully had just scared her.

'The SS man was immediately abrupt and aggressive. He told mum to go back home, and she left in tears, then he marched me back to the admin block, spitefully abusing me all the way. "You swine," he said. "You've been lying to us all this time. Now you'll see a difference. Give me your key, leave everything where it is and go back to your room. This evening we'll see if your partners in crime are willing to have a Jew in their midst."

TORTURE AND KINDNESS

'That evening after rations had been eaten, the SS bully came to our barracks with the most extraordinary command. He told the 15 inmates I shared with that I'd been revealed as a *Mischling* and a Jew, and they all had to vote as to whether I should stay or go. They were all given small voting slips and asked to write "Yes, he can stay" or "No, he has to go."

'The inmates in my barracks had changed over time but none ever spoke about why they had been sent here. I felt sure I would be a marked man. I hardly knew these 15 men, and yet now my fate was in their hands thanks to the SS thug's idea of a cruel game.'

As the SS officer counted out the voting slips, Heini sat on his uncomfortable bed, preparing himself for what was to come. He could hardly believe it when the officer announced 11 of his fellow prisoners had voted for him to stay, with only four voting against. He was told he could remain in his barracks, but he would be given a new job.

Heini felt a strange mix of emotions. He could hardly believe that most of his barrack inmates had come through to support him – he was very touched. He was delighted not to be moved to a worse barracks, like Beck had endured, nor would he miss being *Hofhund* and whistled for like a dog. On the other hand, might his new job be worse, now they knew he was a *Mischling*? He wondered which four men had voted against him, and that reminded him never to let his guard down completely. Caution had got him this far.

The very next day Heini was sent to work alongside his old team, toiling away on the tracks under Sergeant Franke. He'd now been told that Heini was a *Mischling*, but just as Heini had hoped, he behaved exactly as always towards him, for which he was deeply grateful. Heini didn't go in for any grand gestures, but thanks to the vote and to Franke's reaction, a fragment of his faith in human nature was restored, although not quite enough to let him completely trust anyone in Wuhlheide.

8
SURVIVAL AND SADISM

Unmasked now as a *Mischling*, Heini wondered again what his captors had in store for him.

'Just days later, after morning roll call,' he wrote later, 'my name was called out along with 11 others, and we were told we were going to be moved. I took fleeting pleasure in thinking I'd never see the SS bully again, and when we were told to change into the clothes we'd arrived in, I couldn't wait to tear off my scratchy work suit and throw my worn shoes into the bin. I then took great comfort in putting my leather jacket back on again.'

As Heini was driven out of Wuhlheide, he couldn't know that the starvation diet, disease and brutality had meant that 2,000 Berliners weren't so fortunate and had died there.

The SS officer in charge shoved all the young men into a police van and told them they were now under SS command and there was to be no talking on the journey. As the road twisted and turned and they sat in complete silence, all had only one question on their mind – where are they taking us?

MISCHLINGE

When the van jolted to a halt, Heini didn't recognise the building and was told they were in Prinz-Albrecht-Strasse. This was the capital's most feared address, the HQ of the Gestapo and the base of Hitler's elite killers, the fearsome SS, paramilitaries infamous for having to provide rigorous genealogical proof of their Aryan ancestry to join, as well as the Reich Main Security Office prison and interrogation centre. Heini was horrified to be in the notorious building, with all that he'd heard about the place. He found it eerie, and how could he not be anxious?

'It was swarming with uniformed armed men,' he recalled. 'The SS took me immediately to an upstairs room packed with strangers, while those I'd travelled with from Wuhlheide were sent into others, and I never saw any of them again. As the door slammed shut I was on high alert, anxious and angry, yet also paralysed with fear.'

The huge detention cell was crammed full of prisoners, most sitting on mattresses piled high on the floor. Heini found a spot in the crowded, smelly room and tried to take in his surroundings. All day long and into the night the SS called out names: some for transfer, some for questioning, some to report to a medical room. Some people returned to the cell, others didn't. That night, mattresses were laid out on the floor for all to sleep on, but the lights overhead never dimmed.

Heini tried talking to other prisoners to pass the time, but their replies only made him more fearful. Word was that legal process didn't apply within these four walls, and there was talk of missing people and a spiral staircase down to a cellar with a torture chamber. Once again, no one was willing to confide in anyone else as to why they were being held, each suspicious of the other, so while there was a certain amount

SURVIVAL AND SADISM

of small talk, it was mostly about what might happen. Days passed, time dragged.

Night-times were the worst, when the SS would shove someone back into the room, the blood on their face showing the other prisoners all they needed to know. Watching and listening, waiting and more waiting, wondering what would happen to him, for weeks on end, all of this was enough on its own to send Heini into a hellish place. The waiting and not knowing, the dreadful anticipation and imagining were the worst of it for him. Even the physical labour and being outside at the camp began to feel appealing compared with the endless stagnant days on which nothing whatsoever happened.

After several weeks of being cooped up in the same room, when all the other detainees had been called for and Heini was wondering if there had been some sort of mistake, he was at last called to see a doctor. He had to strip naked and was fully and thoroughly examined, perhaps partly to see if he was circumcised, which he wasn't. He wondered whether he'd got through it, but the doctor remained silent and he returned to the monotony of the cell.

Nothing came of the visit to the doctor, and more empty days passed before he was called once again and taken down a corridor. Not knowing what to expect, he was both shocked and thrilled when the door opened and in walked his mum.

Erna had brought her usual parcel of food, and more of his clothes and long socks. Erna embraced Heini with a tenderness he'd been yearning for, and maybe this loving exchange softened the guard. Not only did he allow Heini to keep the parcel, but he also told Erna she could stay a few minutes. Having realised her mistake at identifying Heini as

MISCHLINGE

a *Mischling*, Erna stuck to safe topics and made no mention of Sigi's disappearance or Edie's transfer to slave labour work. Instead, they talked of trivial things, with Erna reassuring Heini that apart from a few broken windows, no one had suffered during the nights of air-raid attacks near their flat. Heini tried to find joy even in this dark spot, and had confided to his mum that his rations here were better than at Camp Wuhlheide. But he didn't tell her the worst part of his confinement was having to wash and dry his clothes in the toilets.

As they chatted, Heini's thoughts turned to the much-loved leather jacket he'd kept by his side this whole time in the hated cell. It was always at risk as everyone admired it, and as it was very cramped and hot in the room, he asked the SS officer if he could take it off now and give it to her. The guard said he could, and as he entrusted it to his mum, he was cheered by the thought that one day in the future he'd be free to wear it again when life in his home city returned to normal.

When the SS man said it was time, Erna's eyes filled with tears and Heini could only look down at her tiny frame and marvel at what courage and determination she possessed in coming to see him at Gestapo HQ. He'd always known her to be a caring mum, but he'd no idea she had such extraordinary daring. For a second time she'd somehow discovered where he was, obtaining permission to enter this dreadful place to bring him useful things and her loving reassurance. He had to admit it to himself, growing up he had no idea that this quiet, gentle woman was capable of such things. As they kissed goodbye, Heini thought his mother looked older and more careworn; these terrible times had taken their toll on her. He squeezed her tight and told her how grateful he was,

SURVIVAL AND SADISM

while vowing to himself he would never take her for granted again.

Heini found the weeks of waiting at Prinz-Albrecht-Strasse hard to handle and was almost pleased when he was finally called for questioning. The guard took him into a small room, where an SS interrogator at a small table told him to sit down opposite him. He saw a file with his name on it as well as his army service record with his picture. The SS man glanced at the file. 'I see you're in good physical shape. And you're not "a real Jew", I hear. What shall I do with you? You're Kv1, according to your service record.'

'Most of all I'd like to go home,' Heini ventured, but the SS man obviously considered it a monologue not a conversation and did not look at or speak to him again. He simply sat there and just read Heini's file, then asked the guard to take him back to the same cell.

'Just days later,' said Heini, 'I was called for again, but this time I was led down to the cellar, the place rumoured to be the torture chamber. There were no windows down there, just skylights whose panes had been painted white so you couldn't see through them. Every small corner had mattresses squeezed into it with people on them. When anyone had to leave the room for any reason, they had to climb over all the people on mattresses. The dim light was left on for 24 hours and flickered irritatingly.

'We waited, listened and killed time, unable to see what was happening. This ongoing inaction, the eternal dawn and the extreme monotony were awful. It was mostly quiet, but sometimes cries of real pain, obviously from torture, rang out which was mental torture for us detainees. In a half-sitting, half-lying position we'd sometimes exchange our fears with

MISCHLINGE

the new arrivals. All sense of time disappeared, and only when our food rations arrived could we tell that it was morning, lunchtime or evening.'

There was no squabbling over food, as in this place nobody wanted to misbehave or draw attention to themselves, and everybody tried to stick rigidly to their own tiny space on the floor. According to one man, this cellar was the last port of call before prison or concentration camp. 'If you end up in Poland,' he said, 'just forget it. You might as well make your last will and testament now. If you end up being sent west, it could be to Buchenwald, where you'll have to work like a slave and where there's an electric fence that stops people from escaping.'

It seemed clear that nobody was released into freedom from 'the cellar'. It was just a route to further imprisonment or forced labour. Heini kept his own counsel and did the hardest thing for him. He just waited.

Heini's 21st birthday found him still being held prisoner – without charge – in the bowels of Gestapo HQ in Berlin. He'd hoped to spend that evening in some Berlin dancehall with his fiancée Margot in his arms, making up a party with his good friend Gerhard, perhaps sitting around a table enjoying some of Berlin's finest foodstuffs. But that was just a daydream now.

Just weeks after his birthday, months of waiting ended when Heini awoke to hear his name being called. An SS guard handcuffed him to two other detainees, telling them loud and clear, 'You're going to Buchenwald. Don't think that you can run off. If you do, you will be shot without warning.'

SURVIVAL AND SADISM

One of the prisoners next to Heini sank to his knees when he heard the word 'Buchenwald'. Wuhlheide was mostly run by the Gestapo, but Buchenwald was run by the SS, whose reputation for cruelty was legendary. The SS man stuffed the stricken man into the middle of the three prisoners and ordered them into the police van waiting in the courtyard. They were packed so tightly with the others already in there that it was difficult for him to fall down or for anyone to move.

And from there, the nightmare journey to a different hell began at a railway siding. 'Men and women of all ages and talking in different languages spilled out of vans and lorries and were pushed onto goods carriages that were built to carry animals or parcels,' Heini said. 'Then the carriage door shut, plunging us into darkness, and the train chugged away to we knew not where. When it stopped at a station, we could hear vehicles outside, and the SS opened the door only to push a new batch of detainees inside. Nobody could stretch out anymore, everyone had to crouch down to find some space, a few stood, but no one could settle. Ventilation slits let in a little light and air, and at one stop the SS pushed a small amount of food through the gap, along with one bucket of water to be passed round and last all of us all day.

'It was a slow journey, as the train stopped to let military trains pass and sometimes to shelter from air raids. The rations were meagre, and we were all hungry and could hear everyone's tummies rumbling and gurgling. With every stop, as more people joined each carriage, we became more and more cramped and the atmosphere increasingly fetid as the smell of sweat – and worse – increased. We were all dirty and, of course, answering the call of nature was difficult and beyond humiliating.'

MISCHLINGE

Eventually the train halted, the doors were flung open and everyone was ordered off. The SS marched them all to a warehouse, their submachine guns at the ready at all times. The floor in the warehouse was bare, but there were blankets and straw – and Heini could at last stretch his legs. The water supply and the toilet were very much in demand, and one detainee said that he recognised the city of Halle. A couple of the young men looked like prisoners of war and spoke to each other in a language Heini couldn't understand.

An older man was rocking himself and seemed to be praying in Hebrew, but it was the two sobbing young women that really moved Heini as they talked of the children they'd been separated from. One told how her little Ruth and Jacob had been holding on to her skirt when the Gestapo had prised them from her – she couldn't forget her daughter's screams or her son's frightened expression. Heini could find no words of comfort, only able to hug her and say they were probably being sent to a different camp, but really, he had no clue as to their fate.

A few days later, everyone was ordered back onto the train, and as it moved off it was obvious that the sealed, stuffy carriages, were dirtier and more unpleasant than when they'd got off. Heini chatted to an old woman from Berlin who somehow reminded him of his mum, but they got separated as new prisoners boarded and were crushed in between them.

Another stop at Jena was probably where they picked up an outbreak of lice, causing relentless itching and making them all hugely uncomfortable. Heini ached all over from standing all day, squashed up next to other people who wriggled and tried periodically to move around. And he was really feeling the effects of crunching up his long legs underneath

SURVIVAL AND SADISM

him in an effort to sleep. Sleep was hard to come by in any case in those conditions, on a hard floor while scratching at bites. After what Heini reckoned to be around a ten-day journey of torment, the train eventually pulled in at the little station at Buchenwald concentration camp.

Back home in Berlin, Erna was beside herself with anxiety, having heard nothing from Heini for months. She'd turned up at Gestapo HQ once more, hoping to see her son again around his 21st birthday, but was turned away. With Sigi also still 'missing', the uncertainty was terrible. At least she knew where Edie was, even if she was constantly worried about her.

Erna knew nothing of the progress of the war. After more than four years of fighting there had been two turning points: the victory of British Empire forces at El Alamein in Egypt, and Germany's greatest defeat by the Soviets after the long and bloody battle at Stalingrad. Yet although Germany was now losing the war, vital resources were still being poured into the Final Solution, the murder of Jews on an industrial scale. The newly created extermination camps across Europe were killing thousands every day, while dwindling numbers of slave labourers were being worked to the point of death for the war effort, in all its varied forms.

Edie's work as a slave labourer, clearing the ever-increasing number of bodies from heavily bombed areas all around the capital, was made tougher by the unusually stifling heat in the summer of 1944. The skinny teenager was doing hard physical labour on reduced *Mischling* rations, being forced to be outside all day for five days a week. Returning to the barn every night to sleep on hay, with no privacy whatsoever and minimal washing facilities, must have made rest of any kind hard. But it wasn't the heavy lifting that saddened Edie. It was what lay under the rubble – the body parts, and the ornaments and possessions that so poignantly told the story of every family's home life.

'When I found a body part, I had to pick it up and put it on the side of the road to be collected by a truck later on,' she recalls. 'I tried to do it respectfully and not think about that person at the same time. I just knew I had to get through it, so I tried to picture my mum's smiling face and getting back to her at the weekend. It was the only thing I looked forward to. Back home with Mum, I loved our time together and we both found some element of peace. We'd tell each other about our week and she'd always have saved much of her ration, going without in the week so she could spoil me at weekends.'

As Heini stepped out of the filthy goods carriage onto the platform at Buchenwald concentration camp that summer, he was amazed at the number of languages he could hear, as all the prisoners disembarked the train and the SS marshalled the bedraggled group inside the fences. He could hear there were very few Germans, but among the many nationalities gathered he could recognise the Dutch, French, Russian, Polish and perhaps other Slav languages, alongside dialects of the Romani language. One thing was obvious – the vast majority of the men were under 30 years old, many of them with soft, unbristled chins.

'We were immediately divided into two lines for no reason I could fathom,' Heini recalled. 'I looked around at the huge, bleak site, with lots of flat-roofed buildings. When my queue reached the SS guard keeping a record, he asked for my name

SURVIVAL AND SADISM

and papers, and another marched my line into the fenced-off quarantine area. I was very relieved to be marched into the shower block, where I could take off my louse-ridden clothing. We were all given the blue and grey prisoners' uniform, and I was given a red badge and a number on a piece of light grey material that I had to sew firmly onto my top and trousers.

'The whole procedure was a shock, as next I was obliged to hand over my hair and my name. From now on I was to be known as Number 3009.'

After the issuing of the prisoner uniform and the identifying badge, Heini had the humiliation of a strange stripy haircut and was then given a rigorous medical assessment, with an official looking into his mouth and under his arms, as if he were an animal being taken to market, with his height and weight measured and his general fitness assessed, before being immunised against a number of diseases and told that quarantine would last for some time.

'The SS guard told us that from now on our names wouldn't be used, only our number. As I looked around for a familiar face I was disappointed not to recognise anyone – but then we all looked so alike with shaved bald heads and a cap.'

Heini bore the strip search, examination and hair-shaving stoically, and showed none of his mounting inner anger. Instead, he was determined to learn about this new place and wasted no time in walking around the quarantine area. As he stood by the internal fence looking into an adjoining section of the camp, he heard someone calling his name, and he couldn't believe it when on the other side of the fence he saw three Soviets who'd been in his work detail at Camp Wuhlheide. After exchanging news in their pidgin Russian-German, they told him to wait, and when they were sure no one was watching they threw him a wrapped-up piece of bread over the wire. His enormous hunger from the horrific journey had left Heini feeling tremendously weak, so this little gift was more than welcome. The Soviets said they had felt the same after their hideous journey, and later on they brought him some cooked potatoes and a swede. They were thrilled when he told them the news he'd picked up of the advancing Soviet and Western armies. The men reminisced about the time they'd spent together, their shared experiences with the ration and cigarette cards, and for the first time in a very long time a smile broke across Heini's drawn face.

His spirits lifted by their kindness, Heini began talking to some of the other prisoners. Now and then he would stand outside and chat with one particular man, a heavy smoker who told Heini that he maintained his supply by swapping his food rations for cigarettes. Heini couldn't understand why someone would want to swap already insufficient life-saving rations for something they couldn't eat, but the man argued that smoking reduced his hunger pangs and suggested Heini try some of his chewing tobacco. Heini succumbed and felt terrible afterwards, sick and trembling. He remembered the bad experience he'd had trying cigarettes as a teenager years earlier, when he resolved never to smoke again. Eating was always going to be of far greater importance to him. He'd always loved his food and now dreamt of the tasty stews of sausage and potatoes his mother had often cooked for him. The meagre rations left Heini constantly hungry, but he resolved always to buy food and perhaps soap rather than cigarettes.

Time hung heavily as Heini sat around in quarantine with nothing to do but waiting to find out what was next. So he asked the senior inmate if he could repair all the dripping taps in their washroom. The man agreed and found him some tools to do the job. This brief respite, with something practical to do, stopped Heini thinking too much and kept his mind off his empty stomach.

When his period of quarantine ended, Heini was allocated to the camp's single-storey Block 45 and as Number 3009 was given the top bunk of three. He was also assigned to a work detail whose job was to maintain lots of areas around the camp: the paths, some green areas and various areas between buildings.

He went straight back to the place he could talk to his Soviet friends to hear what he could learn from them as they had been there for some months. Astute as ever, he wanted to know as much as possible about Buchenwald, what happened there and what he needed to do or avoid. Knowledge, Heini knew, was power, and it would serve him well in this dangerous place.

The Soviets gave him several good bits of advice: first, that he shouldn't venture anywhere near the electric fence surrounding the camp. His friends told him the SS at Buchenwald were known to be fond of committing vile acts, such as taking someone's cap off and throwing it over the fence. They'd then order them to go and get it, before shooting them for attempting to escape. They also advised him to stay well clear of the stone building with painted white windows next to his Block 45, as it was thought to be an area where contagious prisoners or something similarly risky were kept. They were certain that it was not a sick bay, but something more sinister. It looked medical, and it was thought that more people went in than came out.

MISCHLINGE

On his first walk to roll call, Heini saw a grim sight, a clear warning to all new inmates. Near to the main gate were two posts fixed to the ground, joined by a cross-beam. It was a gallows, from which a prisoner was hanging. A loudspeaker announcement that the same fate would befall anyone who resisted the SS was broadcast across the camp. That, and the armed watchtowers, were enough to stop Heini wandering far.

He also arranged a time and place to meet his Soviet friends again, safe from any patrolling SS or inmates that might not be trustworthy. The Soviets brought along some friends they could rely on, posted someone as a look-out, and the small group sat in a circle and listened as Heini told the stories of his ration-card visits to the villages near Camp Wuhlheide and of his 'escape' and return, all translated by a Soviet prisoner who spoke good German. Heini's audience laughed a great deal, despite the terrible situation they found themselves in, and because such humour was so rare in the place, Heini was called upon to repeat it and drew an even bigger crowd the next time.

Somewhat bafflingly, Heini discovered that he was allowed to write home. He'd got used to the idea that most of his captors were at best unfeeling and at worst sadists – with the exception of Sergeant Franke – so this came as a welcome surprise. The camp provided a special form with his 3009 number and a proscribed word limit, and prisoners were allowed to request a parcel from home, perhaps to save them valuable resources. Heini wrote straightaway to his parents, telling them where he was and asking for lots of things. He soon received a postcard from his mum, saying she would send a parcel with all he'd asked for. Other prisoners would

SURVIVAL AND SADISM

fold up the postcards they received and sew them on the back of the red cloth badges they wore to strengthen them, as prisoners were punished if they came off, so Heini did the same.

Buchenwald was expanding fast. Its central position in Germany meant that prisoners of war, Jews, *Mischlinge* and others were sent there from 30 different countries. In December 1943 the main camp housed 37,000 inmates, but by the same time the following year its population had grown to around 63,000, which meant everyday life was deteriorating every week with the constant influx.

Heini had already lost a considerable amount of weight, and he really noticed the difference in the reduced rations, his increasingly crowded barracks and the noisier nights, which, along with all the dirt and smells, made it hard to sleep, especially in the heat of summer. But worst of all were the latrines. With so many people using them, they were quite unspeakable.

Allied bombing raids in the area were increasing, with air-raid warnings sounding during the day and the sky lighting up like a firework display, illuminating the land below. The hilly landscape around Buchenwald meant that Heini couldn't see exactly where the air raids were taking place, adding to the perpetual fear that the explosions might get very close. So, when bombs fell outside the camp, starting a great blaze in the adjacent land, Heini was unsure what to do. The instructions were to stay inside the blocks until the attacks were over, but they had stopped now and everything was quiet. Venturing out into an eerie silence, while others moved tentatively to try to see what had happened, Heini went off to look for himself.

MISCHLINGE

'The SS area in front of the gate had suffered a direct hit,' he recorded, 'the building was badly damaged and the bodies of dead SS men lay on the ground. When the other prisoners saw this, they all disappeared, but I decided to go in closer and spotted a pistol, attached to a belt lying on top of a pile of rubble. Looking around to see if anyone was watching, I pulled out an 8mm pistol with ammunition, put it in my shirt and tied up the cord of my trousers more tightly so I wouldn't lose it.'

It was both daring and dangerous, but Heini thought the weapon could well come in useful. With the arrival of Allied ground forces a distinct possibility at some time in the future, there might be a chance of escape, and who knew what the guards might do to their prisoners if all were lost, so this lucky find could prove very useful for defending himself. He knew he couldn't keep a gun on his person or anywhere near him – that was too risky. So he buried it on the way back to his block, but almost immediately began to worry about what he'd done. This was way more dangerous than hiding a tin of potted meat. For days afterwards he became increasingly nervous and cross with himself for picking up the weapon in the first place. Had he been enterprising and quick-witted or simply foolish? He couldn't sleep, imagining the SS shooting him with the pistol after forcing him to show them where he'd hidden it.

The following day an SS man called out Prisoner 3009 and Heini froze, wondering if someone had seen him bury the gun. It was a huge relief when he was just ordered to join the clean-up party in the extensive area outside the camp that had been reduced to a smouldering expanse of ash and rubble. In all, 400 inmates and 80 SS men had been killed by

SURVIVAL AND SADISM

the Allied bombing, and the camp's disinfection room and many other buildings had been flattened.

Having cut himself off from other inmates for so long, not trusting anyone enough to confide in or befriend in either Wuhlheide or Buchenwald, Heini now felt reassured having the Soviets in the same camp, albeit in another section. He'd already benefited from their kind gift of food on the day he arrived, as well as their invaluable practical advice on survival in this new place. He could now think of them as friends and men he could talk to, trust and even turn to. The camp did not allow any interaction between the separated sections of prisoners, but Heini was prepared to risk getting close to the fence between them just to enjoy their company.

During one of these discreet chats in early September, his Soviet friends told him they were being sent to an external labour camp detachment. Heini was shocked and surprised at how upset he was, but these men had become his first and only friends since his arrest and imprisonment. Over time in Wuhlheide and Buchenwald he'd grown to like and trust them, but now he'd be alone once again. The prospect made him shiver. Of course his Soviet friends were worried about where they were being sent, joking that there could hardly be anywhere worse as they said their farewells through the fence. It was a blow, no question about that, and when the truck carried them off Heini felt tremendously sad.

Not long afterwards Heini was told he was also being sent to an external labour detachment, and he dared to hope it might be the same place as them. As he prepared to leave, Heini remembered the hidden pistol and wondered what he should do with it. He thought it was too dangerous to take it with him, but then again it was too valuable to leave in the ground. The weapon might come in useful sometime in the future; he might be returning here and he'd certainly rather that it was in the hands of inmates, as the frequent bombing had made him think there might be a chance of escape.

'I decided to seek the advice of my senior in my block,' he recalled. 'We'd got to know each other quite well, swapping tools on the same work detail. I asked for a word in private, so we both went to a quiet place and I explained my problem. The senior suggested we should fetch the pistol from its hiding place and he'd hide it in a better spot. We decided daytime was safer if we picked our moment, and with the senior as a look-out, I took the pistol from its hiding place and carefully hid it under my shirt. Then we walked across the camp together, heading for the washroom, out of view of other people. I handed him the pistol, and we swiftly went our separate ways. I returned under cover of darkness and the senior thanked me for leaving him this useful asset, which, as the bombing grew nearer, might well be needed soon. I left feeling reassured.'

The next morning, as Heini took his place on the Buchenwald drill square, he realised that he was just one of many being assembled to be moved elsewhere and they seemed to be the fittest of the inmates. As he marched out of the gates of the camp he felt sure that it was his youth and good health that had got him this far, but he wondered if these would be enough to save his life? Other inmates had left Buchenwald, never to be seen again, presumed dead from back-breaking manual labour, an SS beating or simply being shot.

And even though he'd survived Wuhlheide and life in the main Buchenwald camp for many gruelling months, working

SURVIVAL AND SADISM

outside in all weathers, the starvation rations, sleep deprivation and living in fear so much of the time were taking their toll on every part of his mind and body.

He thought of his loved ones. His fiancée Margot – was she still thinking of him, or had she met someone else and dismissed their love as too risky? And what of his mother, father and little sister – had they survived the recent heavy bombing of the capital?

Once again, as he boarded a railway wagon heading who knew where, he'd no idea what awaited him.

9
DEFIANCE AND PUNISHMENT

The sheer numbers of prisoners arriving in Buchenwald, and the increased demand for armaments as the war entered its sixth year, saw the camp extend outwards, with more than 80 outlying sub-camps being opened. Heini was among those Buchenwald inmates sent from the main camp to work as forced labour for the war effort at Witten-Annen, over 200 miles away in Germany's industrial heartland of the Ruhr.

These young men – united only by the enmity of the Nazis towards them for one reason or another – were marched to Buchenwald railway station, then had to endure an unpleasant two-day journey, packed tightly in goods wagons once again, that delivered them to the bleak, muddy camp at Witten-Annen. On the journey Heini chatted to a Czech prisoner – František – as much as their lack of a common language allowed.

At their first morning roll call in the drill square, the prisoners were divided into a day shift and a night shift, and the SS officer demanded that any cook, locksmith or fitter stay behind. Hoping to avoid more hard labour, and thinking he could do most jobs, Heini remained while the other men were

MISCHLINGE

sent to their barracks. When the cook and locksmith roles had been allocated to others, it became clear that what had really been meant by 'fitter' was an electrician.

'The SS man ordered me to light the drill square by first thing the following day, and carry out electrical repairs as and when necessary,' Heini recalled. 'He explained this would mean having my own workshop.

'I immediately realised that I'd made a mistake, but I was reluctant to admit it as I thought that might bring me more problems. So I resolved to see if my practical skills meant I could rise to the challenge of electrical work.'

Looking around his miserable new sleeping quarters, he could hardly believe he was expected to sleep on a bare-wire bed with no mattress. Heini's spirits sank. He'd volunteered for a job he couldn't do and dreaded being found out the next morning. As he sank onto his new uncomfortable bed he confided this to his neighbour in the adjacent bed, František, the Czech he'd talked to on the train, only to discover that he really was an electrician. The Czech hadn't understood what the SS officer had asked for either, but his eyes lit up when Heini explained the fix he was in. František immediately offered to help Heini do the job. He suggested Heini drill pilot holes for the cables first, then report back to him the task ahead. Heini couldn't believe his luck and went to sleep a little cheered.

The next day when the tools and materials arrived, Heini, remembering František's instructions, began laying the cables via one of the blocks but he was worried about connecting them to the power source. When František returned from doing his electrical shift in the nearby steel factory, they both approached an SS officer and asked if it might be permitted

DEFIANCE AND PUNISHMENT

for the two of them to work together to get the job done a lot quicker. Perhaps because lighting up the SS accommodation was the next task, the officer readily agreed, and from then on they worked as a team on the kitchen, the prisoners' blocks and the area near the fences. Relieved this had worked out to plan, Heini gave his tobacco allowance to František to thank him for his help.

Working around the camp as an electrician brought Heini unexpected opportunities. 'With frequent calls to fix faulty machines in the kitchen, I would seize the chance to steal some of the SS's superior supplies, including carrots, raw vegetables, pudding powder and rice. I would sneak it into my workshop, mix it up with water and cook it, producing something tastier than the thin soup the prisoners were given to eat. I shared it with František, who in turn was teaching me electrical skills.'

Heini quickly grew to like the Czech, and although language differences made things tricky at times, it was good to have someone to talk to and work alongside, as well as them both watching out for each other. František told Heini about his hometown, his family and the food he longed to taste again, while Heini enjoyed reminiscing about his favourite meals in Berlin and his mother's cooking. If either of them had any doubts about ever seeing home again, neither would admit it out loud.

In Berlin, Erna and Edie were spending more nights in cellars, avoiding the heavy bombing. The frequent raids by British Lancasters, Halifaxes and Mosquitos, alongside attacks by Soviet and US planes, were causing immense devastation and deaths all over the city. One raid alone killed 2,000 Berliners

MISCHLINGE

and left 175,000 homeless. The very next day, another raid left 1,000 dead and 100,000 homeless. Berliners thought they had seen the worst, but 1944 saw an increase in the attrition as the Americans sent long-range fighters to escort their bombers all the way to Berlin to drop more munitions.

The Allied bombing raids brought misery to the Witten-Annen sub-camp too. Day and night the air-raid sirens would repeatedly screech their ominous warning; the off-shift prisoners would shelter in the covered trench in the drill square, while those at the steelworks would take cover in the cellar.

Sometimes there was enough space to sleep in these damp, dark holes, but on a Sunday, when all the prisoners had the day off work and remained at camp, conditions were hideous. With the SS stretched out at either end of the trench, the prisoners were so tightly packed that they couldn't lie down, and having to stand for hours on end was painful and offered no rest. Heini tried to sleep standing but ended up exhausted, and even back in the dormitory sleep was hard to come by. The beds were far worse than those at Wuhlheide, and the lack of any padding on top meant their metal springs cut into his perilously thin body, causing sores and extreme pain.

Heini set out to learn more about how things worked at the camp. There were horror stories of inmates being shot for any minor error that annoyed an SS guard. And he discovered that there were two distinct groups of prisoners: those who wore red badges like Heini included communists and political prisoners, Jews and *Mischlinge*, as well as prisoners who'd attempted to escape and gentiles condemned for assisting Jews. Inmates who wore green badges were long-term criminals commandeered by the SS to work for them in the camps as overseers.

DEFIANCE AND PUNISHMENT

'Our overseer was a criminal called Alfred Neumann,' recalled Heini. 'No one knew what his crime had been, but from first meeting him none of us felt he was a man we could trust. He was a senior man in the camp, responsible for giving out jobs and supplies to inmates and running around after the SS, and he behaved more like one of our captors than a prisoner. From my workshop I could see he often swapped his convict's uniform for a civilian suit and could be seen walking around the camp smoking. I soon learnt he didn't mind what he did, as long as it brought him benefits.'

Heini and Gerhard, a fellow prisoner who worked as a kitchen helper, saw a great deal of Neumann as their work took them around the camp, and both experienced his bad temper. Gerhard hated having to share a room with him, and he warned Heini how awful and untrustworthy the overseer was.

'Neumann seemed to move freely around the SS block and frequently left the camp with an SS man to visit Herne, his hometown, and source supplies for themselves. So he could be ready at any time. His green prisoner ID badge and the number on his jacket and trousers – labels that us inmates had to have tightly sewn on – were attached by snap-fasteners so he could take them off in a second. He even dressed in luxury clothes, so he looked just like the SS – sporting jackboots, breeches and a pocket watch. The only thing he didn't have was an SS jacket. He was clearly being used by the SS as a procurer, and in return they granted him plenty of perks.'

What angered Heini was not that Neumann took more than his fair share of cigarettes or rations but that he would promise to do something for the prisoners and then let them down. It was Neumann's job to get the correct forms to write home but he never did. Nor did they receive the straw sacks they were promised to put on top of the beds' metal springs, which would have given their emaciated bodies some comfort at night.

Neumann was a prisoner in name only and had clearly sold his soul to the SS. Everyone saw him as a willing SS tool, treating his fellow prisoners like his own slaves. Being one of them somehow made his actions worse. Yet Neumann seemed blind to the effects of his behaviour on men who had already been dehumanised.

'In the run-up to Christmas 1944,' remembered Heini, 'Neumann's self-interest became clear to me when I saw the scale of his hoarding after I'd gone to his office to repair the electrics. There he was, smoking at a table, with whole sausages and other goodies laid out in front of him. He shouted at me for not knocking on the door before entering. I could see Gerhard was right when he told me Neumann was using his local contacts in the town and their ration cards to get clothing and a supply of Christmas produce for "customers" in the SS who had become dependent on him for highly sought-after goods. We all despised the man.'

In the New Year, Heini received a parcel from his mother. Ripping it open, his joy was short-lived as he could see it had taken three months to reach him from Buchenwald. The bread and cake had gone mouldy, but he was able to make good use of the shaving kit, pocket mirror, three pairs of long socks, long johns, two packets of biscuits and some sweets. There were also 20 cigarettes, which František was very thankful for. Heini thought lovingly of his mother – she'd come up trumps again and would have scrimped, saved and gone without herself to send him that parcel. What a little

DEFIANCE AND PUNISHMENT

dynamo she was. He was so lucky to have her and he trusted that she was still safe in Berlin. One day he hoped to thank her and somehow repay her.

As the Allied raids drew closer and more frequent, Heini and František were impatient to know more about the war's progress. František took it upon himself to build a crystal radio set at his factory workshop, but he needed Heini to translate the news for them.

'So we tuned the radio in my small dark workshop at camp,' recalled Heini, 'and when František came over after his shift, we had a clear view from my window over the drill square and camp gate. I first tuned in to a German station, but we quickly learnt it could not be trusted – the number of ships the German U-boats claimed to have sunk sounded exaggerated, and they hardly acknowledged their defeats in the East nor the advance of Soviet forces. Tuning in to Radio Luxembourg and Radio Nancy, their bulletins in German had quite different reports of the various fighting positions. So we tuned in regularly to hear the news, which made us feel part of the world again, and we even risked listening for longer to hear music, which neither of us had heard for years and gave us a huge boost. It brought back memories of dancing the night away with Margot and made me wonder where she was after so many years.'

When Heini and František heard on their radio that the Red Army had liberated Warsaw on 17 January 1945, they shared the news with the prisoners they trusted, and passing the word around brought many prisoners a little joy.

As winter temperatures dropped, Heini managed to keep his little workshop quite warm with scraps of wood he collected from around the camp. This meant he was never short of visits from some of those he'd got to know and trust. There were Soviet, Polish, Czech, Hungarian and French prisoners, as well as Gerhard the kitchen hand, Günther the cook and Horst, an inmate from Berlin.

Heini was relieved to have another Berliner to talk to and the two men swapped stories about their pasts. Neither of them had ever been charged with an offence, both possessed a service record proclaiming them fit for something. But what? Horst confided that he'd been arrested and sent to Buchenwald for being a *Mischling*, but Heini once again held back on revealing that this was his status too. Ever cautious, he waited some time until he'd really got to know Horst and then revealed that he was in exactly the same position. He even told Horst how his mum's unfortunate revelation to the SS guard had seen him sent from Wuhlheide to Buchenwald. Their similar backgrounds cemented the friendship and trust between the two Berliners.

One evening, two young Soviet inmates whom Heini had got to know a little came to his workshop with a double-edged request. After dispensing with their cover story that the lamp in their barracks wasn't working, they asked him if he'd put a pair of pliers out for them to cut the wire fence. They were planning to escape that same evening, straight after the change of guard when the moon clouded over, and they hoped to be far away by the next change of guard.

Heini explained that it was just not possible. The guards checked his tools every evening after work, and he'd be in real trouble if he lost even one. At the same time he did want to help them, so on impulse he agreed and said he would leave them the pliers. He suggested they break a window to get in, to disguise his involvement. Appreciating his willing-

DEFIANCE AND PUNISHMENT

ness to help them, the men thanked him and asked if he wanted to join them.

Tempted, Heini discussed their offer with Horst. They mulled over the latest news they'd heard on Radio Luxembourg; the advancing Allied fronts were still a way off, and as they both wanted to head to Berlin, their route was not yet open. They both agreed it was too soon to try to escape.

The next morning at roll call the SS found 24 prisoners missing – 22 Soviets and two French. Initially they thought some had overslept or collapsed, and inmates were sent to fetch them. Pacing the drill square, one of the SS men spotted the broken window. Their suspicions aroused, the alarm was sounded and guards dispatched to check the perimeter. After a long search they found a hole in the fence, which the escapees had carefully pushed back together so that it would be hard to spot.

The next Heini knew, the SS man in charge was yelling at him: '3009 – go get *all* your tools and report to me at the SS block.' 'As I walked into the building I feared the worst, as the SS guard was standing behind a counter, glowering and red-faced. He had the inventory of my tools in front of him. I'd been made to sign it when I was given them.

'"Something's not right here," he said. "Where are the pliers?"

'I tried my best to look surprised and said they must be somewhere in the workshop, or maybe they'd been left at my last job.

'The SS went off to search my workshop for the pliers and I was thankful the crystal radio set was at František's factory, but as I waited I became more and more frightened. When they returned empty-handed, they looked very bad tempered and the SS bigwig was beginning to go really wild.

'He pushed his face up close to mine and almost spat at me. "Open your mouth, 3009, and tell us the truth – you'll be saving yourself the whip."'

Heini decided things would probably be far worse for him if he admitted his actions, so he just shrugged and said he really didn't know.

Without pausing, the SS officer shouted his punishment: '3009 is condemned to 25 lashes, to be administered immediately.'

'I was shoved into an adjoining room, where an SS officer ordered me to drop my trousers and lean over a table. Two SS men took it in turns to whip me, telling me to count the lashes and that if I didn't the punishment would be increased. I gritted my teeth through it all and called out the numbers. As I limped away, the SS man shouted behind me, "We've not finished with you, 3009. Now get back to your workshop."

'Back in my workshop, my backside was burning and although I could hardly think straight, I scolded myself for not taking the chance to escape. The SS came over, removed the key from the door and told me that from tomorrow I was to swap jobs with František and work in the factory. Günther came along with cold compresses and cooling cream, and František and Horst visited me too as I lay on my stomach. But despite their kindness I never confided in any of them that I had lent the escapees the pliers. My number one rule was caution. So we all talked of the escapees and hoped they'd all got clean away.

'I was feeling a little cheered until the overseer Neumann turned up, and with a mix of *schadenfreude* and scorn he

DEFIANCE AND PUNISHMENT

chipped in: "You now realise what an idiot you've been. Do you really think I believe that you didn't give them the pliers? You should just be happy that they didn't simply finish you off."'

But the big escape had a dramatic effect on those left behind in the camp. The SS seemed almost hysterical and their behaviour became increasingly savage. Heini's punishment was just part of their wider crackdown after the escape. The slave labour girls from the East that worked in the kitchen were driven out of the camp, to who knew where, and others took their place, while the Soviets who carried heavy supplies into the kitchen were also replaced – by French prisoners. Rumours went around that some had helped the escapees, others said they'd been caught smuggling cigarettes out to prisoners. The SS guards left their usual posts and stopped walking around the camp; instead they began patrolling around the perimeter fence.

Heini was having real trouble sleeping on his front, so, tired and tormented, he decided to ask Neumann if he was due for more punishment. The overseer scoffed and said that the SS had more important things to worry about than him. Heini thought that meant the Allies were drawing close and felt a little cheered. After a few days the swelling on Heini's backside was slowly going down. As he bent to sit down he tried to give himself courage by repeating to himself the rhyming phrase '*Keile vergeht, Arsch besteht*' (Thrashing done, can feel my bum).

Heini and František took the crystal set out of its hiding place as soon as it felt safe to check on the Allied advance. Radio Luxembourg reported that the Allies were indeed getting closer, with the Soviets laying siege to Breslau

MISCHLINGE

(modern-day Wrocław) in the east, the British and the Americans bombing Dresden and Weimar, and the front in the west getting closer too.

It was looking like the beginning of the end, and they dared to hope that their servitude might be nearing its end too. At the factory the workers were never told exactly what they were manufacturing other than small pieces of metal for the war effort. But now their shifts were being reduced, that seemed significant; perhaps bombs were blocking rail and road routes, and fuel and deliveries of raw materials weren't getting through. Whatever the reason, there was much less work to do and both men felt uplifted by the fact, except they were almost too exhausted to feel any emotion.

František had given Heini tips when they swapped jobs and he started working at the factory, including where to find a warm place, out of sight of the SS guards, that he could hide in and sleep when there was little to do. It wasn't possible to lie down there as the floor was covered in oil, but that didn't stop exhausted Heini, hunched semi-upright in a corner. On the night shift with no jobs to keep him busy, he made his way there and soon fell asleep alongside a Soviet electrician. He was woken by a painful body blow when an SS guard opened the door with a bang and thumped Heini with his rubber truncheon.

'Others are working for Führer, Volk and Fatherland,' he told Heini, 'and you, 3009, are sleeping. We'll soon get that out of your system.'

He was ordered back to the lathe to complete his night shift and told to stay behind after the morning roll call that followed. Then two SS men took Heini to the kitchen where he was ordered to fill two buckets with water and carry them

DEFIANCE AND PUNISHMENT

to the drill square. One of the SS placed a stool on the ground, and instructed Heini to stand on it and balance with a full bucket in each hand. 'Here, 3009,' he told Heini, 'here you will stay and go to sleep.'

'How long I stood there,' recalled Heini, 'holding the buckets, I couldn't say. My arms began to feel longer and longer, and the bucket started slipping out of my cramped hands. I was absolutely exhausted, so tired that I thought I would fall over at any minute. I hoped the air-raid siren would sound and spare me, as we'd have to return to our barracks when it did – but the siren never came.

'I wasn't sure whether there was a guard watching, but I didn't want to chance running in case I got shot. So I just tried to stay upright, balancing on the stool. Time became my enemy again, and I could feel myself sway and almost lose consciousness.

'Then I saw another inmate walk towards me, a virtual stranger. He was looking all around to see if guards were watching, and then he said to me, "I'm going to move the stool. Go, go, get to bed. If the SS ask, we'll say you fell and we carried you there."

'With my feet back on the ground I hobbled all the way to my bed, dropped down upon it and immediately fell asleep. When I woke, František was there with my food ration, which I gulped down, and then fell straight back to sleep again until the morning.'

The news on Radio Luxemburg soon brought Heini and Horst some relief. Anglo-American units were crossing the Rhine at Remagen, a strategic victory that let the Allies bring tanks and troops into the heartland of Nazi Germany. And while at first Heini thought that a rumbling in the far distance could be thunderstorms brewing, as the noise continued and grew nearer he realised it was the fighting coming closer. A few inmates thought that they could see flames, which added to the feeling of hope.

Then came an announcement that two shifts were being scrapped, surely a confirmation that supplies weren't getting through. Heini's hopes were raised that liberation might be coming. Exact timings weren't clear, but a news bulletin confirmed the Allied offensive on the eastern side of the Rhine had begun. An inmate climbed on the roof of the camp and reported that muzzle flashes were easier to see.

Then early one morning, 20 laden trailers drove into the drill square and were loaded with food from the camp store. It became clear a big move was planned – but who was leaving and what was the destination? At morning roll call, the SS order was issued: 'Get ready to march off. We're all leaving here. Take a blanket.' The SS gathered in a large group, extra jumpy and trigger-happy, seemingly ready to shoot at anything. They shouted for the prisoners to hurry as they'd be leaving the camp for another part of Germany.

For Heini, the realisation that they were heading in the opposite direction from the Allies – and setting off away from the chance of freedom – felt like the very last straw.

10
LIBERATION

In Berlin, the talk on the streets was of Allied victory and Germany's inevitable defeat. Berliners saw most of the capital was now reduced to rubble, and as Christmas 1944 approached, the quip of the season was, 'Be practical: give a coffin.'

Berliners were full of fear as Goebbels ramped up their centuries-old fear of an invasion by the Slavic peoples from the east. Erna did her best to put a Christmas meal on the table for her and Edie, but after sending some of her rations to Heini in Buchenwald, it wasn't much. She also observed the family tradition and put up a small Christmas tree in their flat, fixing little white candles on its branches and handmade decorations too. It brought welcome cheer to their cold flat, making Edie beam from ear to ear when she returned home and saw it.

As the Soviet Red Army approached Germany borders, Heinrich Himmler, head of the SS, attempted to wipe out any living evidence of the Nazis' war crimes by ordering the evacuation of all concentration camps. Hitler, in a state of denial, now rarely made speeches or broadcasts, but Himmler ordered that camp commandants 'make sure that not a single prisoner from the concentration camps falls alive into the hands of the enemy'.

At Auschwitz, the part-concentration, part-extermination camp in Poland where Sigi had been taken after being discovered in the Berlin pub cellar, his life hung in the balance. After his long period in hiding and the starvation rations, followed by the gruelling long hours of work and the filthy conditions at the camp, Sigi's health was failing, and he looked and felt far older than his 43 years. The gas chambers at Auschwitz that would kill more than a million men, women and children were being extended at around the time Sigi arrived the previous year, but the fact that he was a skilled upholsterer who had once worked for the car giant Opel had seen him put to work around the camp – like others with skills the Nazis found useful at the various industrial concerns in its sub-camps – and not sent to his death.

Just as Heini had heard the approach of the Allies, so did Sigi in Auschwitz. The SS took it as their signal to dismantle the gas chambers and destroy all records of who had been an inmate at Auschwitz and exactly what had happened there. On Himmler's orders, more than 60,000 weak and starving prisoners were marched from the frontlines back into the German interior in temperatures plunging to −20°C. Those who couldn't walk were to be shot. As the raggle-taggle line stumbled out, heading west and away from the Red Army, it was clear that the malnourished, inadequately clothed and desperately weak prisoners were completely unfit to walk

LIBERATION

35 miles across rough terrain in the freezing weather to Wodzisław Śląski railway station, where they'd be herded into freight trucks to take them to other camps. The prisoners themselves named it the 'Death March', and sure enough around 15,000 of them died on the way.

As Soviet forces drew nearer Auschwitz, panic and chaos spread through the camp and the SS guards focused on saving themselves. Instead of shooting the prisoners that were left behind, the SS fled the camp, ditching uniforms and identities and heading off in different directions.

Sigi was one of 6,000 prisoners left behind and who survived, perhaps due to this breakdown in SS discipline. Those lucky enough to have escaped the gas chambers on arrival or a bullet on the Nazi exodus were mostly middle-aged, like Sigi, or young.

The Red Army, led by men on horseback, entered Auschwitz on 27 January 1945 and liberated those who had not perished. The Soviet troops were shocked by what they saw and smelt: the crematoria, the dead piled up in great mounds and the extent of the Nazi genocide. Two field hospitals were established under the Soviets, housing former inmates from 20 countries. Four and a half thousand survivors are recorded as weighing on average 35 kg, or five and a half stone.

Sigi would spend months recovering from years of malnutrition and the various diseases he'd been infected with in the camp. He was assessed and medicated, and could only be gradually introduced to normal eating after having starved for years. Unlike many fellow inmates, Sigi was lucky and survived the first few months, but he then faced a long and painful hospital stay and a lengthy recovery.

MISCHLINGE

At first he was just grateful to be alive and barely knew what he thought and felt, other than wanting to wake up the next day. But as the pain subsided and he started to feel stronger, his thoughts turned more and more to home. Were his wife, son and daughter still alive? Weak as he was, Sigi knew that as well as not yet being fit enough to undertake a journey, it would in any case be impossible while fighting continued across Germany. He was impatient with his body's slow healing process, but when one of the Red Cross nurses told him transport was going to be provided to help him and others return to Berlin, it lifted his spirits hugely. But he needed five months of medication, food and rest to be strong enough to leave Auschwitz's field hospital and start the 350-mile journey from Poland back to his home in Berlin.

Just days after the liberation of Auschwitz, the US Army Air Force carried out a massive daylight bombing raid on Berlin on 3 February 1945. It was either this attack, or another of the frequent Allied bombing raids, that made a direct hit on Erna and Edie's home.

'Walking back from sifting through another bombed-out site,' recalls Edie, 'I turned the corner to see our home wasn't there anymore. It was nothing more than a pile of bricks. I ran over and through the smoke and dust, almost out of instinct, I got down on my knees and began looking under the rubble in case my mum was there. I found nothing, and looking further around suddenly spotted my mum standing there.

'I was so relieved. I ran over to her, and we hugged each other tight for a good few minutes before letting go. When we recovered ourselves, we talked to some of our neighbours,

LIBERATION

who were busily pinning notices to anything left standing, informing family they were still alive and where they might be found. We spent a little while looking through the wreckage to see if any of our possessions had survived, but as it got darker and colder we decided to head to Grandma Emma's flat.'

The two families hadn't seen each other for a while and had been alienated in the past, but of course Emma was surprised and delighted to see her daughter and granddaughter alive and well on her doorstep. The old lady welcomed them in and immediately said they could stay. 'No Nazi could come between them now,' she announced. Erna was keen to spend time with Eva, the daughter she'd seen so little of in recent times. So the four women settled into the little flat and waited to see what Germany's defeat would mean for them.

By February 1945 the Allies were so certain of victory that Roosevelt, Churchill and Stalin met at the Yalta Conference to discuss the inevitability of Hitler's unconditional surrender, carving up the territories his armies had occupied between them and planning the division of Germany and Berlin into four Allied occupied zones.

Heini, weak and half-starved like his fellow inmates, was making slow progress away from Buchenwald on the death march that was to claim many of their lives. Their SS guards, walking alongside them with machine guns and rifles at the ready, from the outset shot those who couldn't keep up, even though they needed beasts of burden to carry their supplies.

'We were divided into two teams of 25, with 14 of us attached to a harness, like horses, to pull a trailer full of food and the SS belongings, with the other 11 inmates pushing from the back and sides. These two lines formed a huge, long convoy moving slowly over hills, fields and meadows, deliberately avoiding every town and village.

'We cheered ourselves by commenting that the SS men, who were unused to any physical hardship, seemed to find it as tough as us and needed to stop if we came across a stream or a brook, where those of us who had them could refill our water bottles. One day we were even allowed to wash in a stream because the SS, despite having better boots, needed to relieve their painful blisters. Every evening we'd stop to spend the night in barns, but swollen, blistered and painful feet – and ever-present hunger – made sleep hard at times. In the morning, after paltry breakfast rations and roll call, we'd set off again, harnessed up to the trailers like beasts.'

As usual, the prisoners found small ways of relieving their hardship, swapping themselves around so they were with their friends. The SS were clearly only interested in checking that everyone was there and that they pressed on, and in any case all the inmates now looked so similar that from a superficial glance they wouldn't have known one from the other. Heini was together with his friends Horst, Günther, Gerhard, František, a few Czechs and a Frenchman. Their chat cheered them and they shared their hope that the Allies might catch them up.

'As the day warmed a little,' Heini recalled, 'the delicious smell of bread reached Horst and me from inside the trailer and made us hungrier. So while Horst acted as look-out, after several attempts I was able to steal a loaf of bread from inside the trailer, stuffing it down my roomy trousers as the march continued. Later, when the SS made themselves comfortable

LIBERATION

at one end of the barn, Horst and I took our tiny rations into a corner and shared the loaf we had stolen. Depriving our captors of it added to the flavour.'

But the comfort of snatched food didn't compensate for their rapidly deteriorating physical condition, with aching backs and legs, and ever-present blisters. Demoralised by the fading sounds and sights of warfare, the men realised that each painful step was taking them further from the Allied advance, and with some men dropping exhausted by the roadside, Heini and his crew felt utterly ravaged and were beginning to lose hope.

Yet their slow march lumbered on, the country paths now turning into paved roads, and at last a road sign revealed their location two miles from the town of Lippstadt.

'As night fell,' Heini remembered, 'our convoy reached a cinema on the outskirts of town, where the SS said we'd stop there for the night. They took their luggage upstairs to the gallery, while we slept on the rows of cinema seats, in the corridors or by the emergency exits, anywhere that offered comfort for our bleeding and aching feet.

'In the middle of the night an explosion shook the cinema, and then constant shelling stopped some of us from sleeping. When I woke in the morning, I thought perhaps the whistle wake-up call was late, but as I crept around looking everywhere, I found no SS guards, only their discarded uniforms. I ran around shouting, "The SS have gone, all gone." At first nobody believed me, but after several inmates checked upstairs and outside, it was clear the previous night's bombing had sounded the alarm that the Allies were close, and the SS and the hated overseer Neumann – clearly one of them – had made a run for it.

MISCHLINGE

'The clock in the cinema foyer no longer showed the correct time and the folding calendar no longer showed the correct date. One of the men made us laugh by correcting them. It was Sunday, 1 April 1945, and it was not an April Fool's joke. The SS had disappeared, and it was 9 o'clock.'

For now, there was a huge, palpable sense of relief. The SS had clearly set off in civilian clothes and had taken their weapons but left some of their superior rations in the trailers. The prisoners helped themselves to a feast of sausages, butter, margarine, and there was also tobacco. Unsupervised for the first time, the men could relax, resting in the luxury of the cinema seats, smoking, eating and speculating as to what had happened. There was a plentiful supply of water in the cinema, so everyone was able to wash and then just sit.

Their respite was short-lived, however, as members of the Volkssturm – men aged between 16 and 60 conscripted on Hitler's orders the previous autumn to be a German Home Guard – entered the building, armed with rifles, announcing they'd be taking the prisoners elsewhere. Heini and Horst felt angry, cornered and fearful of walking with the Volkssturm into the eerie-looking wood ahead. The pair spoke briefly and resolved that now was definitely the time to escape.

'As these new captors drove our straggly band forward towards a wooden bridge,' Heini recalled, 'Horst and I exchanged a glance and when we reached the bridge we jumped to one side and hid underneath it, out of view of the Volkssturm. When the clattering of the prisoners wooden-soled boots overhead subsided and we saw the long column of men disappear into the woods, we headed out in a different direction from the convoy, elated at our success.'

LIBERATION

The two Berliners soon found a country path to a farmhouse and knocked on the door, hoping for water and directions to the nearest town. No one answered, but as it was ajar they just called out and stepped into the kitchen. Still nobody came, but the pair were transfixed by the big bowl of potatoes on the table, the delicious smells coming from pots on the warm stove, and knives and forks laid out on the table. They hadn't seen anything like that for a long time.

'This freshly cooked meal was too tempting to resist. Without being asked, we just sat down and ate the whole meal; finding a fruit compote that we thought was very exotic, we ate that too. It was a real event and we savoured every mouthful. We sat there, waiting for an old farmer to appear, but he never did. Horst and I decided that our shaved heads, awful clothes and grubby appearance had more than likely frightened the family off, and they were hiding nearby. After some more calling and exploring, it was clear no one was going to show up, so we took some ham and sausage, only a fraction of what was in their well-stocked larder, and headed out again on our onward journey.

'As we reached the edge of a wood, we saw a tank half concealed in some bushes. At first we stood motionless and petrified, but after a while we noticed that one of its caterpillar tracks was broken, the hatch was open and the monstrous machine appeared to be unmanned. The gun barrel wasn't pointing in our direction and we noticed lots of straw packed around it, as if someone were trying to hide it. We edged closer, and seeing no sound or movement we both dared to climb up and look down through the tank's hatch. There was

MISCHLINGE

nothing scary to be seen, just a lot of terrycloth flannels. Neither of us could figure out what they were doing there, but we both decided to quickly move on.'

As they jumped off the tank, they saw two small bundles of bank notes on the forest floor right in front of them. Needing no invitation to seize the money, they congratulated themselves on their good fortune. After having counted it, they were giddy with delight as the 1,200 Reichsmarks would easily pay for their rail tickets home to Berlin. Despite feeling that this was their lucky day, the two friends were also aware that they could come across German or Allied soldiers at any time, and they had no idea of the military situation or their exact whereabouts. So they moved cautiously as they emerged from the cover of the woods.

It wasn't long before they had another shock. Several uniformed men walked up to them, guns in their hand.

'You,' shouted one of the men, in what sounded like broken German. 'Where from?'

Horst, who spoke a little English, replied, 'Concentration Camp Buchenwald. Where are we now?'

The soldiers said a word they didn't recognise, just pointing to a nearby path, then asked whether the two of them had seen any German troops. When Heini explained they hadn't, but they'd found an abandoned tank, the soldiers asked to be taken to it. After a quick look around the machine, the soldiers seemed satisfied, and they set off in one direction and directed Heini and Horst to a path leading to the nearest village.

Alone again, Heini and Horst discussed the foreign soldiers for a while and eventually agreed they were American GIs, as they knew from the radio that they were the nearest Allied

LIBERATION

force. Heini told Horst, 'Our strange striped suits and scary hairstyles, the wooden soles on our boots, our very brief shorts and shabby jackets would give scarecrows a run for their money.' As they continued walking, more slowly and with slightly more confidence now, they saw a convoy of American army lorries. Surely they were now behind Western Allied lines. They both breathed a sigh of relief, overjoyed to have escaped the death march.

Soon they reached a small village that was swarming with US army personnel. Suddenly tired and thirsty, they just sat down at the village's central fountain and drank lots of water while trying to take in the scene. A US army doctor appeared, and without saying much made them both undergo delousing, which they found quite amusing.

But then an officer who could speak German perfectly arrived and bombarded the pair with questions, asking them to account for themselves: who were they, how had they slipped away from the other inmates on the Buchenwald death march, and could they point on a map to where they had left them?

'And I'm sorry to say, boys,' he told them, 'but I'm going to need proof. You say you're escaped prisoners. Your clothing, prisoner number, red collar, wooden-soled boots and your strangely shaved heads alone are not sufficient. You could easily have stolen this get-up and under your disguise could lurk a dyed-in-the-wool SS officer.'

Heini was startled and confused. He and Horst were taken to a house, and in a service room they were ordered to remove their tops. 'We're looking for a tattoo underneath your upper arm,' the officer told them. 'We need to be certain that you're not actually SS.'

MISCHLINGE

Heini felt angry and insulted, and asked why they should take any of their clothes off. As he spoke, a higher-ranking American officer entered the room and in perfect German apologised to the young men.

'I'm so sorry,' he said, 'but we must ask for your understanding in this matter. We've had plenty of bad experiences with the SS so far and we must make every effort to come to the correct decision with each individual case. The SS are keen to disappear, and they're using disguises to do so. Looking like a concentration camp prisoner is, I'm afraid, an ideal disguise. These brutal men are capable of anything to save themselves. They have no scruples.'

The US soldiers explained they were searching for a specific tattoo that identified its wearer as SS. These were *Blutgruppentätowierungen* (blood group tattoos) on the skin of members of the SS to identify blood type. They were taken as prima facie evidence of being a member of the SS; if a person had such a tattoo they were liable to arrest, prosecution and possible execution.

After their arms had been checked and cleared, Heini and Horst were allowed to get dressed, but the officer still wanted to know if they had any paper identification or letters to prove their story. Heini smiled, as he remembered what his proof was – he asked for a knife and split the collar of his jacket open, revealing the postcard his mother had sent him. Horst also had a letter from his family, the postmark of KZ Buchenwald and a detainee number, and all of these bits of evidence legitimised the pair of them. They gave silent thanks to their old Buchenwald comrades for advising them to reinforce their badges and hoped that they would soon be using their letters to prove their identity.

LIBERATION

The high-ranking US officer asked the very relieved Heini and Horst for their help. Would they guide a US convoy back to search for their companions from the death march? They were both happy to agree and soon set off in the first of a convoy of jeeps, a medical car and lorries, all marked 'US Army'. Heini and Horst showed the way, followed by the rest of the vehicles, all of which were armed.

They found the woods where they had escaped, but there was no sign of their fellow prisoners, only abandoned weapons on the ground and hanging in a tree. The officer in charge said they should go back to the last place they had spent the night – the cinema. Sure enough, their companions from the march were there, in a weak and feeble state. Heini and Horst were overjoyed to see them, and the prisoners were more than delighted to see the American army contingent.

Their fellow former inmates explained that when the Volkssturm guards heard the Allied forces drawing close they simply melted away, just like the SS had done before, abandoning their prisoners to save themselves. They were all very pleased to catch up with each other, and even more so when the Americans immediately dispensed medical treatment. František and Gerhard had their painful and distorted feet properly treated, while Günther and other more seriously ill men were taken to Lippstadt Hospital to be treated for dysentery and other acute ailments.

The US officer in charge asked Heini and Horst if they'd be prepared to return with him and the convoy to the temporary American headquarters and help him further, and both readily agreed. At the base they heard how US forces had liberated Buchenwald. In the first ten days of April, the SS had tried to force the last of the prisoners out of the camp onto another

MISCHLINGE

death march. Two inmates still at the camp, a Pole and a Soviet, were sending out Morse code messages in English, German and Russian, repeating the plea:

> To the Allies. To the Army of General Patton. This is the Buchenwald Concentration Camp. SOS. We request help. They want to evacuate us. The SS wants to destroy us.

Within minutes the US Third Army responded:

> KZ Bu. Hold out. Rushing to your aid. Staff of the Third Army.

The prisoner who received the message is said to have fainted.

Heini heard how some of the emaciated inmates found the strength to storm the watchtowers and kill the remaining guards using guns the resistance had collected over the past couple of years. Heini wondered if his hidden gun and the senior he'd given it to had found the strength that day to exact revenge on one of their tormentors.

There were still 21,000 prisoners in Buchenwald on the day they were liberated by the US Third Army on 11 April 1945 at 3.15 p.m., the time now permanently set on the clock at the camp's entrance gate.

US infantrymen, President Barack Obama's great-uncle among them, were sent the following day to take control of the camp and some journalists were admitted to report on what they saw. CBS reporter Edward R. Murrow broadcast his eyewitness account:

LIBERATION

I asked to see one of the barracks and was shown a building that had once held 80 horses. There were 1,200 men in it, five to a bunk. The stink was beyond all description. They called the doctor. We inspected his records. There were only names in a little black book. Nothing about who these men were, what they had done or hoped. Behind the names of those who had died, there was a cross. I counted them. They totalled 242 – 242 out of 1,200 in one month.

As we walked out into the courtyard a man fell dead. Two others, they must have been over 60, were crawling toward the latrine. I saw it, but will not describe it.

The day after liberation, the Allied and US Commander General Eisenhower and Generals Patton and Bradley visited Buchenwald. Eisenhower wrote:

The visual evidence and the verbal testimony of starvation, cruelty and bestiality were so overpowering as to leave me a bit sick. In one room there were piled up 20 or 30 naked men killed by starvation. George Patton would not even enter. I made the visit deliberately to be in a position to give first-hand evidence if ever in the future this should be dismissed as propaganda.

A quarter of a million people passed through Buchenwald and its many sub-camps, where it's thought that more than 56,000 died. Those who survived probably did so through a mixture of youth and health, resourcefulness, enterprise and maybe a little luck.

MISCHLINGE

The camp liberators discovered that in the block next to Heini – block 46, the one his Soviet friends had warned him to avoid – thousands of inmates had been the subject of medical experiments, injected with typhus and other diseases, and died painful deaths.

Heini had suffered from both physical and mental torture in both the slave-labour and the concentration camps. He'd been forced to do hard labour on starvation rations in both the freezing cold and in heatwave conditions for months on end. He'd been called a dog and treated much worse than one, and used as a beast of burden to pull heavy wagons. He'd been deprived of his freedom, deprived of his name, deprived of food and clothes. Even his hair had been taken from him. For more than two years he'd been starved, tortured and humiliated throughout what should have been his childhood and maturity to manhood.

Yet as the war in Germany was ending in the spring of 1945, aged 21, he still had the precious gift of life. Now his thoughts focused on his family – could his mother, father, sister and grandmother have all survived in Berlin under Hitler's nose? Was his fiancée Margot still waiting for him? Haunted by thoughts of what they might have endured, he wondered if he might ever see any of them again.

11
SOVIETS AND RETURNERS

Berliners woke every day now fearing the inevitable Soviet invasion, as foreign radio stations brought news of a massive fighting force marching towards the city from three sides. Stalin was determined to take Berlin and beat his American and British allies, ordering his two senior commanders – Marshals Zhukov and Konev – to lead a pincer movement from the east, south and north, encircling the city before launching a massive attack. When the Soviets entered Berlin on 15 April, in tanks and on horseback, they were a terrifying sight, massively superior to the defending German forces in both numbers and firepower. The highly trained Wehrmacht and SS had only 45,000 troops, while the poorly trained, younger Volkssturm and Hitler Youth had just 40,000. This small army took up positions to resist an invading force of a million and a half Russian soldiers.

An atmosphere of gloom and fatalism pervaded daily life in the city, and Erna, Edie, Emma and Eva felt extremely vulnerable. The street below their flat was a feral place, with

MISCHLINGE

groups of soldiers huddling around bonfires through the night, as Erna saw from their window. Everyone was watching and waiting, and only Erna dared venture out in a quick dash to get their rations.

A massive barrage of shells, tanks and machine gun fire hit the city, and fighting went from street to street, house to house, with a huge loss of life that by the time the battle was over had claimed the lives of 300,000 Berliners. There was strong resistance in many areas, while in others civilians put out white flags of surrender, only too pleased to see the end of hostilities. Many senior Nazis quickly fled the capital, but SS execution squads roamed the city, executing any defeatist 'traitors' and fighting on.

Erna was pleased to find that for the first time since the war began, Jews were allowed into air-raid shelters. These were always crowded, but with water, toilets, plenty of candles and sometimes a nurse, they were stronger and much better equipped than domestic cellars. The first time they took refuge in one they were shocked to see several former Nazis down there too. They had swapped their uniforms for civilian clothes in an obvious attempt to hide their party membership. No one dared challenge them and anyway it wasn't the Nazis that they feared now, but the invading Soviets on the prowl for young women. More gallows humour began to appear. Air-raid shelters were known as LSRs, and some joker wrote that this abbreviation now stood for '*Lernt schnell Russisch*' – 'Learn Russian quickly'.

Bombs still fell on Berlin, and when they did Erna and Edie were pleased to at last take cover in one such air-raid shelter alongside most of their neighbours. 'All of a sudden we heard shouting and yelling,' says Edie, 'and for the first time Mum and I saw Russians – four young soldiers came clattering down the stairs, brandishing their guns. Mum immediately stood in front of me trying to hide me, but one of them spotted me, pointed his gun at me and yelled, "You!" Then he grabbed my arm and pulled me along to another room in the cellar.

'I was certain I would be raped and I froze as the soldier lifted my dress. He saw immediately that I had my period and only messy rags between my legs in the absence of sanitary towels, and he recoiled. I was very frightened then and felt sure he'd shoot me, but he just raised his gun, pointed back the way we had come and marched me back to my mum.

'Back in the main shelter, right next to Mum and me, was a young woman with a couple of kids sitting on the bunk beds against the wall next to her husband. The soldier let go of my arm and grabbed her, dragging her away from her husband and children. He took her back to that same room and obviously raped her instead. Mum and I could hear her crying for what seemed like a long time. All we could do was wait for the horror to be over. Silence fell over everyone sheltering down there. The poor woman didn't come back to where we were, but soon afterwards all the soldiers left the cellar and as soon as it was silent, people began to leave and go back up. Once we saw the coast was clear and there were no Russians to be seen, Mum and I almost ran all the way back to Grandma Emma's. Once inside the flat, Mum just held me and we both sobbed, at once grateful and guilty for such a lucky escape, and so sad for the woman and her family that didn't.'

The Soviet army's extended victory celebrations, fuelled by alcohol, saw the rape of women on a massive scale. The two main Berlin hospitals estimated that they treated between

MISCHLINGE

95,000 and 130,000 rape victims. Some figures suggest that perhaps 10,000 of those raped died, many from suicide. Berlin women soon learnt to disappear during what were called 'the hunting hours' of night-time as sounds of these attacks reverberated around streets that no longer had glass in their windows. Mothers hid their daughters for days on end, as did Erna, and after her 'lucky escape' 17-year-old Edie was only to happy to comply and not leave the flat.

Around the city, reports circulated that many of these Soviet soldiers were uncouth peasants from the poorest parts of the country. A neighbour told Edie that they'd witnessed one who'd never seen a toilet and didn't know what it was for. They had seen soldiers trying to wash potatoes in it, and when they pulled the chain they lost them all. It was another rare moment of laughter in thoroughly grim times.

Food was scarce and Berliners resorted to cutting meat from horses that had been killed in the fighting, but neither Erna nor Edie had the stomach for it. The sight of butchered, rotting horses on the street was enough to make them feel sick, so they eked out their meagre supplies, although their hunger was constant.

Historians estimate that 80 per cent of the city was destroyed by the bombings and the battle to capture Berlin. Meanwhile, Hitler was holed up for months in his underground bunker complex near Berlin's Reich Chancellery. He was still issuing orders, 'the battle should be conducted without consideration for our own population' being among his last. Regional commissioners were instructed to destroy 'all industrial plants, all the main electricity works, waterworks, gas works', together with 'all food and clothing stores' in order to create 'a desert' in the Allies' path.

SOVIETS AND RETURNERS

On 29 April 1945, when Soviet forces entered the heart of Berlin, Hitler's military commanders told him that no relief was coming and there was not much time left. Early in the morning of that day, just after midnight, he married his mistress Eva Braun in the bunker with Joseph Goebbels and Martin Bormann as witnesses, followed by a small champagne reception. Having said his goodbyes to them, all the remaining inhabitants of the bunker had been given poisonous capsules to end their lives. The following day Hitler shot himself in the head and was found shortly afterwards, his pistol by his side. Eva Braun lay next to him, having taken poison. As per Hitler's instructions, their bodies were taken to the Reich's Chancellery garden, where Goebbels and Bormann watched as their corpses were doused in petrol and set alight. Days later, the Soviets identified their burnt remains through dental records.

A wave of senior Nazi suicides followed, among them Berlin's mayor Goebbels, who administered poison to his wife and six children, as well as Wilhelm Burgdorf, Hitler's adjutant, and General Hans Krebs, Chief of the Army General Staff.

The news that Hitler had committed suicide on 30 April was a relief to many, but life for Berliners continued to be tough, chaotic, full of uncertainty, fear and without hope for the future. So much so there was an unprecedented wave of suicides across Germany, particularly in those parts that had been invaded by the Red Army, including Berlin. In Friedrichshain, where Edie had been based as a slave labourer, more than a hundred people were said to have committed suicide on the day that the Soviets entered the area.

MISCHLINGE

Erna and Edie were still cramped up living in her mother Emma's flat, and although Erna had enjoyed seeing more of her other daughter Eva, their relationships were also different now. They were all getting on each other's nerves and yearning for a return to normality, although they all knew that was a way off as fighting on the capital's streets dragged on. Living so close to the centre, their neighbourhood still rang with gunfire from the remaining pockets of German resistance. On 7 May news finally came of the German surrender. It had been a dark and dangerous spring.

Erna ventured out alone at first to look for food and firewood, but after a few solo trips she judged it safe for Edie to join her. At night their thoughts and conversation focused on Sigi and Heini. Had they survived the war? Where were they now? Everything was still in a state of such chaos, with so many buildings having collapsed, no post, no newspapers and no one in charge whom they could ask about the current situation. They could only be thankful that the bombs had stopped, and picking their way through the destruction they did meet some familiar faces to talk to and find a few local buildings that were still standing.

With hostilities ended and peace declared, Erna heard that local officials in the town hall were allocating properties to homeless Berliners. She was delighted when they allocated her family a flat in Lichtenberg, as she'd told the officials she was hoping that her husband and son would return soon and she'd need a home for them all. And she hoped beyond hope that this was true.

Edie remembers walking into the flat and saying out loud, '"Mum this is heaven." Because the first thing I saw in the kitchen was a larder full of food. Food we hadn't seen for

SOVIETS AND RETURNERS

years. Mum explained to me that the flat had belonged to a Nazi, and he and his family had fled as the Soviets approached the city. The larder had sausages hanging in it, there were tins of meat, ham and other things in bags we couldn't wait to open. Mum's face lit up as she explored the place.

'Between the kitchen and the bathroom there was a large hole in the wall where a bomb had hit the building. The Nazi family had left all their possessions behind when they'd run away, and as we'd lost everything when our home was flattened, we didn't let a single thought about whom they'd once belonged to bother us in the slightest.

'We were so delighted to have our own place at last, despite the holes in the wall and its horrid former occupants, and we tried to make it homely. Mum got started straightaway, sorting through what was there to make it as comfortable as possible for us. "And who knows when your dad and your brother will be back," she'd sometimes say. "It's good we're near Lichtenberg railway station." I think we talked about Heini and Dad often, to keep them alive in our hearts and minds.'

Three hundred miles away, Heini was also experiencing a little luxury, thanks to the US army. Now satisfied that they were who they said they were, the US officer had offered Heini and Horst temporary accommodation at the US base. Mentally and physically exhausted from the stresses and strains of their return to the concentration camp with the US soldiers, they were shown to two beds in a little gabled room. It was so luxuriously decorated, with fresh towels and sheets and pillows, that the two men were overcome.

MISCHLINGE

'We just sat in the room for a while, admiring it,' recalled Heini. 'It had been such a long time since either of us had slept in a proper bed. Our American hosts gave us white bread, butter and tins of corned beef. When we went to collect it, we were surprised that they seemed familiar with the Westphalian ham we had taken from the farmhouse. They were keen to swap, and we gave them our ham and got chocolate in return. As we began to eat in our quaint little room, we both said we could hardly remember ever having eaten better. We then took turns to take a long, hot bath, and before climbing into our beds that night I told Horst that the whole day had seemed like Christmas all day long. And when he woke, Horst declared it his first proper night's sleep in years.'

Over the next few days, as they ate three good meals a day, bathed daily and slept on thick mattresses, they began to feel a bit more normal, keen to get out and do things. The one thing holding them back was their emaciated appearance, along with their strange striped prison haircuts, and of course their tatty prison clothes and uncomfortable wooden-soled shoes. They both hated the idea that they stood out as ugly and odd. So when they next reported to the US commander, Heini asked if it might be possible to have some new clothes and shoes.

'Not only was it possible, but we were given huge choice when we were shown into a room full of US supplies: suits, coats and jackets, shirts, pullovers, socks and shoes. There was so much to choose from, it looked like a small department store. We didn't know what to choose first, trying on all sorts of different combinations until we found what suited our thin frames. We couldn't believe it when we were invited

SOVIETS AND RETURNERS

to take a suitcase each and fill them with whatever clothes, underwear and everyday items we needed.'

Now, their only concern was their dreadful haircuts. Both men had a bald strip in the middle of their head from their foreheads to the back of their necks, with about a centimetre of growth on the sides. So Horst chose a beret and Heini chose a jaunty hat, and when both men reported back to the commander, he hardly recognised them. '*Kleider machen Leute*' ('clothes make the man'), he told them. He then told them, 'This is the last thing I can do for you,' and handed them both a proof-of-identity document, written in English, recording them as prisoners at KZ Buchenwald and Witten-Annen labour detachment. This would stop anybody doubting their identities again, he assured them. Finally, he asked them if they'd stay awhile at the nearest American HQ and provide the Americans with details of their experiences in Buchenwald, as part of the official records, which they readily agreed to do before thanking him and making their goodbyes.

Heini and Horst were then given generous rations and small packs of chewing gum before being driven to the nearby town of Soest, the regional US headquarters. Both kept their old prison clothes at the top of their bags just in case they needed another proof of identity.

As the US army jeep dropped them off, the two GIs waved and shouted good luck, attracting a few locals who wanted to see what was going on. An elderly man with a limp came up and introduced himself as Herr Schulte, and they asked him for directions to the mayor's office, where they had to report. When they explained that they were former camp inmates due to help the US, Schulte explained that the office

MISCHLINGE

was now shut for the day, but he'd happily put his caravan at their disposal for the night and take them to see the officials in the morning. Having never been inside a caravan, Heini and Horst were 'struck by the charm of something new', in Heini's words, and accepted the offer. The next morning the old man arrived and insisted on taking them to his sister-in-law's home for breakfast.

At Frau Schulte's breakfast table they learnt that the Nazis had arrested her father for the 'crime' of having Romani ancestry, and he'd also been sent to a camp. The fact that Heini and Horst had survived a similar camp gave her hope that her father might also be home soon, and as they talked and shared their stories, they decided to trust one another a little.

'We were touched when Frau Schulte offered us a room in her house so we didn't have to remain in the caravan. We gladly accepted her kind offer, but – before we went off to see him – we asked her if we could trust the mayor. Might he be a Nazi sympathiser? We were reassured when we were told that the Nazi mayor had fled town the previous week and his deputy was now in charge and could be trusted.'

When they met him, however, and showed him their American papers, he had no idea what to do with them. Apologising, he said that for the moment he'd give them a double ration card and 100 Reichsmarks to help them. He was happy for them to stay with Frau Schulte, but said he'd try to sort out more permanent accommodation and asked for their patience.

'Walking around Soest, we felt in a whole new world,' Heini recalled. 'Walking around the town together, free from all pressure, was amazing. The town seemed to have with-

SOVIETS AND RETURNERS

stood the ravages of war and not a single destroyed house could be seen. A few days ago we still looked subhuman, but today we looked and felt like normal citizens. Here we were not being watched and acting as free, equal men. It was hard to believe any of this was real.

'Life had returned to some sort of normality here, with civilians being asked to hand in all weapons, to obey a night-time curfew and where possible report back to work. Our only worry was it made us think: *What could be normal in Berlin? What damage had the relentless bombing attacks on so-called important military targets caused to our families? Had they even survived?*'

The next day, Horst and Heini reported to the US command centre as requested. An American officer took their details and then asked them to complete their registration with the German authorities at the police station. Before they left they were surprised by his next request. Would Heini and Horst be prepared to help the US authorities to search for, apprehend and arrest former SS and Nazis, given their experiences? Neither hesitated and immediately said that of course they'd be willing to help.

At the police station the deputy mayor had arranged for them to be issued with ID cards, but Heini was horrified when asked to pose for a photograph. Both he and Horst loathed their strange, deforming haircuts, and so they asked the army commander if they could postpone having their pictures taken until their hair had grown a bit. With touching understanding the commander agreed, and issued the pair a temporary ID card with their last known address – KZ Buchenwald, Kommando Annen. And with that, Heini and Horst were officially made citizens of Soest.

MISCHLINGE

Heini and Horst were more than happy to help the US military catch Nazis, but Heini also wanted to earn a little money for whatever the future held. It was obvious that very few men remained in Soest – they had seen only the elderly, ill or disabled who couldn't fight, and the few French prisoners of war who'd been put to work in the local farms. It was clearly a town of female householders, whose businesses and homes were in need of repair. So many jobs needed doing – roofs with holes in, walls to be rebuilt, electrical problems, water leaks, plumbing damage, roof repairs, the list was endless. Heini and Horst agreed that they'd knock on doors and offer their services.

The two Berliners found not only work, but numerous acts of random kindness. The women who lived near Frau Schulte took it upon themselves to look after these two young newcomers.

'Our emaciated bodies and odd appearance told our story better than we could,' Heini said. 'And as the story of who we were and where we had been was understood around the neighbourhood, our desire not to talk about our past was respected. If we'd had nicer memories, we'd have been more willing to share them, as we were asked round for meals from breakfast right through to supper, hardly needing to use our ration cards. All the attention could be a bit overwhelming at times, but we were also enjoying the company of so many women for the first time in a long time and feeling more optimistic about the future.'

One afternoon, walking past the hairdressing salon, Heini was teased by some young women that his last barber had done him no favours, so he stopped to share a bit of banter with them, saying he preferred female hands to a barber's.

SOVIETS AND RETURNERS

The owner, a Frau Erni Knipsel, heard the chatter and asked whether Heini might be prepared to do some jobs around her hairdressing business in return for one of her spare rooms and a decent haircut. Heini thanked her, but said that as the authorities were finding him a room he would have to consult them and let her know. Ever cautious, he wanted to check out the political sympathies of those who lived in the building. Having been reassured that Frau Knipsel and two other tenants in the building – a French prisoner of war and his wife – weren't Nazi sympathisers, Heini thanked Frau Schulte and moved out the next day. Horst wasn't upset as he'd found a girlfriend and was spending most of his time with her when he hadn't any repair jobs to do.

Frau Knipsel was older than Heini and she soon took him under her wing, preparing him hearty farmhouse breakfasts and tasty suppers, while Heini began with small jobs around the salon as he was still weak. The two hit it off, and as Heini began to trust his landlady, he told her that he and Horst were awaiting a call from the US army to help them track down Nazis. Keen to help, Frau Knipsel fetched a small record book.

She explained that Soest was a small town and the townsfolk, including the new mayor, had helped her keep a record that might one day be useful to bring about a reckoning. Her book contained details of those who'd been members of the Nazi Party, along with their rank and medals, including those who'd been awarded the Iron Cross. She gave the book to Heini to take to the US army commander, in the hope that it would help bring justice.

As he gained more strength, putting on weight and sleeping well, Heini got to work on the repairs needed everywhere. All

MISCHLINGE

over the building, in the house and in the salon there were jobs to do: and all were increasingly urgent as Frau Knipsel's customers began to return. In the daytime, Heini was never short of jobs. He dismantled the ugly blackout curtains and boards, which were no longer required. Little by little he worked his way through the list of things that had to be repaired, the sinks, the hairdryers and the leaks in the water supply, taps and washbasins.

As his health improved, Heini's good looks and easy charm were surfacing through the bad haircut and thin frame. Frau Knipsel was delighted with his work and their relationship was developing apace. She insisted he called her Erni and not Frau from now on and said that he could stay as long as he liked; his skills were so useful that they paid for his board and lodging. And as the bond between them grew, Heini confided in her about his *Mischling* status and his concerns for his family in Berlin as the war dragged on.

When the shop closed, Heini and Erni would get together with the other occupants of the house: the former French prisoner of war and his wife and son, who was a master locksmith and now worked out of the courtyard workshop. They'd listen to the Anglo-American radio station together for news, then tune in to some good music. Conversation was usually about the present or the future – they'd all had quite enough of the war. They'd even sometimes go out to neighbours' houses or the local pub, making sure to return home before the 8 p.m. curfew.

It wasn't long before a romantic affection developed between Erni and this handsome young stranger, despite the fact that she was older and her status uncertain – her husband had gone to fight in the war but had now been missing for more than two years. The salon was becoming busier as Erni gained more customers and her family and friends visited. Heini certainly seemed to charm the ladies with his gentle manner and ever-improving appearance. Erni joked that she'd never had so many visitors and couldn't think why so many girls wanted to drop in all of a sudden.

'Soest was proving a haven. It was almost possible to forget the war was still going on because it hardly touched us,' Heini remembered. 'I was enjoying life again: work kept me busy and there was laughter, time to relax and friendships.

'At weekends, Erni and I would walk in the countryside near the Möhne Reservoir [famously breached by the RAF Dambusters in 1943 with their bouncing bombs], and what I saw there, in a spot that remained a beauty spot, made me very angry. To see the numerous luxury villas where the Nazi bigwigs had lived and contrast them with how we'd lived not far away in the labour camp made me very emotional. Their luxurious and comfortable lives were in stark contrast with ours: worked like slaves, sleeping on bare-wire beds and given only starvation rations.'

Sometimes these experiences sparked darker conversations between them, with Heini's concerns for his family, friends and his home city when the fighting stopped and at what point it might be safe enough to make the return journey. Bit by bit Heini shared a little, but by no means all, of his experiences in the camp with Erni.

Despite his freedom, hugely improved eating and periods of relaxation, Heini had not by any means escaped his recent past: 'As the months passed, dark nightmares came, at first occasional, then every night, becoming worse and worse. In them I relived horrific events, I'd shout out and sweat so profusely that my sheets became literally drenched. Several times Erni would check on me, often changing the bed in the middle of the night while I took a cooling shower.

'I was angry at myself and embarrassed that my nightmares woke up everyone in the building. I reasoned that this sudden change of circumstances had been a shock to my system. I hadn't adjusted as well as I thought. I no longer had to put up with being abused and worked hard all day long and imprisoned, but with freedom had come its own difficulties. When I was miserable, all I yearned for was the chance to be on my own, to use the toilet alone and to sleep in a normal bed. But now I did feel a little lonely in my room.'

Heini and Erni decided – just for the time being – to live in the moment. He resolved to put Margot and worries about his family out of his mind because, with the war still continuing, they were all out of reach, just as Erni couldn't know if her husband was alive and would ever return to her. And having Erni close was comfort indeed. After several nightmarish nights, Erni suggested they share a bed and both hoped Heini's nightmares might disappear.

One Sunday Erni suggested a visit to her parents' farm to help Heini's transformation. Herr and Frau Föhrer had a mixed farm, a restful, beautiful place that they were finding difficult to manage as they aged. When Heini offered to help with the repairs, tending their crops, as well as looking after the pigs and cows, he'd no idea how much he'd enjoy it. He loved the work, and as he did more and more, he felt valued and pleased to help those who were being so kind to him.

Heini began to spend more days in the countryside on the farm than in the salon, having completed all the repairs there. He enjoyed working with the animals and learnt new skills

SOVIETS AND RETURNERS

tackling all the jobs around the farm. He'd bike over there early in the morning and return to Erni in the evening, often bringing fresh vegetables that she cooked for supper.

The combination of this friendly town and farm, in an area almost untouched by war, which had welcomed and nurtured him, together with the care of this kind woman, was having a cathartic effect on Heini.

Quite unexpectedly, all the church bells rang throughout Soest for a good half an hour on 8 May, bringing news that the war had finally ended and peace had really come. German forces had unconditionally surrendered and the Allies proclaimed 'Victory in Europe' – VE Day. Heini was deeply touched by the moment and the words 'The Day of Liberation'.

Heini and Horst were improving physically and mentally with the peacetime delights of Soest. It brought back thoughts of all his comrades who had been incarcerated in the concentration camps, their lives reduced to the role of slaves. He felt sure it was a remarkable day when he'd regained his rights as an equal human being.

Heini thought about his future: as happy as he was with Erni in Soest, he'd never lost his desire to get back to Berlin to his sister, his parents, his grandmother, Margot and his friends. But as the radio news made clear, there was no infrastructure in Germany now – no post, no trains, no way yet to find out about his family or return to Berlin to them.

At times he felt as if he were living on an island, in a sort of parallel universe in Soest. Now that there was peace, the curfew was lifted completely, the cinema showed Hollywood films and there were dances where bands or records invited everyone to take to the floor. As comfortable as life was, and as much as he was enjoying it, Heini knew he had to return to Berlin, although he didn't know how or when. He whispered that to Erni; she must prepare herself.

Slowly the men from the town returned, Wehrmacht soldiers, coming from the front or from prisoner-of-war camps. There was no sign or news of Erni's husband, but she'd long presumed him dead.

To Heini's surprise, Günther, the Buchenwald camp cook, turned up on their doorstep one day, having been released from hospital and told by US HQ where Heini was. He'd decided to visit his old friends on his way home to find his family in Kassel. They found Horst, and the three young men spent a happy day together, with Günther promising them he'd test the postal services en route to see if they were working better than from Soest. And when a few weeks later a letter did get through from Günther, saying he'd found his family in good health and his flat still standing despite the considerable damage to Kassel itself, Heini had to know if his parents had survived. He immediately wrote a letter to their last address and began to make enquiries about how he could travel to Berlin if and when he received a reply.

First he needed ID documents to travel. That meant returning to Buchenwald to get his papers upgraded from temporary to permanent by the US authorities and have those postponed photographs taken. In July, shortly after his 22nd birthday, the US commander gave Heini the go-ahead to return to Buchenwald with Horst, as soon as an army vehicle was going that way. That month was dominated by news of the Potsdam conference in Berlin where the three Allied leaders – Joseph Stalin, Winston Churchill and Harry S. Truman –

SOVIETS AND RETURNERS

were discussing terms for the end of war and the administration and division of Germany and Berlin between the great powers.

Before Heini set off for Buchenwald he asked Erni to give him a haircut that would be smart enough for him to face the camera for his identity photo, and her styling restored his confidence. All the care and good food he'd received had seen his weight bounce back a little, and he felt ready. Erni thought him most dashing.

The US commander had kindly loaned them a swanky Mercedes V170, which had been confiscated from one of the Nazi bigwigs' villas above the Möhne Reservoir. Neither Heini nor Horst had a driving licence, but with a written authorisation document from the commander, and their papers in hand, the two of them set off in what they hoped would be another step towards home.

As they drew close to the infamous camp, both felt a sense of dread, the words on the entrance gate – '*Jedem das Seine*' ('To Each What He Deserves') – sending shivers through them. Inside the camp they spotted some of their former comrades who had been too unfit to travel and were now just waiting for transport to go home. As clothing supplies were short, they were wearing a mixture of prison and civilian clothing. They talked about the final days of KZ Buchenwald and how the SS guards had simply vanished. Although the camp had changed and only the weakest of inmates remained, along with those caring for them or those waiting to leave, both Heini and Horst felt the same oppressive atmosphere and couldn't wait to get out.

A man in the International Camp Committee tent said it would take a fortnight to process and release Heini and

Horst's paperwork, as priority was being given to non-Germans who were keen to travel home. While Heini understood, he explained they had neither the money nor the rations to stay that long in the area. The man was sympathetic, offering them another temporary set of papers that could be picked up the following day.

Heini felt a deep empathy for the foreign prisoners he saw, taken from all over Europe, ill and weak, desperate to leave the place, but waiting on either paperwork or transport. He completely understood why they had priority, and he knew how fortunate he was to be in the safe haven of Soest.

On their return, Horst was thrilled to find a letter from his parents in Berlin, and relieved to discover they were well and still in their flat. Heini was pleased for his friend but bitterly disappointed to have no news from his family. But with proof that post was getting through to Berlin, he wrote to them again, and to his great childhood friend Gerhard hoping he'd survived the war and was back home again.

As autumn turned to winter, Heini received no news from Berlin, either from his parents or from Gerhard, and he was becoming increasingly anxious and uneasy. He resolved to wait a little longer and spend the yuletide period with Erni in Soest, then set off for Berlin no matter what. So Christmas 1945 was Heini's first for a very long time without air-raid warnings, the fear of bombs, starvation, humiliation, cold or abject misery. And he loved celebrating it with Erni and her parents, as well as his new friends the locksmith, his wife and young son, who'd all helped restore him in body and mind. But thoughts of his own family were never far from his mind, and he smiled at the memory of their movable Christmas tree.

SOVIETS AND RETURNERS

In Soest everyone was celebrating in the traditional way at home, enjoying home cooking. Even though there was little to buy in the shops and food was rationed, people had generally become more optimistic. The war was over and its terrible events were behind them. This, Heini knew, was the best Christmas present. Things would settle down gradually, the economy would recover, and he and millions of others could now view the future with hope.

Radio broadcasts revealed that Germany's infrastructure was gradually being restored or rebuilt, and transport links were opening up. Heini knew it was now time to make his way back to Berlin and his own family.

'Erni knew it too,' he recalled. 'She'd always known it. We talked about my life in Berlin before and after our relationship developed. I'd told her about Margot, my sister and all my family, and she understood that I'd return to Berlin as soon as the war was over and the journey feasible. That didn't mean she wasn't upset when I told her I'd resolved to leave, as soon as practicable, in the New Year. But she understood.

'I first said goodbye to those I knew in the town, then I cycled over to her parents' farm one last time and thanked them both for making me feel like part of their family. Erni and I spent a last quiet evening together, and I told her how grateful I was for all she'd done to restore my battered body and tortured soul. We both agreed we'd never forget the happy times we'd had together. Erni even said that if I didn't find what I wanted in Berlin, I was welcome to return.

'The next morning Erni and I said our emotional goodbyes at her home, and she waved me off with some food for the journey. I set off alone for the railway station, my head full of anticipation and anxiety about what I might find in Berlin. Had my little sister, Margot, my parents, my grandmother, Gerhard and my other friends survived the war and the flattening of the capital?'

12
REUNIONS AND BEGINNINGS

It was a mild day in October 1945 when Erna answered a knock at the door and saw another shocking sight on her doorstep. There stood Sigi. Thin, worn, gaunt, shrouded in silence. She hugged him for a long time, then led him into the flat. It would take weeks and months before Erna was able to piece together from him that he'd been in Auschwitz. And that being an upholsterer had saved his life.

At first Sigi did not say a single word about his time in the camp or the death march out of it. The trauma and humiliation of the whole experience had made him shut down, and he barely spoke about it, even to his wife Erna. His physical deterioration was obvious – he was 45 years old but looked more like 65. What was going on inside this shell of a man no one could really fathom. Erna had heard on the news about the atrocities at Auschwitz, but she'd never ever hear any details from her husband. He simply told her that they were treated worse than beasts. He never talked about it then or in their future years together.

'I won't discuss it. I'm here now, and that's the end of it,' is all he'd say.

Sigi chose to keep silent about the two years of his life away from the family, first as an *U-Boot* and then in the most notorious extermination camp of all. It was clearly his way to save his own dignity and self-esteem after a subhuman experience.

This was to prove the case with very many Holocaust survivors – not looking back and never talking about it were their ways of coping, if not healing. Erna was only grateful Sigi's upholstery skills had proved lifesaving, as reports were now surfacing that more than a million had been murdered at the camp in less than five years, and very few Jews survived. Erna could hardly believe her husband was home at last, but it was often like treading on eggshells as he didn't find adjusting back to life in Berlin at all easy.

Sigi was often grumpy and short-tempered, but neither Erna nor Edie could blame him for it. He was still in physical pain, could only manage small meals and couldn't sleep through the night. Years of poor food, forced labour and terrible living conditions would take years to reverse Erna reasoned. Sigi would get up in the night and pace about the flat for hours, and if Erna tried to comfort him he'd simply insist she went back to bed.

The family survived on rations until Sigi had sufficiently recovered to start his trade again. His tools had been lost when their home was bombed, but he picked up a few essentials and pinned a sign to their door saying 'Repairs and Reupholstery Undertaken'. Many people had furnishings that had been damaged in the bombings, and work started to trickle in. Buying new materials was impossible, so Sigi scavenged broken-down bits of sofas, armchairs – whatever he could find on the streets – that he could work with. He found the restoration work helped heal him a little too; returning to his old craft restored him to his old self. Edie would sit with

REUNIONS AND BEGINNINGS

her father, and he began to teach her how to do upholstery, giving her the job of stuffing chairs and sofas with horse hair. The two of them would sit in companionable silence, as Sigi began the long journey back to a kind of normality.

The Bernsteins felt lucky to be living in a comfortable flat, even though it had once been home to a Nazi family. If Sigi harboured any misgivings about eating from the plates once used by supporters of Hitler's regime and sleeping in their sheets, he never shared them. Like Erna and Edie, he soon got used to these superior comforts as his life acquired some kind of rhythm. Edie would often catch her father looking at her and smiling; he'd shake his head and say, 'I've missed so much.' One or other of the family would mention Heini every so often and say that because they'd not heard any news to the contrary, he must be alive and would come back to them. But as other young men returned to the area and he didn't, they couldn't help starting to fear the worst.

Across the country, Heini had begun the journey towards Berlin as soon as his January ration cards had arrived. Station staff had warned him the rail network was in chaos, with huge ongoing repair work, and sure enough at Duisberg he discovered there were no onward trains. There was nothing to do but wait. He spent a couple of miserable days walking around town, trying to pass the time, at night bedding down in an unsavoury bunker with other itinerants, unable to sleep for long for fear his suitcase might be taken by one of them. Then at last, just as his rations were starting to run out, he heard the train link to Hannover had been repaired. He was relieved he could now resume what looked sure to be a very tricky journey.

'Hannover station was a wreck,' he recalled, 'but full to the brim with hundreds of returning men and women looking for people and places. Despite the police presence, the station was full of dubious-looking individuals trading cigarettes, cameras and clocks. Everyone was hanging on tight to whatever they were carrying. The information desk was busy directing the homeless and those in transit to people who were offering lodgings.

'As the centre of Hannover had been heavily bombed, I was given an address in a suburb, and after a long tram journey during which I saw the terrible devastation, I was greeted by a friendly young couple and shown a clean room. They told me about the division of Germany and Berlin into zones by the winning Allied powers at Potsdam. I realised I'd have to travel through the Soviet zone to enter Berlin and wondered if there was any public transport, but the helpful young couple didn't know how these new divisions worked. It had all happened so recently that nobody seemed to know, even at the station.'

So Heini travelled on to Braunschweig, changed trains again and then continued on through Helmstedt and Marienborn. 'At Marienborn, lots of people got on the train with luggage. So many were climbing on board that all the wagons were full to capacity, and men and women were now clinging on to the steps, the brake area, even climbing up on the roof, and on the buffers. It was all so precarious that many tied themselves on with rope, straps or belts. This was absolutely necessary because in the cold their fingers froze a few minutes into the journey, making it almost impossible to hold on tight. Indeed after one sharp jolt we saw someone lose their grip and fall off the train. Those up on the roof had

REUNIONS AND BEGINNINGS

to lie down to avoid any obstacles overhead, and we were thankful the train moved so slowly.

'As we approached the River Elbe, you could hardly call the structure that spanned it a bridge anymore. I was horrified. It must have been so badly bombed that the rail track across this wide river looked like a skeleton. We passengers could see the water below through the gaps, yet this bridge was what our overcrowded train had to travel across. Admittedly the train slowed down as we approached it, but we all felt queasy at the prospect, especially those hanging all over the outside who could be heard gasping and moaning. I wondered whether this fragile bridge would be where I met my end.'

Relieved to reach Magdeburg railway station in one piece, Heini was asking about his onward train to Berlin when a small patrol of Soviet soldiers marshalled him and a crowd of others to their commanding officer. No explanation was given – they just had their ID papers taken and were shown down to a cellar to wait. Heini tried to speak to the soldier, but none of them understood German. Being imprisoned in a cellar again was traumatic for Heini and he felt utterly miserable that he was having to wait once again. He reproached himself for thinking about even trying to get home while Horst was safe in Soest, without a care in the world, having sensibly put off his trip to Berlin. He was trapped underground, with just cabbage soup and a chunk of bread to eat, facing another night sleeping on an awful bed and waiting to be questioned again.

The day passed into night and Heini watched and listened to the other men held in the cellar with him. 'I came to the horrifying realisation that they were most certainly Nazis.

MISCHLINGE

Once again I kept my own counsel, neither speaking to nor trusting anyone, but I hated having to live alongside these Nazis for ten long days and nights before I was brought before the commanding officer and his interpreter. They examined my identity card and Buchenwald papers, then ordered me to strip to the waist, examining my body for those SS tattoos. They asked a few questions and then told me my papers were in order. After more hours waiting, I was given my papers back, along with a new document with a Soviet stamp on it, and released. The stress and the poor food while I was being held meant that I'd lost several pounds in just a few days. The one-day ration card they gave me did little to help, as I could only cash it in for a very mediocre bowl of soup at a nearby inn.'

At Magdeburg station, Heini boarded the final train link to Berlin, wondering if any other cruel surprises lay ahead. The train journey was an eye-opener. Most of its windows were nailed shut, and it was full of people and potatoes. He eventually worked out that people were foraging for food outside of Berlin, either to eat, sell or barter and supplement the meagre supplies inside the city.

The journey ended at Berlin-Charlottenberg and Heini followed the foragers to the S-Bahn overground and took a local train to Alexanderplatz. This was a place he knew well, but like everywhere else he'd travelled through on the train it was barely recognisable after very heavy bomb damage. The whole glass roof of the station was missing, both the Alexanderhaus and Berolinahaus showed signs of considerable damage, and the police headquarters next door was barely recognisable, with no outer walls and an unobstructed view of the cells from the street. There was just rubble where

REUNIONS AND BEGINNINGS

the restaurant, cinema, shops, offices, flats and a dance café used to be, and as he looked round, all the other familiar buildings, including the Hertie department store, were in ruins. It was a wretched sight, and once again the fear rose in his stomach that his family might not have survived.

Heini jumped on a tram heading homeward, saddened by the views he saw of familiar streets and buildings, many with no roofs or no walls. At the final stop on Elisabethstrasse, he immediately saw that his old home – the building he'd last lived in – lay in ruins. He quickly went and looked through all the notes pinned onto posts with forwarding addresses on, but hard as he looked, he couldn't find his parents' name. He shivered when he realised he might be standing in front of his family's grave.

'I walked on through the streets that, despite being strewn with boulders and debris, were still so familiar to me. Among the destruction people were still living in every semi-decent space, which gave me hope and made me press on. I arrived at Gerhard's house at Prenzlauer Tor and found it empty, scarred with bomb and bullet damage. Missing walls revealed rooms laid bare to the elements and strangers' eyes, rooms I remembered fondly. As I stood wondering what to do next, I saw a neighbour I knew, who said Gerhard and his family had survived the bombing and been allocated new accommodation nearby.

'I rang Gerhard's doorbell, and when he opened it there was a great hullabaloo and much excitement as we close friends saw one another again after all we'd both experienced. "Bear" and "Mouse" hugged each other, and Gerhard's wife hugged me too. I could only marvel at the size of their two boys, but it made me grasp the reality of three years away. After we'd all sat down, I asked Gerhard if he'd any news of my family and was overcome with relief when he told me that both of my parents and my sister were living in a flat in Lichtenberg. My greatest fear had been unfounded – it was such wonderful news.

'We had a lengthy catch-up at the kitchen table, with Gerhard explaining how he'd been captured by the enemy and held at a prisoner-of-war camp until hostilities ended. Although I'd no intention of going into too much detail about my captivity, I shared with Mouse a little of my time in Buchenwald, my escape from the death march and my recuperation in the haven of Soest. After a few hot drinks and some laughs about old times, Mouse insisted on accompanying me on the S-Bahn to Neu-Lichtenberg and walking me to my parents' new home. We hugged and arranged to meet again in a few days, and Gerhard said he'd wait to see me reach the front door before leaving.'

It was a sunny day, and Edie was cleaning the front doorstep of her father's workshop when she saw a tall man walking towards her with a big bag in his hand.

'At first I didn't recognise him,' she says. 'He looked familiar, but I wasn't sure who he was. He was so very, very thin that he didn't look like the brother I'd last seen. I wondered why this man was staring at me, but as he got closer he just dropped the bag and ran towards me. Then I realised – a wonderful moment. It was my Heini, my big brother, lost to me for so long. We didn't speak, we just threw our arms around each other and held on tight for what seemed an age. I think I started crying, but Heini just cuddled me and told me everything was all right, he was fine and we were together again.

REUNIONS AND BEGINNINGS

'As we walked inside, Mum let out a scream when she saw Heini and then started kissing him over and over. Then Dad appeared and looked completely overwhelmed and dumbstruck. Heini and Sigi sat down, and Mum rushed about putting almost everything in the larder on the table, and we all sat together around the kitchen table, eating, talking and sometimes pausing to just stare at each other in disbelief.

'There were many, many questions. Heini asked after his grandmother Emma and Eva, and was relieved that they had made it too. It was incredible that a family of *Mischlinge* had all survived persecution, bombing and street battles in Berlin, the capital of the Reich, as well as forced labour and concentration camps. It felt like a miracle, he kept saying.'

Like his father, Heini did not give a full account of his experiences then – or indeed ever – and, as he came to realise years later, neither did Edie. For now, the family wanted to concentrate on just being reunited.

Heini laughed at the idea his father had spent part of the war hidden in a cellar, earning his place by sometimes making schnapps. Then Heini asked about a subject closer to his heart – had they heard anything of Margot? They all shook their heads. 'What of my beloved leather jacket?,' he asked next.

Edie told him, 'I know how much it meant to you, my darling brother. I did look after it and always took your leather jacket with me to the cellar and kept it safe there when there was an air-raid warning. But later, when we all had to go to the bunker in Alexanderplatz, it was too much of a hindrance; it kept getting in my way, so I left it at home. It was destroyed when they bombed our home. I'm so sorry that it happened like that.'

MISCHLINGE

Heini did nothing to show his disappointment, telling her he was happy the Nazis didn't get it and he was happy to swap it to be back with his little sister again.

The next day Heini registered again with the police and collected his ration cards. The suit they issued him was gratefully received, and, hoping to look his best, he went to seek out his old love and fiancée Margot – the engagement that had so enraged the Nazis.

'I was relieved to find Margot at her old address, alive and well. When she opened the door I thought she looked much the same as the girl I left behind, but she looked shocked to see me and there was something in her manner. I could tell almost immediately that things had changed.

'She smiled and said, "How wonderful to see you, you're alive!" She invited me in, and after a brief exchange with her parents she ushered me into another room and shut the door. "I'm sorry," she said, "but I've met someone else. I didn't know if you'd made it, and he was here and it just kind of happened."

'It was a blow, but I wasn't entirely shocked. It was wartime, after all, when no one knew who would return to them. I'd prepared myself for the possibility, so I told Margot I understood and wished her luck. She hugged me and said it was still so very good to know I'd survived, and she hoped I would find a good woman. I walked out of her place sad but not completely down.'

Edie fussed over her brother and insisted on taking him to meet her new friends in Café Schmidt. Heini was soon part of the crowd and going to dances, where it was clear, especially with the black-market alcohol on sale, that everyone was letting their hair down after years of being restricted by the

REUNIONS AND BEGINNINGS

war. He became a regular at the Schweizergarten dances and sometimes the Babylon cinema, finding it all such a welcome break from the terrible events of recent years. He saw a lot of his old friend Gerhard the Mouse, who in turn introduced him to his circle of friends, the young families in his new block who'd withstood the terrible bombing raids and burning buildings together.

Pretty swiftly, Heini and Edie were living the carefree youthful lifestyle they'd been denied. Life was different without the pressure of carrying their *Mischlinge* label: cinemas, libraries and parks were open to them now. Heini sometimes bumped into old friends who were curious about his past in the labour and concentration camps, but he'd never talk about that period of his life. He felt silence was the best medicine for him. Brother and sister both found it rather liberating to be living in a new area, where their neighbours knew nothing about them.

Finding food was still an issue, and the Bernsteins were once again grateful for the parcels sent by the Jewish charity based at the synagogue in Oranienburgerstrasse, although, of course, none of them ever went there. Eating well was still a daily challenge. Everyone had grown weary of the terrible diet of dried potatoes, which they got on the ration cards and only ate when they absolutely had to. But they could buy all kinds on the black market, in doorways, pubs, on the street and on the various squares. Foraged produce changed hands at high prices, as people were desperate to get certain goods, such as proper bread. The fake lard was horrid, and when maize bread became available on the ration cards it was a struggle to digest; their stomachs were getting hungrier and hungrier and needed something more nourishing than just *ersatz* cake.

MISCHLINGE

Finding a job was even harder than finding food. Heini registered with the employment office, as was required by law, but he received no job offers other than clearing rubble. More and more people he knew earned a living by dealing on the black market, sourcing items that people needed. And it wasn't long before Heini's thoughts turned back to his return to Berlin, when he'd stared at people with their sacks of potatoes on the train without realising why they had them. These trips were now widespread and named 'hamster runs' by Berliners, as city dwellers travelled out of the city to farms and returned with their pouches stuffed with food, just like hamsters, to enjoy and to sell.

Earning money from these trips and reconnecting with his friends, Heini was beginning to recover from the disappointment of losing Margot. He began seeing Ruth, a young friend of Edie's from Café Schmidt, and they'd sometimes go out as a foursome with Gerhard and his wife. Still, it was hard to make enough money to buy the train tickets for foraging outside the city, supplement his family's rations and have some left over for fun himself. On top of that, their flat was cold as the gas supply hadn't been restored and fuel to keep warm was hard to come by, electricity was limited only to lighting, with frequent power cuts, and even candles were in short supply.

Heini was on the look-out for another way to make money when a man he met at Café Schmidt suggested a more profitable trade than potatoes. Arno, a tall, handsome man with a handlebar moustache, convinced his new young friend that there was considerable money to be made in selling seafood. He knew where to buy marinated herring, a nourishing and tasty fish you couldn't buy in Berlin, that would fetch a good price. But to buy it they'd have to illegally cross over into the zone occupied by the Western Powers. Arno explained this involved a long and tricky journey – by train, by foot, and then wading through the river that separated the Soviet and Western zones – and they'd have to make the journey at night to evade the many Red Army and Allied patrols. They'd take black-market schnapps from Berlin out in their rucksacks to bribe the guards, if need be, or to barter with, and return with them full of fish to sell. For Heini, the danger of it added to the thrill and adventure of it all, so he readily agreed.

'We got off the train at Oebisfelde, then walked through woods and over a meadow to find a shallow section of the River Aller to wade over, while watching out for any armed patrols. Guided by Arno's knowledge of the area, we reached our destination and traded our schnapps for herring and other smoked fish. On the train home we took turns to sleep, with one eye open for the railway police while we waited for our connecting train. Crossing the border illegally was dangerous, but we both somehow thrived on the challenging trip, which took a day and two nights. Our fish-buying trips were so successful that we dared to travel further – to Hamburg, Bremerhaven and Cuxhaven. We found more foods to trade there and brought some home for our families. They were delighted and our enterprise also gained us a bit of a reputation in our circle.

'When my girlfriend Ruth heard about them, she asked if I'd take her across the border to see her grandparents, who lived near Oldenburg, as she really missed them. Because we were living under martial law, to leave Berlin without permission was a serious offence, but when Ruth explained that her grandparents were farmers who'd make them all welcome and I was sure to do good business with other farmers, I was persuaded. When Edie heard us planning the trip she asked if she could come along too, and I couldn't refuse my little sister a chance to escape to the countryside.'

Edie was excited to be leaving the city for the first time in her life. 'Heini told me to be ready early in the morning and to dress in dark clothes. Then we two sneaked out, just leaving a note of explanation for Mum and Dad. We met Ruth and headed for the night train towards Oldenburg.

'After the long train journey across the border, we reached Ruth's family farm, deep in the countryside. Her elderly grandmother welcomed all three of us, and she cooked us a big plate of country ham and eggs as soon as we arrived. It was delicious.

'I loved waking up in the big farmhouse bedroom, looking out over green countryside. The air smelt clean and the surrounding meadows were blooming. The whole area seemed untouched by the war and so much nicer than the ravaged city I'd left behind. Ruth and I spent idyllic days in the fields and helping her elderly grandparents around the farm, while Heini headed out alone most days in search of deals and food to sell back in Berlin.

'We were now in the British-controlled zone of Germany, so it was no surprise that one day as the three of us strolled down a country lane, we met a British soldier in uniform, wearing a long overcoat, walking towards us with a bag on his shoulder.

'Heini spoke no English but gestured to the soldier. Did he have any cigarettes to trade? The soldier, who spoke a little German, introduced himself as Jimmy and produced packs of

REUNIONS AND BEGINNINGS

cigarettes from inside his overcoat. Heini paid cash for them and the two discussed what else they might trade in the future, communicating with a mixture of words and gestures. Heini pointed to the farmhouse where we were staying, and Jimmy said he'd see us there the following day.

'The very next day this English soldier turned up at the farmhouse, but he hadn't just come to trade. He'd brought us many gifts and treats. We were all transfixed as he produced tinned food, nylons, cigarettes and chocolates from pockets inside his overcoat. Ruth's granny was tearful as she hadn't seen some of those things for years, and she thanked him profusely for his kindness and being their liberator.

'This soldier kept looking over at me, and I noticed how smiley and outgoing he seemed to be. He was very keen to talk and communicate. Perhaps my brother's and my skinny appearance, or some of Heini's words, had touched this young soldier. Jimmy explained he was a Londoner called Jimmy Ring, a staff sergeant, and said there was plenty of these sorts of things to spare at his base. He stayed talking to Heini for a couple of hours, and despite the linguistic challenges there seemed to be an instant connection between the two of them, with both making a concerted effort to understand the other. Jimmy offered to bring more cigarettes if Heini wanted, which he did.

'All through their conversation Jimmy never stopped smiling at me, and when he got up to leave he asked Heini if he might take me for a walk the next day. Heini turned to me and said he'd learnt whom to trust in recent years and had a good feeling about this British soldier. If I wanted I could go, but I wasn't to stray too far from the farmhouse. I knew my dear brother wanted to get rid of me so he could have time with Ruth, and I liked Jimmy's nice smile and easy, open manner, so I agreed.

'Jimmy dropped off the cigarettes as promised, and we went for a long walk, Jimmy doing his best to talk in his pidgin German and somehow or other making me laugh. Heini went off to negotiate with the locals, paying them for fresh produce like butter, sausage and bacon. In the evening we all met back at the farmhouse and Ruth's grandparents were only too happy to feed us all.'

Jimmy, with his easy, jokey manner, went all out to woo this skinny, dark-eyed girl, but Edie was shyer and more cautious. He was eager to communicate and break down the language barrier, and from their very first date began to teach Edie English.

'Jimmy never let go of me really from the moment he first saw me,' says Edie. 'I met him every moment he wasn't on duty. On our first night out alone together, Jimmy took me to the army base recreation centre (the NAAFI), where there was music as well as lots of food. We hadn't been there long when he jumped on the stage and in this lovely, melodic voice started singing "I'm confessing that I love you", the Perry Como song. He didn't show a hint of embarrassment, but I certainly did.

'Five days after we first met on that country road, Jimmy looked me straight in the eye and said, "I'm going to marry you."

'I was taken aback and replied, "But I don't know you."

'He just smiled and said, "You will."

'For him it was love at first sight, he told me later, but it took me a little longer. I liked him from the moment we met, but I suppose I was – like Heini – cautious. There wasn't any doubt he was very keen.'

REUNIONS AND BEGINNINGS

After a few weeks Heini had completed his trading and told Edie and Ruth that it was time for them all to return home, but the girls had other ideas. They felt safer in the countryside, away from the rubble of Berlin. Edie also confided to her brother that she was increasingly charmed by this young soldier who was paying her a lot of attention and she wanted to get to know him more. They had good reasons to stay on at Ruth's family farm.

Heini mulled it over and decided there was no harm in his sister having a little holiday, with Ruth and her family by her side, enjoying far better food and unrestricted by their mum's over-protectiveness. So they said their farewells and Heini headed back to Berlin alone, crossing the river at a different spot to avoid detection.

Edie gave her brother what she called 'a reassuring letter for my mum, saying I'd met a lovely and trustworthy young man.

'I liked it that Jimmy loved and respected his mum as much as I did mine. He told me that the Rings were a large and loving London Catholic family with Irish heritage, that he was the youngest of six children, spoiled and adored, and still living with his mum when he was called up to fight in the army as a 19-year-old.

'Neither of us wanted to discuss the war, but Jimmy told me he'd seen a lot of action and lost friends in action at El Alamein in Egypt, and in many battles throughout Italy, France, Belgium and into Germany. He was one of the first British soldiers to enter Berlin after the Soviets, and he'd been part of the Allied victory parade in the city in July 1945 that my mum had forbidden me from going to watch.

'Jimmy came to see me at the farmhouse every day he could and became a familiar sight around the place in his

MISCHLINGE

long overcoat, even in warm summer temperatures. He called the coat indispensable as it had several inside pockets that came in handy to transport bits and pieces to trade and barter. I couldn't find fault with Jimmy. If I was worried about anything, he'd play the clown and defuse my anxiety. He was kind and patient, and slowly my affection for him grew. And it was obvious why he'd got on so well with Heini – they were both resourceful entrepreneurs and providers.

'All initial caution I had about this British soldier soon disappeared. Jimmy quickly won my trust. I was very soon as in love with him as he was with me'.

As their relationship grew stronger, Edie confided more to her young suitor about her troubled childhood: being labelled as a *Mischling*, being excluded from school, working as a slave labourer and the disappearance of most of her family, but only in the briefest of terms without too much detail or reflection.

Jimmy and Edie when they first meet in the countryside near Oldenberg in 1946.

REUNIONS AND BEGINNINGS

'He was kind and didn't press me to say more than I was willing to talk about. I nicknamed him my little fella,' she recalls, 'and in my regular letters to my mum I told her all about this 23-year-old who was really looking after me and teaching me to speak English with a Cockney accent while I was extending his German with a Berliner twang.'

As the months went by, Staff Sergeant Jimmy Ring was told he was essential personnel, needed to remain at his barracks and was not to be discharged for another year.

'Jimmy turned up one day beaming from ear to ear, saying he'd submitted a formal request to his superior to marry his bride and take her to live in London. "I told you from the first that I'd marry you, didn't I?" he teased me. I was then called for interview by a British army officer who asked lots of questions to establish that I was sincere and committed, and part of the process was a full medical examination. Our marriage application was then submitted, but it was not a quick process and we had to wait a while for a decision.'

Both now had to tell their families. Erna and Sigi knew quite a lot about Jimmy Ring from Edie's letters and Heini's good account of him, but they had yet to meet him. Edie was more worried what Jimmy's family would make of their baby marrying a German-Jewish girl – how would they feel about his returning home with a girl whose countrymen were undoubtedly responsible for the death of some of their sons and fathers, friends and neighbours?

'When Jimmy was given a fortnight's leave, I understood he wanted to go home to see his family and tell them about me. Five days later I was shocked to see him back at my door – he said he missed me too much to stay away any longer.

MISCHLINGE

'That's how we were from the beginning and for very many years to come. In love and inseparable.'

Jimmy found only good news in London. Back in the family home in Highgate his mum had heard from his two brothers, Micky and Tommy. They had survived the war and were in good health. They were still serving in the Commandos and Royal Navy respectively, and not due home yet. His mum Ellen, who ran a floristry business from Floral Street in Covent Garden, said she was happy that her youngest had fallen for a lovely girl and wasn't against them marrying, but she did suggest he took Edie to visit his brother Tommy, who was still in Germany as a naval petty officer in the port of Kiel. Clearly, elder brother Tommy was to check Edie out.

Edie's confirmation certificate, detailing her christening in 1936 and her religious education and confirmation in 1941, was copied in 1946 – possibly to allow her to marry Jimmy in a church.

REUNIONS AND BEGINNINGS

Brothers in uniform. Army recruit Jimmy Ring and his brother Tommy, who served in the Royal Navy and would vet Edie for their mum.

Jimmy soon received an invitation to tea on board his brother Tommy's ship, and he and Edie set off for Kiel on his next spell of leave. Edie's English vocabulary had come on enough for her to chat easily and the brothers laughed at her enthusiasm for what she called the biggest cream cake she'd ever seen. When the brothers hugged each other goodbye, Tommy whispered his approval to his baby brother and said he'd write to their mum.

Back in Berlin, the British army had yet to give *their* permission for these two youngsters to marry as there officially needed to be what was termed a 'cooling-off period', which meant waiting a whole year. Jimmy told Edie not to worry about an outfit as he'd brought her some smart grey cloth back from London and a tailor at his camp was going to make it into a smart suit for her. Edie was delighted but less pleased with the heeled wedding shoes, a gift from his sister – they were two sizes smaller than her feet.

'On the first day of July 1947,' remembers Edie, 'very first thing in the morning, Jimmy came rushing around to the farmhouse door, all smiles and excitement. He shouted that our permission had come through and that we needed to be ready to marry that evening at six o'clock in the local Catholic Church of the Holy Ghost. He'd fixed the wedding after being told he'd soon be demobbed, discharged and sent home – he didn't know exactly when, but he wanted to marry me straightaway so that I could return with him to England as his wife. He rushed off, saying he'd return to collect me later.

'That evening I put on the lovely grey-striped suit and the new shoes that were so tight I could barely walk in them – there were no others to be had, and fortunately they looked good. Jimmy knocked on the door, looking very smart in his uniform, with his two army mates as witnesses and a huge bunch of white flowers he'd picked from the hedgerow on the way over. I couldn't wait to marry my "Little Fella".

'Jimmy held my hand and Ruth followed as we made our way to the local church as fast as my shoes permitted. Inside, the man with the white collar asked me some questions in English that I didn't fully understand. Then came the short but very special ceremony, which was deeply moving for me.

'I did understand that having married in a Catholic church, I'd now promised to bring up any children of ours as Catholic. I had no problem with that as I'd want them to have moral principles. The exact details of the religion seemed less important to me than teaching children to "love their neighbour", whatever their religion – that was important. I understood that I'd made a promise and I intended to keep it.

REUNIONS AND BEGINNINGS

'There was a curfew that night so we didn't spend our wedding night together, but that didn't matter – we were so happy. I've always believed that just meeting Jimmy on that country lane was *the* most romantic of meetings, and so was our wedding. Our different backgrounds, nationality, religion – none of that mattered to us, we truly loved each other.

'When I'm asked why I married him, a foreign soldier, I can only say I fell in love and I took a chance. In life you have to make a judgement, but you also have to take a chance. I trusted that it would work out and we'd have a happy life together, and we did. I never regretted it for one second. My happiness began the day I met my little fella. He rescued me. It's as if my life began on the day I met him, and he allowed

Edie in her wedding suit, July 1947.

me to relegate all those bad memories to the back of my mind.'

From that day on Edie always described Jimmy as her 'rescuer'.

Weeks later Jimmy was granted leave and the newlyweds returned to Berlin to finally meet Sigi and Erna. Edie was apprehensive about heading back to the city she'd left illegally what seemed like a long time ago. When Soviet soldiers boarded the train at the border of their zone and began walking through the carriages asking passengers to show their ID papers, Edie was instantly terrified.

'But my "little fella" grabbed my hand and with him beside me, that fear gradually subsided. He showed the soldiers my papers identifying me as a British wife and citizen, and they nodded us through and the train moved on.'

That first meeting with their new son-in-law went very well for Erna and Sigi. Not only had Jimmy brought them a selection of food and clothes, but he chatted away in his pidgin German, accompanied by his customary smiles and jesting, putting their minds at rest about their daughter's choice.

After watching them together, Erna winked at her daughter and said, 'It's *treue Liebe* with you two, isn't it?', and when Edie replied, 'Yes, true love,' Erna told her how proud she was that she'd learnt to speak English so adeptly. When it came to parting there were tears all round, and Erna gave her daughter a parcel to take to her first marital home containing a damask tablecloth, a few plates and bowls of quality china, small glass dishes and pretty glass coasters. These had all belonged to the Nazis who'd fled their flat, so Jimmy jokingly named them 'Edie's Nazi trousseau'. But Edie was just grateful to have something from her mother, something to

REUNIONS AND BEGINNINGS

bring with her from her family home to a new one in another country.

At their tearful farewells Edie told her mum these items would be treasured, '*treue Liebe*' would become a family saying and she'd always have a Christmas tree wherever she lived. Mr and Mrs Jimmy Ring were all set to make a new life together in London, just as soon as he was demobbed from the army.

13
REFUGEES AND PROMISED LANDS

Sigi made an emotional return to his childhood home in Schönhauser Allee in search of his mother, brother and his wider family. But he could find no trace of them or anyone he knew. He glimpsed men he didn't recognise in the business part of the building, but he was too fearful to question them as they were probably the Nazi Party members who had bought the business for a pittance.

Sigi tried asking about his family at the local council offices, but he was told that records were still sketchy about missing people. Back home, Sigi confided to Erna that he was realistic about their chances of survival. Perhaps Georg his brother might still be alive, as he'd have been a useful worker, but after what he'd witnessed he didn't have much hope.

Only around 1,700 Jews and *Mischlinge* like Sigi, Heini and Edie are thought to have survived in Berlin throughout the war, either through the protection of a Christian spouse or as *U-Boote* in hiding.

MISCHLINGE

Schönhauser Allee, Berlin – the Bernstein family's home and business address in the 1930s, from where some of them were seized by Gestapo, pictured in 2005.

In the febrile chaos of the postwar period, the Jews were still an easy scapegoat to blame. Sigi, Erna and Heini were now living in a different neighbourhood, but their name was still Bernstein and they soon discovered that ardent Nazis continued to openly express their opinions. One day Sigi hadn't gone far from home when a man spat at him on the street. 'Dirty Jew!' he shouted. On another occasion a teenage boy swore at him so viciously that, fearing for his safety, Sigi dived into a shop until the boy moved on. Erna warned Sigi to change his route home after she saw a gang of young men menacing those they could identify as Jews at a nearby crossroads.

Berlin was a bleak place. Wounded troops were returning to the devastated capital to find themselves among a million homeless people. They were forced to sleep on the streets or in cellars, searching for family and friends, mourning loved ones and having to hunt for both food and fuel alongside everyone else. Amid the relief that the war was over, there was huge anxiety about the future under occupation and the city's division by the four Allied powers. Food and fuel had been sent to the capital from the surrounding occupied countries during the war, but now with its own land decimated, Germans were reliant on slow and inadequate Allied food aid, while Berliners depended more and more on the 'hamster runs' bringing in food from the countryside.

According to Heini, Erna told him: 'Dad is finding it very hard to settle back to life in Berlin. Quite apart from the continued threats, after some initial work making basic repairs to furniture, his paid work has dried up. He's out all day looking for work, returning empty-handed and depressed. We're so grateful to receive the Jewish Aid food parcels once again.'

At the Jewish charity's offices Sigi heard the World Jewish Congress announcement advising all Jews to leave Germany. A rabbi who survived Theresienstadt said, 'The history of Jews in Germany has found its end. It's impossible for it to come back. The chasm is too great.' When a national poll showed that more than a third of the population felt it was better for there to be no Jews in Germany, it confirmed what Sigi and Heini already knew: antisemitism hadn't disappeared simply because the war had ended.

At the charity's offices Sigi talked to other Jewish men. They said to stay in Germany meant being silent and invisible, and the only alternative was to think about a new life in Palestine, which was being touted as a haven for Jews across Europe. Sigi listened with interest, telling Erna that some families he knew were planning to go there, although he had to admit he knew nothing about the country.

Heini recalled his dad coming home and suggesting that he and his mother watch a film presentation about the country at the global Zionist agency in Joachimsthalerstrasse. 'The film promised a wonderful social structure in a beautiful country where Jews from all over the world could live and work together without the threat of persecution,' said Heini. 'The images of its natural beauty gripped and impressed us and others in the audience, and we went away with a lot to think about.

'Like Dad, I wasn't earning much money. I'd been running a little transport business with Gerhard, having rebuilt an old car with second-hand parts, and we were doing deliveries, but the car needed constant maintenance to keep it on the road and we barely made a profit.

'So I began to take stock of my life and I realised that if my parents emigrated to Palestine, with my sister married and living in London, my only family in Berlin would be Grandmother Emma and "sister" Eva. I had some affection for my grandmother, but I couldn't entirely forgive either of them for distancing themselves from me, Edie, Mum and Dad in the past. I thought if my little sister can act so decisively, I can too. I need to do something different, given the trauma of the past few years. Mum was also keen to leave Berlin. She hadn't had much happiness in the city of her birth – not for a very long time – and she loved the idea of a fresh start in a warm, welcoming country.'

But it was Sigi's visit to the Jewish charity's office that finally made the family's mind up to leave Germany. Records of the disappeared were emerging and there was at last news

REFUGEES AND PROMISED LANDS

of his family, taken from the family home in Schönhauser Allee. Sigi wept as he read the tragic news. On 4 October 1942 his 73-year-old stepmother Tinchen, Heini and Edie's grandmother, had been taken to Theresienstadt, a ghetto and transit camp where 33,000 people died from disease and starvation. Incredibly, she'd survived in that dreadful place for what must have been three hideous years before her death was recorded there on 17 July 1945, just a couple of months after the war in Europe had ended.

The newly published records also showed that Sigi's younger brother Georg, who'd appealed to Sigi to hide him and his family, was loaded onto Transport 27, Train Da13 from Berlin to Auschwitz-Birkenau on 29 January 1943, along with his wife Susi and their daughter Anita, Edie's little playmate, together with Sigi's sister Charlotte, known as Lotte, and her husband Heinz Goldstein. All in all, six of Sigi's family members had been murdered by the Nazis.

Sigi had neither seen or heard of them when he was prisoner in the same camp. Did these two families even survive the hideous journey and reach Auschwitz? Was Anita shot on arrival, deemed too young to work? Were Georg, Susi, Lotte and Heinz worked to death long before he was taken there? The exact manner and date of their death was marked unknown. And of course, there were no bodies to mourn or bury.

Sigi couldn't help brooding over the dreadful night he'd turned away his brother when he appealed for shelter; he had no alternative than to protect his own family. He'd long feared they had perished, but he always harboured some small hope that they might have survived, just as he and Heini had. This confirmation – along with the details of their fate – was incontrovertible truth and painful to face. He hated the fact that the bald facts of their deaths left out so much. He would never know the whole story of what had happened to his family once the Nazis took them. Sigi spent some time walking and grieving alone before he could face going home and telling the family.

Heini was horrified and appalled at the news, while Erna, who'd never really known them, was shaken and extremely upset. This was all the impetus the three remaining Bernsteins needed to decide to leave for Palestine. So the family planned to emigrate, without giving much thought to the fact it was illegal. 'We began the formalities with the Zionist organisation,' remembered Heini, 'with only a vague idea it was not a straightforward journey. We were ill-informed and ignorant of the complicated political situation we were about to enter into.'

Palestine had been under British control since 1920 and since then Jewish immigration had grown increasingly rapidly, with the Jewish proportion of the country's population growing from a sixth to a third thanks to the rise of Nazism and antisemitism. Unsurprisingly, this caused widespread anger among the Palestinian Arab population, who had shared rights to this land, and both Jewish and Arab nationalist movements were gaining in strength. The British imposed a controversial quota system, limiting the numbers allowed to emigrate to Palestine, but this did nothing to quell the tide.

After the war, the British refused to give Jewish survivors sanctuary in Palestine, but there were around 250,000 displaced Jews from all over Europe living in refugee camps hoping for just that. Like so many others fleeing from the grim legacy of the Holocaust, although that word was not coined for some years after the war, the Bernsteins were simply hopeful of a better life.

'Because Germany had been divided between the four powers,' said Heini, 'those wishing to emigrate were told to make the journey across the country independently and report at a given time to the Jewish Agency in Munich. So, with a mixture of sadness and excitement, we started packing our few belongings, ready to leave Berlin for Munich in early December 1947.

'Dad sold his upholstery tools for a pittance and I handed over our pretty defunct transport business to Gerhard after a lovely evening of sad goodbyes with his whole family, to whom I'd become so close. Mum had tried to persuade her mother Emma to join us, but she was adamant she didn't want to. She wasn't Jewish, of course, and Eva followed her carer's choice. There was an extended emotional farewell when they promised to write frequent letters, but in truth we'd all led separate lives for some time and grown apart.

'As usual Dad and I clashed when making plans to travel the length of Germany to Munich, and it was left to Mum to calm the tension between us as we set off in winter on an unknown route. When we reached the border of the Soviet zone at the River Aller, a place I'd crossed so often on my runs to buy and barter fish, I picked what I hoped was the safest place and time to cross. I felt for my parents as it was both dangerous and frightening for a man and a woman as short as them to wade across a fast-flowing river, holding all their worldly goods up high above the water. The fading light protected us from the guards' attention as we made our way across, but we were mightily relieved to find the river low, and to reach the other side safe and half-dry.'

MISCHLINGE

Sigi remained extremely on edge until he was certain they'd left the Soviet zone and reached the Western one. But the journey was long and fraught, with Heini guiding them through Velpke, Braunschweig, Hannover and further south to Munich. In Munich they had to pick their way through the rubble of bomb damage to find the Jewish Agency, where they had to complete the formalities needed for departure. Sigi and Erna were told they'd be flying to Palestine, but young men like Heini would have to make the journey by boat later. They joined groups of others with their bags, boxes and children, all boarding a bus to a camp near Bad Tolz outside Munich, where they were told to wait in readiness for departure.

Arriving at the refugee camp the Bernsteins were struck by the number of nationalities that surrounded them, families not just from Germany but from Poland, Czechoslovakia and the Soviet Union too. Little groups of all ages – men, women and children – speaking a variety of languages, banding together with their own kind. After completing formalities the Bernsteins were allocated a room in a block, which they found basic but perfectly acceptable. They had a bed each, a wardrobe, a table and chairs, with bathrooms and toilets down the corridor that were shared with several others.

Waiting around in the refugee camp turned from days to weeks once again, and Heini in particular became fretful – he'd spent too much of his life waiting.

Erna befriended some of the other German women in the block, but Sigi kept to himself, still bruised by the terrible news about his family. Heini explored the camp and found it scruffy and cramped. As it was some distance from the city of Munich, there wasn't much to occupy those living at the camp. The Poles, Czechs and Germans in the various barrack-like buildings mainly stuck to their own – language was a barrier, of course – and the only thing they had in common was being Jews.

'Many around us celebrated the Jewish festival of Hanukkah together,' recalled Heini, 'with what passed for feasting with our rationed food. I could see it was a special and emotional experience for many, as it was the first time in many years they had done so without fear. But our family had never celebrated Jewish feasts, and now for the first time living in the Jewish tradition we couldn't celebrate Christmas either. It felt odd not to have a Christmas tree. Once again I felt a strange sense of being an outsider, not celebrating Hanukkah or Christmas. We Bernsteins never seemed to belong, wherever we were.'

Early in January 1948 Sigi and Erna got word they were to fly to Palestine. They felt apprehensive but excited too. Sigi was tense and anxious as always, but Erna couldn't wait to board the plane, although of course neither of them had ever seen a plane before that wasn't military. Heini waved them off, hoping his turn would come soon. When he asked, he was told he'd be going by train to Marseilles and then taking a ship to Haifa. But not yet. He needed to wait. Heini felt suddenly vulnerable, alone in a strange place, without a pfennig to his name.

Pained by boredom, Heini helped out in the clothing depot at the camp – unloading, folding and arranging men's and women's items according to size and giving them out to the many immigrants who were arriving regularly from all over Europe dressed in rags. He was able to swap his clothes occasionally, and thought of himself as paid in shirts and trousers. As the wait turned from weeks to months, Heini, alone in his room, became restless and lonely until he found two kinds of company. He began a relationship with a girl who worked in the camp kitchen, and she found him a German shepherd puppy. Heini was soon smitten by both the girl and the puppy, walking and training the dog, which he named Rolf. Then a letter arrived from his mum, sent from a large assembly camp in Ramat Gan, which explained that they were waiting to be moved to a home, and this cheered him again.

Three long months after Erna and Sigi's departure, Heini was at last called to board the train for Marseilles. When asked to hand in his ID card, Heini lied and said he'd lost his, his bad experiences having made him distrustful. Perhaps it was illogical not to declare his name as Bernstein, but somehow he didn't want to trust anyone with his card. Being able to prove who he was had saved him once, so he wasn't going to let it out of his sight again. He and Rolf boarded the long, crowded train, packed with families and their earthly belongings, all heading to the same place. There were so many babies and young children on board that they were sleeping in the nets meant to hold luggage, with all bags and cases having to be stacked in the corridor. There was a collective holding of breath when the train was stopped by guards, but after what must have been some kind of financial inducement the train continued.

Heini chatted to a lot of Germans on the train about where they'd come from and what work they were hoping for in Palestine. All around him families were lying down in huddles, trying to keep their children amused, while others were playing games in the little floor space available. Heini didn't recognise any of the stations they passed through, but he was grateful for the well-organised supply of drink, biscuits, fruit and cigarettes he received every morning, and the children particularly relished their delivery of milk. He got off the train at every opportunity to get water, walk Rolf and let him play with all the kids.

'When we reached Marseilles,' said Heini, 'we were all allocated to different buses, and when we arrived at what was called the Colosseum camp I could hear I was the only German among Poles. Someone made a welcome address, which I only partially understood as it was in Yiddish. Then I was given an identity card with the name "Adek Weiss", which appeared to be the general name they were handing out to people with no identity cards. It was a little strange: not understanding the language and being given a different name.

'But our new location had fascinating and impressive views over the Golfe du Lion and the Mediterranean. It was in a wine-growing suburb of Marseilles, and when the sky was clear you could see the harbour and pick out the individual boats that were anchored there. It became an ideal play area for Rolf and me to explore, as another period of waiting for a ship to Haifa loomed.'

Heini welcomed any diversions and was soon chatting to a local Frenchman, René Noirtier, who'd been a prisoner of war in Germany and enjoyed speaking German. He owned all the vines around the camp, and after a few chats he invited Heini to his vineyard for Sunday lunch with his family. Heini was keen to explain to René that he wasn't one of the Nazi barbarians he might have come across and for that reason explained the bare facts of his *Mischling* experiences.

MISCHLINGE

After that chat, René insisted Heini tasted some of the wine he produced. It was Heini's first ever taste of wine, which although a fraction of what his host drank, went straight to his head. He had to rest after lunch but was invited back the next day and given a tour of the vineyard, with his host's tales of his successes, failures and emergencies in the wine trade fascinating the young man. And when he explained his problems with irrigation, Heini immediately saw an opportunity.

Heini offered to overhaul and extend the watering system as long as he could bring Rolf with him. René readily agreed and even offered a few francs in payment when Heini spent day after day at the vineyard. It also meant that he was out of the camp most of the time, especially during the Jewish Sabbath. This was warmly celebrated by the Poles, but it meant nothing to him and he resented its strict rules. He'd waited months now in the refugee camp, although he had to admit he'd also enjoyed a good summer, having been treated like one of the family and spoiled at the vineyard, where he shared their fresh and tasty food and only returned to the camp to sleep.

Heini was absolutely delighted when asked by René to accompany him and another worker on a delivery run of wine barrels and bottles to Paris, as this wouldn't only give him a chance to see some of France but to spend a couple of days in the capital. They saw all the major sights in Paris, ending up with a night at the Moulin Rouge, as René had declared that any visitor to the capital should experience the world of Henri de Toulouse-Lautrec, the 19th-century painter of bohemian life. Heini refused his host's offers of wine this time, and later proved his worth by driving the empty truck and two trailers much of the way home the following day along the quieter back roads (he had no lorry licence), while his companions slept off their celebratory evening.

Back in Marseilles, Heini was fretting again as there was still no news of a ship that would take him to Palestine, let alone any departure time. It had been months now. When René showed Heini a news report about Palestine it suddenly became clear why. The country had been at war. How did he not know this? There had been rumours in the camp, but as most of the men were Polish, Heini couldn't understand them.

The newspaper explained the reality of the place he was heading to, and it came as a rude shock. Hours before the British mandate expired on 14 May 1948, David Ben-Gurion, the head of the World Zionist Organization, had declared Israeli independence, establishing the State of Israel. That was after six months of virtual civil war between the Jewish and Arab populations of the mandate, and triggered a wider international conflict with Israel's Arab neighbours, but the new state was quickly recognised by the US, the Soviet Union and others.

Heini reflected, 'My first thoughts were for my parents. Without realising it they'd emigrated to a country at war. What will the war be like and what weapons are being used? Will it be like it was in Germany, with everything being destroyed? Are thousands of people being killed and families torn apart? Are people homeless, with hardly anything to eat? Are my parents even still alive? I felt the torturous uncertainty of it all happening all over again, just like I'd felt in the concentration camp. And here I am, waiting for the signal to travel to Israel, without knowing whether I want to go.'

The situation in Israel clearly meant further delay, and Heini made himself useful, replacing the primitive hole-in-the-ground toilets they used at the farm with modern versions. These were such a hit with the locals that they were declared 'throne-like' and visited by many of the neighbours, who'd never seen such things.

When Heini was finally given a departure date of mid-September, he was sad to be told he couldn't bring his dog Rolf and still had misgivings about emigrating at all. But he decided his concern for his parents, his desire to see something of the world after years of seclusion and the exciting prospect of a sea voyage were all driving him to plump for Israel, despite his concerns about the war and the country's unsettled state. René's wife saying she'd happily have Rolf to stay was a comfort.

With the francs he'd earned, Heini bought clothes for a warm climate: a light pair of trousers, a sports jacket and a pair of shoes. Full of confidence and hope, he said goodbye to the Noirtiers, thanking them for being such lovely friends, and, close to tears, handed over Rolf. They wished him luck and said he was always welcome to return.

At Marseilles harbour Heini joined the crowds walking across the gangway to board the SS *Galila*, a large refugee ship. 'There were perhaps six hundred or more of us from all over Europe. I could see three decks. We were told the open upper deck was reserved for crew and we were shown to the two lower ones, which housed huge dormitories with washing and toilet facilities. We soon discovered there was so little space that we'd be crammed together like sardines in tins. We were all told to stay below deck until we'd pulled away from land, since our journey was an illegal one.

'Each person had a hammock that hung from the iron girders overhead and could be taken down in the morning to give a little more space, and everyone also had a stool to sit on. But as the temperatures warmed up, the number of people, the noise of children crying and the smell made it unpleasant for most of the day and night.

'When we hit open water and could go up top into the fresh air it was pleasant to look out across the water, but I never felt comfortable having nothing to do all day.'

So when Heini heard a sailor speaking German, Heini headed straight for him and explained he was a lone and lonely traveller and would welcome a job. The sailor took him straight to see the chef, who asked if he could do anything apart from washing-up and peeling potatoes. Heini quickly replied that he could make scrambled eggs. The chef told him to demonstrate, and if they were edible, he'd give him a job. Once made, the chef declared them tasty and hired Heini on the spot to cook breakfast for the officers in their mess, order supplies and do other kitchen tasks. There would be no wages, he explained, only a space to sleep on the crew deck and the promise of better food. Heini was delighted at the prospect of working in the kitchen and sleeping on the airy upper deck, and soon he was even happier when he was able to eat heartily.

As the ship neared Israel, the chef congratulated Heini for never being seasick, like some of his staff, and asked if he wanted to stay on as full-time paid crew on the *Galila*. Heini thanked him for the offer but explained that he was keen to find his parents, and while he was certainly concerned about the war situation, he felt rising excitement as their arrival in the Promised Land approached.

When 'land in view' was shouted, Heini was full of anticipation. Arriving at the port of Haifa, the passengers

MISCHLINGE

disembarked in orderly fashion and queued up to register their personal details. Heini showed his temporary ID card with the name Adek Weiss, and when he asked an official if he could go directly to his parents at the refugee camp at Ramat Gan, he was told to collect his luggage and directed to a specific bus singled out for young men to board. He assumed he was heading for a holding camp where he could ask more about his parents' whereabouts, and thought nothing of it when the buses all headed off in different directions.

When they arrived at their destination, he was horrified to see it was obviously a military camp, and as he stepped down from the bus a man in uniform told him that he'd been conscripted as a reservist.

Heini was stunned. *'This just can't be happening,'* he remembered thinking. *'I've just got through the war and all its hideous events, as well as the Nazi concentration camp, and now they want me to fight in an army. Nobody said a word to me about the militarisation of Palestine or anything similar back in Berlin when the Jewish authorities enthused about the founding of a new country.'*

He felt a little bewildered as he was billeted into a Nissen hut that was to be their temporary accommodation and asked to report for a medical. He just about understood that the panel of doctors pronounced him to be in good health and fit to serve in the Haganah, which he understood was the temporary Israeli army and soon to become the Israel Defense Force. He was then given a khaki uniform and, still in a slightly dazed state, went wandering around the camp, familiarising himself with its layout and rules. He was issued with a passport-like document but didn't sign it as he couldn't read it. He could understand some Yiddish, because of its similarity to German, but he couldn't read or understand Ivrit, modern Hebrew, which nobody seemed to notice.

'To the armoury' was the next order. As Heini recalled, 'When we arrived there I was handed a German 98 rifle [Israeli forces were prolific users of the Gewehr and Karabiner versions]. Between the barrel and the lock I could see the stamp of the former German national emblem, an eagle perched on the Third Reich swastika, part of the period I'd just managed to survive in Germany. That on top of everything else! It enraged me.

'"*No!*" I said to myself, dropping the weapon and walking away from it. An officer tried to persuade me to pick it up again, but I wouldn't.

'I just couldn't understand it. Here I was, in a Jewish state and being asked to use a weapon that once belonged to the very people who had once persecuted us. How could that have happened? Israel was not at war with Germany. This murderous instrument was being handed out by the Israeli army and brought back to life, without even a thought given to disguise or sand off the markings of its previous owners,

'Was I being overly sensitive, after my time as a concentration camp prisoner? I'd often had these weapons pointed right at me, and yet now I was supposed to use the thing to threaten others? For the first but not the last time, I wondered if I should have stayed on the *Galila*.'

After his emotional initiation, Heini made it his business to talk to other Germans in the camp, asking them if the Jewish agencies back home had mentioned being called up to fight. No one said that they had. Despite his reservations, Heini joined all the other refugees on the parade ground and swore allegiance to the Israeli flag. He was, however, delighted to hear that there were peace talks going on and a ceasefire had been agreed, and so they were to be granted leave and given a few Israeli pounds to cover their food.

Heini was at last free to go and find his parents. He hitched a lift on an army truck, but when he arrived at the holding camp at Ramat Gan he learnt they had moved to Gimmel 1, just outside of Jaffa. He hitched again, but asking around the area, nobody knew the address or his parents – everyone in the place was a newcomer. The tarmac road surface itself had petered out and become a dusty desert track when Heini finally found a letterbox with the name Bernstein on it, in front of a small, unusual-looking dwelling, with no windows looking out onto the road and barbed wire on the top of a high wall. No one answered his knock, so Heini spent his time waiting for their return and thinking what 'a naive twit' he'd been, while mulling over the upsetting discovery that he was expected to fight in an army.

Erna and Sigi eventually appeared, apologising that they'd been out at work. Erna was almost speechless with shock and joy after so many months of uncertainty, and she hugged her son close.

'My goodness,' said Erna after the long hug, holding Heini at arm's length and looking him up and down, 'you're dressed well for the climate. Did you buy new clothes or were you given them?'

Heini was a bit surprised. 'Can't you see that I'm in military uniform? Where would I get the money to buy all of this lot?!' Then he just had to laugh at his mum's unworldliness.

Sitting outside in the shade, Erna and Sigi explained that they'd both found work, Erna as a cleaner in various shops and houses, while Sigi did occasional work as an upholsterer.

REFUGEES AND PROMISED LANDS

Heini was pleased for them, but when they showed him around their new home, he thought it rather miserable, the walls unplastered, the design like nothing he'd ever seen before, rather makeshift and rough. The rooms were small, with a single bedroom, a kitchen, toilet and shower, and a small courtyard and garden. So, as Erna prepared a meal, Heini suggested to his father that while he was there on leave he could build walls and a roof around their little patio, which would give them more space and provide a room for him when he was discharged from the army.

Sigi had been testy with Heini since he'd arrived, as was often the case between them, but he was touched by his son's concern, so after obtaining the necessary permission from the authorities, Heini spent his days building an extension to their home. Their evenings were spent meeting his parents' neighbours, all Berliners with grown-up children. Everyone at these get-togethers was a Jewish refugee and survivor, and they fell into two distinct groups: the few who wanted to talk about the hideous events they'd experienced, and others, the majority, who didn't. Most were eager to forget the past and

Sigi and Erna in Israel.

only talk in the broadest, most sentimental terms about Berlin and their life there.

There was no talk of religion and only occasionally, as they got to know each other better, a few stories about the past: the hunger and the clever ways they'd managed to find food and fuel, along with anecdotes about a cruel workmate or neighbour they were glad never to have to see again. If one of their number told a harrowing tale, there was immediate recognition and empathy from the others, but these were rare moments, and no one really opened up about their past. There was deep sorrow for those they had left behind, and relief that they had survived.

'We talked about Israel and the current war, and how we might all be affected. For some this was a safe place, with its cinnamon sand and the very hot temperatures that took some getting used to. For others it was an awkward, odd spot, very different from their lives in Berlin, which they still missed, despite their experiences there.

'Dad relished being surrounded by Berliners,' Heini observed, 'and thought that it felt like the old days at times, except for the heat. Mum loved having me there, showing me off to her friends, but as time passed she became increasingly anxious about my returning to the army camp and being called on to fight.

'As the time came for me to leave, I'd finished the extension and was pleased with it. I said goodbye to my parents, not knowing what the future held.

'I was most reluctant to return to camp and resume training for a fight that I'd no appetite for. I had no wish to risk my life again. In truth, I'd no idea what I would do if and when the time came.'

14

OLD HABITS AND NEW STARTS

To Heini's huge relief, when his military training with the Israeli Defense Force commenced in earnest, the instructor accepted that he refused to carry a Nazi rifle, and instead he was given a bar to use in drill practice. Everyone was now ordered to learn their first words of Hebrew.

Heini found several reasons to be cheerful. 'I was pleased to be housed with other Germans and in the evenings be able to speak my own language, even if many conversations involved a lot of moaning about conscription.

'The kitchens served excellent fresh food, including a constant supply of fresh olives that I'd eat sitting out in the sunshine. There was even a little cinema on site, and although I couldn't understand either the soundtrack or the subtitles, sometimes there were slideshows about the country and kibbutz life. One that showed huge plantations by the coast of lemon and olive trees, along with melons, seemed to offer an ideal job for me, working on the collective's irrigation systems. I gave it some thought and discussed it with others, but the idea of not keeping my wages and of surrendering control of my life to a commune didn't appeal.

'There was still a lot I was learning about this new "Jewish" way of life we were being introduced to, such as the Jewish calendar showing the year as 5709 instead of 1949, and the Jewish festivals of Pesach, Yom Kippur, Sukkot and Hanukkah replacing Easter, Whitsun and Christmas. Only my dad had any clue about these celebrations from way back in his childhood and teenage years, and I think they were far too painful reminders of his parents, brother and sister – now all dead and lost to him – for him to share with anyone.'

Heini never claimed to have much interest in any religion, but when the opportunity came to visit Jerusalem he was happy to volunteer for a few hours' work loading and delivering goods to see the sights.

A young, handsome Heini in his early 20s.

OLD HABITS AND NEW STARTS

'As I walked into the city it was clear it was divided and I was only able to see the western part, not the path of Christian pilgrimage along the Via Dolorosa, the route of Christ's suffering, but I did see the Wailing Wall. There were many devout Orthodox Jews praying at this site, used as evidence of the Temple of Solomon and now part of the border. In the distance I could see the Dome of the Rock mosque and hear the muezzin calling Muslims to prayer.

'Standing in this ancient city, home to the world's three great religions, was a moving experience. But seeing such devotion only made me more certain that I didn't feel the deeper connection of a religious soul. I was a sightseer not a scholar or a believer. But I was enjoying the sights and smells of this historical crossroads, the aroma of a roast mutton kebab with garlic and herbs called me to try a kebab and drink a fruit juice. Once again I was instantly recognisable as a foreigner, my short-sleeve shirt marking me out, given that the locals, particularly the native *Sabras*, found it cold and were wearing coats, scarves and gloves against temperatures that had dropped from 40°C to 25°C – nothing to a Berliner.'

Back at the camp, Heini noticed the range of commitment among the military recruits he trained alongside: some were eager Zionists, keen to fight for their country, passionate about establishing a new Jewish homeland and all that it stood for. Others, like Heini, didn't feel the same passion for the cause and complained bitterly that they had been misled by Jewish organisations that had encouraged them to emigrate here.

Among them was another Berliner conscript who'd just arrived at the camp. Norbert and Heini had a lot in common – they were of similar age, both had travelled under the cover name 'Adek Weiss', both shared the same parentage of a Christian mother and a Jewish father, and both were non-believing, non-practising Jews. But Norbert had been luckier than Heini; his straight blond hair, bluish-grey eyes and non-Jewish-sounding surname had protected him from the kind of malice that Heini had encountered. Norbert, like Heini, had decided to emigrate and been just as shocked to find himself conscripted into the IDF upon arrival in his new 'homeland'.

'We felt we were almost related and spent our off-duty times together. The camp was lively in the evenings, with live music, dances and folk music. And to our delight we found the camp had an all-female unit and there was a lot of mingling between the two camps. I used my dancing skills to attract women, and I soon started dating one or two of the female conscripts. The nights were long and warm, and we were allowed to walk outside the camp through the eucalyptus, oak and pistachio woods past the giant cactuses. I'd many interesting chats with several girls in this lovely setting, but none seemed to develop into a steady relationship.'

Heini was puzzled as to why these were just dates and he wasn't attracting women beyond a single dance and a walk. One of the women in the camp, herself a German immigrant, explained to him why he was being rejected.

'As a person of mixed race,' she told him, 'you're a foreigner – and I think if you cannot change your views, you'll always be one. Settling down in our country is our patriotic duty. You have to be prepared to help build up the country further and try to see beyond the imperfections. The impression I have is that you've not really left Germany in your mind and that you're just here, passing through. You emigrated without

OLD HABITS AND NEW STARTS

any conviction. You simply joined your parents, without having your own goal, and you're not inclined to distance yourself from your Christian customs and traditions. Our Jewish festivals have no significance for you; they mean nothing to you. You're not trying hard enough to learn Hebrew. Even in the armoury with the rifle episode, you should have been more level-headed. You should have got yourself issued a different rifle without a swastika on it. We all thought that you were being really provocative, although I don't think the duty officer dealt with it well either.'

This conversation was a touchstone for Heini, making him think deeply about who he was and where he belonged. 'I've never said that I'm a Christian,' he told Norbert. 'I've never confronted this issue of Christianity and Jewishness in a Jewish state. And here is the root of the problem. As a Christian I've emigrated and haven't made an issue of my religion. I'm not certain about it myself, not clear that I've got to decide and devote myself to being Jewish. I'm not a religious person. I just can't see the necessity in doing this. I owe my own survival to the fact that I'm a Christian, but I've received such kindness from Jewish charities. The conflict between these two religions remains with me still and wouldn't just disappear if I were to convert to Judaism, the faith I was born into but have never been a part of. I haven't experienced anything here in Israel that has inspired me to yearn to belong. I can see wretchedness and misery in many parts.'

Heini had to admit he felt a little homesick for Germany and on one of his Saturday visits home he confided to his mum, 'I still feel like an outsider here, just as I was in Berlin. There I was too Jewish, here I'm not Jewish enough. I've been shouted at as a *"Jekke putz"* ["Stupid German"]. Another Israeli said to me, "What do you want with us? Your persecution is over. You'd be far better off in your own homeland, recreating that, rather than being here." Perhaps they're right to say that.'

Erna could only empathise with her son and his misgivings, and she tried to comfort him with regular news of Edie, whom they all badly missed. Edie's letters home to her mother with titbits of news about her new country reassured them that she was happy in London. She wrote that Jimmy had remained an attentive husband and she was settling well into life in England. For their part Heini and Erna hoped Edie wasn't hiding any unpleasantness from them, but they couldn't help but worry that the British might treat a German woman in their midst as 'the enemy' so soon after many had lost husbands and sons in the war and in the Blitz.

Sigi brought some welcome good news when he turned up at camp one day with a contract to work, of all places, in the Israeli parliament building – the Knesset – telling his son that it was too much work for one man, and asking him to join him. Heini welcomed the escape, and after some negotiation and paperwork he was given a temporary release, but told he'd have to return if his unit were mobilised. So with nine months' leave to work, father and son worked side by side carpeting the parliament hall, corridors, offices and lounges, and managed to get along well together.

As Christmas approached, Heini was keen to celebrate it as he hadn't the previous year, surrounded by Jewish migrants in Munich. In the unlikely desert setting, with warmth and no chance of snow, Sigi and Erna wanted to celebrate it too, because for them Christmas was a German tradition, not a religious one, and had been a family event throughout their marriage.

'I told Mum and Dad I was on the look-out for a reasonably sized fir tree to cut down under cover of darkness. Dad tried to dissuade me, concerned that if I were caught we might all be in trouble, just as would have been the case back in Berlin. But Mum and I pointed out that this time we wouldn't have to hide our Christmas tree, as the house was surrounded by a wall and no one could see in.

'I found and felled a fir tree, built a stand for it, and Mum made stars and tinsel from coloured and silver paper, just as she'd always done, then arranged them and some small candles in wire holders on the tree. It looked a treat. Our earnings from the Knesset work helped put more food on the table, but there wasn't enough to stretch to presents. We talked a lot about Edie and wished she were with us too, but it was a special family celebration nevertheless. And we were really cheered by her news when her Christmas card arrived from London. Edie planned to visit us in Israel – she and Jimmy were saving hard to buy just one ticket, and as soon as she'd saved enough for the flight she would come. Grandma Emma wrote too, saying she and Eva were well and had swapped their flat for a smaller one. It was the best Christmas gift to hear from all the family and know that they were well.

'On Christmas night, Mum, Dad and I were invited to visit our Berlin neighbours, Herr and Frau Ruben. We couldn't help but laugh when they opened the door and the first thing we saw was their Christmas tree – as we sat around it, we were all full of the Christmas spirit, despite the heat. My father enjoyed drinking Jägermeister, like the schnapps he'd made in the cellar.'

MISCHLINGE

Heini enjoyed working in his parents' small garden and vegetable plot on his day off, and he became more and more interested in the land he could see beyond it, where a small orange plantation was struggling to thrive. The trees looked sad and dried up, and they only yielded small fruit. Heini decided to trim and water the trees in the hope of reviving them. The trees responded after a while and produced a much bigger crop, and although a kilo of oranges was cheaper than a kilo of potatoes in Israel, it did provide a little extra income.

The neglected orange grove set Heini thinking about the men and women who had carefully planted each orange tree in rows in the first place. Who lived here before us migrants?, he wondered. They must have been people who were born here and probably still would be here if they hadn't been driven from their home and plantation. The Palestinian Arabs had had to move so that a Jewish state could be created. Nobody spoke about it, but it made Heini think. He felt for them because he knew only too well what it was like to be displaced from the place where you were born, the place where you felt you belonged, with just a simple twist of fate changing all that and turning you into an outsider. It seemed an irony that just as his family had been forced out of their homes, his family's arrival in Israel might have done exactly the same to another family.

Heini had no answers. 'I could see why surviving Jewish families would want the safety of a new homeland after the mass murder of their people across Europe. Israel seemed like a place of safety for those who didn't want to return to the areas where they had been persecuted in the first place. But I still wondered what had happened to those people who had

OLD HABITS AND NEW STARTS

once lived here. Were they living in a refugee holding camp somewhere like I had once done?'

Following a long ceasefire, the end of the war in Israel was announced in February 1949. Heini was relieved that there was now no prospect of having to fight people he had no argument with, and he couldn't wait to be demobbed. He was keen to earn money, and a friend advised him that the best way to get a job was to show his German ID card, have a photograph taken and apply for an Israeli civilian card. With his new civilian card in hand, Heini went again and again to the Histadrut offices (the national trade unions centre), asking for work as a plumber or upholsterer, but he was only offered temporary work as an orange picker and transporter, loading oranges at the port of Jaffa.

'The job meant carrying heavy crates of oranges from lorries over gangways to boats all day long in the intense heat of 35°C, with no shade. You could earn more by carrying two crates at a time, strapped together. It took me a while to manage carrying two crates along the narrow gangway, still leaving enough space for the other two men to get by with theirs. At the end of the day my back was painful and I felt utterly exhausted, good for nothing except my bed and sleep. Life became just constant hard work and then sleep, reminding me of my days in Wuhlheide and Buchenwald. I felt I'd lost all the fun in my life, so I started looking for a different job.'

His parents' neighbour and friend, Herr Ruben, came up trumps with the offer of a job as a kitchenhand and dishwasher at the restaurant in Tel Aviv where he worked. It was a large coffee house called Herlinger on Allenby Street run by Frau Herlinger in the style of her hometown, Vienna. Once more it was extremely hot work – the kitchen was far too small for all the petrol stoves on which the elderly chef cooked and the thermometer often touched 50°C. Heini enjoyed the change for a while, but after working long hours again in the heat, he admitted to himself that he wasn't enjoying this job either, nor, indeed, his new life in Israel. He began to consider the idea of returning to Germany.

Events were soon brought to a head by the government announcement that thousands of soldiers were to be discharged from the army and by law would be entitled to their old jobs back. Heini talked over the situation with Norbert, who'd been medically discharged from the army. What chance did they have of finding work? Heini felt he'd have little luck getting a plumbing job, he didn't want to go back to hauling oranges nor did he possess the ideological beliefs for life in a kibbutz. He also saw no prospect of finding a wife and starting a family, despite his mother's best efforts. He accepted the German immigrant woman's argument: the reality was, he was Jewish only by birth through his father's bloodline. He'd never been brought up as a Jew, knew little of their traditions or beliefs, would never be Jewish and therefore didn't really fit in to Israel. Although he was disappointed at what Israel had to offer him, he admitted to himself that this was partly his own fault. He'd been so preoccupied with just surviving, ignorant of what was going on in the world for so many years, that it was naive of him to emigrate just because of the Jewish authorities' encouragement and to accompany his parents.

His circumstances had forced Norbert to live at the Rubens' house and rely on eating the leftovers Heini brought him back from the coffee house. Together they went to see

OLD HABITS AND NEW STARTS

the Jewish Assistance Agency and asked how they might return to Berlin.

'To our great surprise,' related Heini, 'the gentleman there was sympathetic, and he understood that we hadn't taken to life in Israel and wanted to return home. We weren't the only ones – many others felt the same, he told us. When he said that our return passage would be arranged at no cost to us, we felt as if a great weight had been lifted.

'I put off telling my parents, as I knew they'd try to dissuade me, and started saving as much of my earnings from the coffee house as possible to prepare for my journey. For not much money you could pick up a smart dark suit and heavier shoes than the ones I usually wore, so I bought some and prepared for my return.'

Their documents arrived: tickets for a boat leaving Haifa, a temporary photo-passport that would run out in six months, a visa covering them as far as Genoa in Italy and $15 of currency. Heini was surprised and relieved when someone translated the Hebrew words on his passport; it said that he was German, not Jewish. 'Now,' he told Norbert, 'I have written confirmation that I'm not Jewish, despite being persecuted by the Nazis for being a Jew. And they'll never be able to send me back here with these words in my papers.' All of a sudden his situation felt less precarious and more secure.

With his departure date confirmed, Heini broke the news to his parents. They were both upset, of course, but accepted his choice. Sigi said that it had crossed his mind to leave too, as work had dried up after the Knesset job and he was worried about earning enough to pay the rent, but he believed he'd find more work soon. Erna had an inkling that

MISCHLINGE

her son might leave and told herself that the family had been split up before. War had done that to so many families, but they'd managed to find each other and keep in contact, and she'd make sure that they'd do the same in the future. Nevertheless, she was in floods of tears as the date of her son's departure drew near, but she told herself he was a young man now – 26 years old – and it was his choice to make. For her the huge worry was his safety when he disembarked from the ship, then had to face travelling across several countries, all the way from Genoa to Berlin, with no visa and little money. But Heini reassured his parents he was resourceful, could work his way and was determined to go.

So on 16 September 1949 Heini and Norbert waited at Haifa port and were surprised to see the very same ship dock that had brought them there almost two years before, the *Galila*. They strode back across the gangway, full of hope for a better life back in their homeland.

Far away in London, the newly married Edie was discovering that the city was also recovering from trauma. It had seen nearly half of Britain's civilian deaths in the war, with around 43,000 civilians having been killed during the eight-month-long Blitz, one in six Londoners being made homeless, and more than a million homes damaged or destroyed. She understood that they had little choice but to move in with Jimmy's mum, and were fortunate to have been given the attic room in her large Edwardian home in Highgate village in the north of the city.

Jimmy, like thousands of other returning soldiers, went straight out to look for a job, but having been conscripted as

OLD HABITS AND NEW STARTS

a teenager, he had no qualifications or experience to offer. And for Edie, being German and with her pidgin English, finding employment would surely be even harder.

The newlyweds discussed the issue, just as they did everything in their lives. Jimmy was adamant from the beginning about how they were going to handle any anti-German backlash. 'We're *not* telling people you're Austrian,' he insisted to Edie. 'We will tell the truth and say you were a slave labourer because of your Jewish blood. The Germans treated you dreadfully – and would have murdered you too. If people don't like it, they don't have to mix with us.'

Edie Ring adored her mother-in-law from the day they met, and the feeling was mutual. 'Ellen welcomed me into her home and her heart,' she says. 'She was short and plump and very warm in her manner, and she had a strength about her. She'd lost seven babies in childhood and brought up the six surviving children virtually alone after her husband's stroke, while also running her own flower stall at Covent Garden market. I soon saw how she loved to cook big meals and fuss over us, and she promised to teach me how to cook. She could see Jimmy and I loved and looked after each other, and that's all that mattered to her. She was never anything but kind to me, telling me bluntly, "You weren't one of them, so your nationality doesn't count."

'Jimmy was the youngest in the family, and as I got to know them all it was obvious his sister Julie found it hard to accept me. I suppose it was because I was born German, but there was nothing I could do about that. Perhaps she resented anyone marrying her favourite baby brother. She never said anything to me in front of the family, but she'd play cruel tricks on me, like putting me on a bus in the wrong direction or just teasing me constantly. I resolved not to let it spoil my new life and just stayed out of her way whenever possible.'

To Jimmy, the occasional disparaging remark he heard about his wife were water off a duck's back. He was so very proud of Edie, and would often say to friends that he wondered how on earth he'd managed to land such a beautiful woman, one who'd survived the horrors of being a *Mischling* and was still able to look forward and just get on with her life.

With her dark skin and hair and her brown eyes, Edie did have the advantage of not looking like a stereotypical German woman, so when she went around London looking for work, nobody guessed she was German, either from her appearance or her accent. Many thought that she might be South African. But once people did know her nationality, either from her job applications or just from asking simple questions about where she was from, their reactions could sometimes be cold, nasty and downright hostile. One clerk looked her in the eye and asked her directly, 'Why would I give a job to one of the enemy, whose father or brother might have killed one of mine?' Even with her minimal education, Edie understood that Germany had been the aggressor in two world wars and there would probably be two generations in some families who would always resent Germans for the loss and heartache they'd suffered. She knew only too well you couldn't fight deep prejudice.

But the response from most people she met was far more nuanced, and overall her experiences were more good than bad. When challenged, she'd sometimes explain that she was not a Nazi but half-Jewish, that she'd been forced into slave labour and was rescued by a British soldier. Whether it was

OLD HABITS AND NEW STARTS

Jimmy and Edie, the newlyweds, 1948.

her gentle manner or the growing awareness of the atrocities of the Holocaust, the majority of people she met could tell the difference between the German aggressors and their victims. But she recoiled from the word 'victim', saying, 'I never saw myself as a victim – that would mean they were the victors. They didn't win. I won, because I haven't let them ruin my life.'

But just like her father and brother, no amount of confrontation or abuse would make Edie reveal much about her persecution to strangers – or indeed even to Jimmy. 'I did have dark moments,' she says, 'but Jimmy always seemed to notice the signs, and before I knew it his laughter, teasing and affection just put me in a better place. I was so lucky to have him.'

Jimmy had proven in the army that he possessed his mother's entrepreneurial spirit, and back in his home city he soon found a job on the railways in the goods yard behind King's

Cross station on York Way. He drove a delivery cart, pulled by a Clydesdale horse that he also had to care for, and he enjoyed driving around the city he knew well. With the help of his sister-in-law, Edie found a job at the Imperial Tobacco factory in the East End, just weeks after she arrived in London. She was relieved to find her workmates accepted her, once they knew her background, and as time went by her English came on in leaps and bounds. Again, she didn't talk about her experiences in any detail to anyone.

But she couldn't entirely escape the trauma and ordeal she'd experienced for so many years. What she'd endured was beginning to show physically and mentally; she experienced bouts of crippling diarrhoea and stomach cramps, then her periods stopped and she had times of huge anxiety.

'Jimmy made me go to our local doctor, and he was very kind. He said the years of near-starvation food, getting rickets because I was hidden in the dark and then the hard physical labour had taken their toll on my body, and it was now getting the bill and paying the price. It would take my body time to recover.

'The hardest thing to hear was that my body wasn't fit enough to carry a baby, and that the much-longed-for child Jimmy and I both wanted was unlikely to happen for some years – and perhaps not at all. That was a blow.

'He also explained that some of these physical symptoms were the result of my mental fears and anxiety. He said I was "holding it all inside me" and it would take time to leave me. Everything he told me made sense, but it still made me feel ashamed. I'd survived when so many hadn't, and now I had the love of a wonderful man, my Jimmy. What more could I want? How could I feel sad when I had so much?

OLD HABITS AND NEW STARTS

'The doctor said all my feelings were entirely understandable and it was natural that I'd feel depressed at times. His words helped me put my experiences in perspective. He also said depression was a physical illness that often ran in families – a chemical released into your body – and I wondered then if that explained some of my dad's behaviour. Certainly being cast out by his family and then being persecuted for years would seem ample justification for Dad's bouts of depression. I accepted everything that the doctor told me and with great reluctance agreed to take antidepressants. To my surprise, they worked.'

Jimmy took the news about no children in his stride. Whatever his private thoughts were, he reassured his wife that they'd be just as happy if they didn't have children.

'This was just further proof that Jimmy was my rescuer and my saviour. Within weeks of coming to England we had a roof over our heads and he had a job. He wasn't a drinker and he didn't have a temper. We had a proper loving home, we ate together and laughed together. He was a gentleman who looked after me – I was so blessed to find him, and I knew it. If it was a gamble in loving and marrying a young foreigner and moving to England, it was the right choice. His unconditional support gave me strength. We didn't have much, but really we had everything we needed and we were living the good life.

'I didn't miss Berlin – there had hardly been anything good to miss, but I did miss my lovely mum, who had always been my protector. I wrote her long letters and relished hearing her news, and how Heini and Dad were finding life in the Promised Land. Jimmy, thoughtful as ever, said if we saved hard we could afford *one* plane ticket. I'd thought that it would be way out of our reach – I'd never heard of anyone flying anywhere – and the idea that it might be possible cheered me up no end when I really missed Mum.'

Neither of them knew then that on the other side of the world, Heini was going to leave Israel and cross continents to return to Berlin.

Heini was finding it strange returning to Europe on the same ship he'd arrived on, the *Galila*. For a start there were fewer than a hundred passengers stretched out on the spacious decks, playing cards, gambling like it was an ocean liner, but he welcomed the chance to rest. He'd lost so much weight hauling oranges and in the heat of the coffee-house kitchen that he was almost back to the state he'd been at Witten-Annen. Virtually all the passengers were men, from a variety of countries, who'd spent time in Israel but like him were now heading back to their homelands.

'Norbert and I talked of working our way back to Berlin, but as we were docking in Genoa, we were intrigued when a Brazilian passenger who could speak German suggested that as we were in Italy, why didn't we visit Rome and Milan before returning home to Berlin. "You may never get the chance again," he said with a smile. He seemed very knowledgeable and told us he was heading for the Jewish Agency in the city to get funds to continue his journey. We weren't sure if we were eligible for anything, but we went along with him anyway. At the agency they asked for our passports and Israeli military identity cards, and after filling in some forms we were amazed to be given Italian currency to cover three days' food and lodging.

OLD HABITS AND NEW STARTS

'*Why not explore while we are here?*, we thought. With money in our pocket, we decided to do just what the Brazilian man had suggested and enjoy Italy a little before we left. It's not as if we'd ever had the chance of a holiday before. We bought a night train ticket and arriving late in Rome, found cheap beds for the night. We spent the next day seeing the sights – we were amazed by the Colosseum, albeit only from the outside to protect our limited funds. We sampled a bowl of spaghetti in a backstreet café before wandering around the Vatican until our feet ached. Then we tasted our very first ice cream, sitting on a low wall, watching the world go by, enjoying every moment.'

The Brazilian man had given them an address for Rome's Jewish Agency, and once again they were given money, more than back in Genoa. So they took the night train to Milan and before they set off exploring, Heini sent a postcard to his grandmother and his friend Gerhard, telling them he was on his way back and that he hoped to see them both soon in Berlin.

'In Milan we had our first proper meal in a restaurant,' recalled Heini, 'although what a sight we must have been. Norbert only owned shorts, so I lent him some trousers, and as he was 5 foot 4 and I was 5 foot 11, they almost reached his armpits, and together with my jacket he looked most peculiar. We savoured the lunch and toasted the Brazilian whose advice had enabled this adventure. We called in at our third Jewish Agency office, where there were many others like us being given money to fund their journey home. The cash they gave us would cover living expenses for two days, as well as a bed for the night. We were relieved and most grateful.'

MISCHLINGE

Having enjoyed what felt like a holiday, Heini and Norbert now faced the serious business of getting from Milan through Austria to Germany without a visa. They bought a map of Bolzano to help plan their crossing to Austria and what was likely to be an unpredictable route across the Alps. As the Four Power status of Austria meant there were no diplomatic relations between Italy and Austria, they knew that if they wanted to go further, they'd have to cross the border at the Brenner Pass without a visa.

'At Milan station we found we could send our suitcases ahead to the nearest Austrian city – Innsbruck – and we boarded the train towards Bolzano. Getting off at the nearest stop to the Brenner Pass, we walked towards the barrier and showed our Italian visas to the Austrian border guards, explaining we were German nationals. We were asked to go inside, and to our shock we were ordered to strip completely, then bend over with our backsides in the air while our clothes were searched. One guard took hold of our walking map of Bolzano and tore it up, but none of them even asked to look at our ID cards, which remained in our pockets.

'Back you go,' said the border guard. 'If you leave illegally, it's up to you to get back in illegally.'

This was an unexpected and worrying development for the pair of them. 'We were deflated but determined not to fall at this hurdle,' Heini recalled, 'and we decided to try again a bit later in the day, when the guards had changed shifts. But the same thing happened; we were strip-searched and once again sent back. It was getting dark, so we knew we needed to find somewhere to sleep, and we headed for the village inn. At the bar we started chatting to a local man from the Tyrol mountains, who spoke German and couldn't

OLD HABITS AND NEW STARTS

have been more helpful. He sketched an illegal route we could take to cross the border from Italy to Austria, pointing out places we could use as marker points to find our way up to a high-lying meadow. He said we'd most likely meet a dairy maid and her cows there and to pass on his greetings. He even exchanged our Italian currency for some Austrian schillings. Crossing his fingers, he wished us good weather and safe passage. We were both so grateful at this very useful act of kindness from a stranger that we bought him a large double schnapps.'

They set off the following morning, armed with optimism and a little food. They followed the mountain man's sketch, and after walking for a few hours they reached the high meadow, where they saw the dairy maid and explained who they were.

'Have a good break here,' was her advice. 'You'll be best off descending later in the day. Whatever you do, you don't want to get to the main road until dawn at the earliest, and you'll need to be really careful when you get there. Austrian border guards patrol the area, so avoid the nearby village too. I'll give you a few reference points, which will make it easier for you to work out where you are on the way down. Find a place to rest, and I'll bring you some milk later.'

'We found a good spot to eat and lay down in the grass in the summer sunshine. The sounds of the cowbells and cows mooing were peaceful and relaxing. Lying on the ground cooled them down a bit. Summer on the mountainside was coming to an end and the dairy maid was preparing to bring the cattle down. She returned with the freshest of milk for us and showed us the best way down the mountain, avoiding the Brenner Pass border point. "Once you get down there stay in the wood, follow the road and then cross it," she told us. "That's the most dangerous bit – you don't want to be seen there. You'll have to be careful there as you won't know the paths, so you'll need to go slowly and not make any noise."

'We were both focused and a little frightened now about what we were about to do. We set off, allowing ourselves plenty of time. At first it was so peaceful; it was as if we were the only people on earth. We saw deer, rabbits and birds. We recognised all the reference points that the dairy maid had mentioned and soon reached the decisive bit. We got to the wood as darkness fell and we suddenly felt more tense and fearful. We were very much on edge as the border approached and both began to stumble over things, making slow progress. Our eyes were getting used to the dark but our other senses were working harder.

'Knowing that all the effort we'd gone to evading the border control could be thwarted in one stroke if we were spotted by a patrol made us both very cautious and careful. We took breaks on tree trunks or stumps.

'We didn't see a soul, which gave us the confidence to walk through the village. Then as we approached a streetlight it lit up – there was a man in uniform with a rifle on his shoulder. Our hearts dropped into our boots as he immediately asked for our ID. I showed him my German identity card.

'"Where are you going?" he asked.

'"We're Berliners, heading home to Berlin," I told him.

'"Go on then," said the soldier. "Off you go, I haven't seen you." He didn't even ask to see Norbert's ID.

'We couldn't believe our luck as we walked out of the village. We said, "God Bless the Tyrol and all those kind

OLD HABITS AND NEW STARTS

strangers." Then we spotted a sign to Innsbruck confirming we were heading in the right direction, and as soon as we reached the cover of some woods we stopped to rest for a while. Despite all the excitement and tension, there was still a lot of night-time lying ahead. When we saw a road coming up and a car's headlights whizz past, we decided to sleep in the woods, as we could better identify who was passing in these cars and lorries in daylight.

'As dawn broke we gave each other a pep talk and set off again. Watching from the side of the road we saw a bright red sports car approach, and on the spur of the moment I ran out and waved it down. I was dumbstruck when the driver stopped.

'"Where do you want to go then?" the driver asked.

'"To Innsbruck," replied Norbert.

'So we climbed in.'

Bedraggled and exhausted after their arduous journey, the pair were nevertheless excited when the driver dropped them off near Innsbruck station. Heini darted into a telephone box to see if there was a local Jewish Agency listed in the phone directory. Overjoyed to find the number, Heini put some coins into the slot, the ones the mountain man in the Tyrolian village had given them exactly for this purpose. Heini then described what happened next.

'"We're on our way back from Israel," I told the woman who answered, "and are asking for your help to get back to Berlin."

'Incredulous, she then asked, "And where did you say you've come from?"

'"From Israel," I repeated, "you heard it right the first time!"

MISCHLINGE

'After what seemed like a very long pause she directed me to the agency's offices, where a small crowd was waiting for us. We were clearly something of an attraction, as they'd never seen people returning from Israel before. We had a lot to explain about our illegal journey and crossing the border. We obviously looked exhausted because the woman dealing with us broke off and said she'd found us somewhere to stay at no charge while they investigated our claim for visas.'

In the days that followed, the agency wanted to hear the young men's stories in full, and they asked numerous questions about their experiences at various borders. They said they'd never encountered anyone like them before, nor had they ever seen Israeli military ID cards or the time-restricted passports with the visa for Italy. But when Heini and Norbert produced the left-luggage ticket for their suitcases as another bit of proof about their story and identity, the staff at the Jewish Agency finally believed them. They agreed to provide visas to Germany, but explained that it would take a few days. Meanwhile, the two of them would receive free accommodation and a small allowance for food, as well as a temporary document confirming their identity in case they were stopped by anyone.

Heini thanked them profusely, and then he explained why he had so much to be grateful for. 'Jewish charity has always helped me at crucial times in my life. As a child me and my family were given food and clothing, after the war they gave us free passage to Israel, and now they've funded my journey across Europe to return home to Berlin. It's true to say my life has been both threatened and helped by Judaism.'

Now Heini and Norbert caught up on missed sleep and gathered strength for the last leg of the journey, which seemed

OLD HABITS AND NEW STARTS

less frightening as it would be on German-speaking soil. They walked into Innsbruck to collect their cases from the station and buy more postcards to send to their families.

'As we browsed in the shop,' recalled Heini, 'our accents drew suspicion and before long the police arrived and took us to the police station. If it hadn't been for the Jewish charity and our identity documents, we'd have had a problem. As it was, they phoned them to verify that our IDs were genuine and then released us with an apology. Soon enough, we received a postdated visa for Austria and another for the tri-zone area of Germany, as well as our rail tickets from Innsbruck to Munich via Kufstein.

'We crossed the border with no problem at all. Back on home soil in Munich we walked into the very same Jewish charity offices we had departed to Israel from, what seemed a very long time ago. We were again given funds for board, lodging and food. This was Jewish Aid's very last gift to us, and despite my disappointment with Israel, I left their offices feeling quite emotional and indebted to them for the opportunity to try out that new life.'

Norbert telephoned his parents in Berlin, and learnt that his stepfather had arranged for them to stay near the frontier with family friends, who would show them the best route to take to the heavily controlled border town of Gutenfürst in the morning. They bought plenty of cigarettes to take with them, a tried-and-tested currency. After a long walk the following morning, they at last crossed a border for the final time and headed for the first railway station on their route in what since 7 October 1949 was a newly founded country – the German Democratic Republic (GDR). At Gutenfürst they sold their cigarettes to buy rail tickets, not recognising the money they were handed – the 1948 currency reform had brought new notes into existence. They were now on the home straight, only needing to change trains at Plauen, where they boarded the service for Anhalter Bahnhof Berlin, their final stop.

'Stepping off the train in Berlin,' said Heini, 'I felt at home, even if I was actually homeless. October 1949 marked the end of an emotional journey, as well as a physically demanding one. I'd left the city I was born in to make a long illegal journey to the new state of Israel, where I hadn't fitted in either. And after another long illegal journey back again, my home city was now in a new country – part of the Soviet Bloc – and renamed East Germany, officially the German Democratic Republic.

'Norbert insisted I stay at his parents for a few days, and they spoiled us both. But I needed to register with the authorities as living at a Berlin address to get my all-important ration cards. I'd need to get to my Grandmother Emma's, and to register I'd need a new identity card and a new photo. The old card was unreadable and I no longer looked like the person in the photo. In truth I felt like a different person too.'

15

THE BERLIN WALL

The new country to which Heini had returned, the German Democratic Republic, was of course neither democratic nor a republic. It was a dictatorship with no free elections and its inhabitants weren't allowed free movement. Most people called it East Germany, and East Berlin was its capital. But Berlin was now divided into four sectors: the Eastern sector was controlled by the Soviets, the other three parts controlled individually by British, American and French forces. The whole city was within East Germany and could only be accessed from West Germany via a 'corridor route', controlled and patrolled by the Soviets. Once you reached Berlin, access between all four zones was relatively easy, at least at first.

'Grandmother Emma was surprised to see me in Berlin so quickly after receiving my postcard from Innsbruck,' recalled Heini. 'She welcomed me with open arms and was happy to let me stay with her and Eva until I could find work and a place of my own. I only hoped the city of my birth would prove as welcoming.'

MISCHLINGE

Initially Heini settled back in the city with ease, living centrally in what was now East Berlin, the Soviet sector. He no longer had itchy feet, his earlier yearning for adventures having passed. He quickly found work as a plumber, as there were still massive rebuilding programmes going on throughout the city.

'I met up with many old friends again and found everything I'd missed in Israel, namely security and a higher standard of living. Most of all I loved the fact that I could understand what people around me were saying and enjoy the pleasure of reading. I felt like I belonged again – for all its faults and the trauma I'd experienced in Berlin, this was the place I knew best.'

At his great friend Gerhard's house, Heini met the woman he'd marry. Gerda Wolter was a tall, elegant woman with high cheekbones and dark, shiny hair that fell almost to her waist. She worked as a secretary, but her sewing skills transformed her into a smart, well-groomed lady at a time when clothes were hard to come by. Sharing a love of clothes and good food, they made a handsome couple, both tall, dark and well turned out.

Gerda had been left a war widow after only three years of marriage, and Heini felt an instinct to protect her. They fell deeply in love, marrying in 1950 at a small affair with just two friends as witnesses. Grandma Emma was too old and frail to come, and Eva wasn't invited, having long been considered an outsider by Heini.

For a while life was good for the newlyweds. Both had jobs and spent their earnings turning his little flat into a comfortable home, the only cloud on the horizon being Heini's increasingly painful back. Years of hard labour had clearly

THE BERLIN WALL

Gerda and Heini's wedding photo, 1950.

damaged it, and now his physically demanding work as a plumber was making things worse.

To add to Heini's physical deterioration, in the 1950s East Berlin was becoming a much less attractive place to live for its citizens. The victorious Allies had poured money into West Germany, regenerating its economy, in what was named the '*Wirtschaftswunder*' (economic miracle), but the Soviets saw their zone as the spoils of war and plundered major industrial assets, taking them all the way back east. The huge differences between the economic boom in West Germany and the greyer, poorer life on offer in Soviet Bloc East Germany gradually became apparent to Berliners in all sectors of the divided city.

Heini and Gerda found that although they both worked hard in full-time jobs, they couldn't afford the little luxuries and comforts that made life enjoyable. Life in East Berlin under Soviet-imposed restrictions had a bleak, drab and

MISCHLINGE

*Heini, Gerda and their daughter Angela
(aged 9 months) in 1956.*

deprived air, the choices open to them in everything from food in the shops to clothes, home comforts, cars and holidays being severely limited in comparison with what was available in the West. At one point, Gerda resorted to cutting and selling her long, shiny hair to a wigmaker to supplement their incomes.

East Berliners and East Germans were leaving in droves, heading for a better life in West Germany. By 1951 the monthly emigration figures were running at between 12,000 and 17,000 people a month. But Heini had no desire to change country again, so he and Gerda tried to focus on the positives in their lives: the fact they both had jobs, an affordable flat near the city centre, and access to a free health service and each other.

Over in London, Edie and Jimmy were flourishing. 'I loved my life in London from the very beginning,' recalls Edie. 'My English was expanding daily because I never, ever spoke

THE BERLIN WALL

German after I moved to London. Jimmy teased me about the Cockney twang I'd picked up from him and our friends said I sounded like a local. And having been confined to the flat in Berlin for so long, I really enjoyed going out to work and mixing with people. Jimmy took me out to the cinema and to a show sometimes, and at weekends I'd watch and learn as his mum cooked his favourite meals like steak and kidney pie, and apple tart and custard.'

Edie Ring had mostly dispelled much of her childhood and teenage years by never revisiting them or talking about them. It was as if her life only began with Jimmy, so successfully did she relegate those bad memories to the back of her mind. But physically she was far from recovered. Like Heini she was finding the years of malnutrition, rickets and hard labour were now taking their toll on her body. Her dream of having a child seemed unattainable, although her sympathetic GP continued to advise that her inability to conceive was the result of Nazi persecution and the legacy of her poor diet,

Young Edie's passport photo.

rickets and mental anxiety. Now she was safe and eating well, he said, time would heal her. So Edie continued with the anti-anxiety pills, went to work and never stopped hoping to get pregnant.

As she remembers, 'My little fella worked overtime to raise the money for me to visit my parents in Israel. In 1952, the day came when we'd saved enough and my work colleagues were shocked when I showed them my plane ticket, as none of them had ever flown before. It was wonderful to visit Mum and Dad, and I was so joyful to see them again after five years. I would just sit with Mum in their little garden in Jaffa chatting for hours. I was surprised that Mum seemed to be enjoying Israel more than my dad. She didn't mind her job cleaning the

Edie on an Israeli beach with her mum and dad during her 1952 visit.

houses of richer folk. But Dad, although at last feeling safe from antisemitism, talked of missing his old lifestyle in Berlin, his neighbourhood, his local pub and old friends.

'I made the most of every minute with Mum, who had always been my protector and had done so much to keep me safe before and during the war. We had much to share, with Mum wanting to know all about my new life. I told her how happy my life with Jimmy was. And she'd smile and say, "I know it's *'treue Liebe'* with you two."'

When Edie returned home to London, Jimmy hardly recognised her – her normally olive-coloured skin had turned a darker shade of chestnut in the Israeli sunshine. He was thrilled to have her back as he'd struggled without her. Love at first sight had matured into a deep bond, and they both knew how much they had to be grateful for.

All was not so good with Heini and Gerda, however, and cracks had begun to appear in their marriage. Heini had gradually become an unhappy man, changing from a charismatic charmer to someone Gerda scarcely recognised. The long years of persecution and imprisonment were now manifesting both physically and mentally; he was plagued with nightmares about his past, his torture and degradation, and the ever-worsening physical pain from his spine. He'd never shared the burden of his experiences during the Nazi regime with his wife, his best friend Gerhard or indeed anyone at all. This 'haunting from the past' had begun to drag him into depressive periods and change his personality.

At first Gerda only noticed her husband going missing for short periods of time. She was not in good physical health herself, having been diagnosed with TB, but she found his unexplained absences increasingly frustrating. When she was medically retired from full-time employment and at home much of the time, she discovered with great sadness that Heini was indulging in bouts of binge drinking, with his behaviour becoming more and more erratic, despite the fact he'd rarely drank alcohol before the war. Heartbreakingly, she then discovered that there were brief dalliances with other women. He was now a very different man to the one she'd married and he'd even taken up smoking.

Gerda felt the man she'd married was disintegrating in front of her eyes. Ill and weak, she was in no mood to put up with his absences and bad behaviour, and after a period of intense strain they divorced in 1952, just two years into their marriage.

Yet despite everything they still retained a great deal of affection for each other, and with homes hard to find, they continued to live together. They even made occasional attempts at reconciliation, and when Gerda became pregnant the pair decided they *must* try again. Their daughter Angela was born in December 1953, and they made a new start.

In Israel, Erna wrote to Edie in London to say they were giving up on their new start – she and Sigi had decided Israel was not for them either. Sigi had once been persecuted for being a Jew, but he now found that he couldn't live as one. 'It's too Jewish out here,' he told people. 'We don't really fit in.'

Sigi hadn't lived as a Jew since they married over 30 years ago, Erna explained to Edie. He felt an outsider – just as Heini had – in this exuberant new Jewish state. He couldn't wait to get back to Berlin with its cold temperatures, German food and the lifestyle he'd known for most of his life. Erna

THE BERLIN WALL

Heini, Gerda (sporting the long hair she later sold) and Angela.

would have stayed, but Sigi told her he was too old to change his habits now. So together with their friends and fellow Berliners, the Rubens, they returned to Germany.

The Bernsteins found a small flat in the district of Wedding in what was now the French sector of Berlin, just a few miles across the city from Heini and Gerda in the Soviet sector. Heini was pleased to have his parents within reach again, regularly travelling across the city and through the checkpoints to stay with them. On one of these visits, Heini was shocked to bump into the man who had been his guard in Wuhlheide – Sergeant Franke. It was a strange moment that immediately brought his memories from that place right to the front of his mind. 'We just stopped,' he told Gerda, 'shook hands and asked each other if we were all right. We had a bit of a laugh about the cigarette and food cards that had fallen from the sky, but no more than that. And then we both walked on.'

But life was still harsh in East Berlin. Every time Heini left the Soviet sector to visit Sigi and Erna in West Berlin, he was only too aware of how his living conditions were so much worse. He could only do his best for his family, going out to work, resisting the temptation to drink when he was down, and try to be a good husband and father.

In 1954 rationing was finally lifted in Britain. Edie, bright and ambitious, fluent in English now and with an aptitude for figures, left the tobacco factory behind for an office job in accounts. And when Jimmy found a job that came with a centrally heated flat, he jumped at the opportunity. He was to help run the central-heating systems in new-build blocks of flats in Hackney. Delighted to have their first home together, their only sadness was there was still no sign of a baby. Edie tried to accept childlessness as her fate, but she couldn't deny the fact that they both still longed for a child.

Then, in the spring of 1955, after nine long years of being together, when they'd both almost given up hope, Edie discovered she was pregnant. Her body had taken its time to recover, but she was now in much better shape physically and mentally, surely thanks to the life she'd led with Jimmy and perhaps the end of rationing the previous year.

Twenty-eight-year-old Edie had defied the odds, and after a normal pregnancy gave birth to a healthy baby girl in a London hospital, just before Christmas 1955.

THE BERLIN WALL

That's me, Sharon, the author of this book, and this is where I enter the story …

I was born on 21 December 1955 – the winter solstice, and therefore the shortest day of the year. From when I was very small, Mum told me, 'Each day gets a little brighter after the shortest day. That means the world actually gets brighter after you were born – and it certainly did for me, Sharon.' It was a phrase she'd repeat to me, family and friends throughout her life.

When I was older, she explained: 'I had you to care for and focus on, and you pulled me out of any backward-looking sad thoughts. I chose the name "Sharon" because of its Jewish roots, and apparently it means fertility out of barrenness.'

English was the only language spoken at home, and Mum taught me to read before I went to school because she didn't want me, as the daughter of an immigrant, to lag behind. She and Dad took on extra work to send me to a fee-paying Catholic prep school, both to give me the kind of education she was denied and honour the promise she'd made at her Catholic wedding ceremony to bring up any children of hers in the faith.

In another of life's little ironies, my local convent school lay at the centre of one of London's largest Orthodox Jewish communities, in Stamford Hill. My schoolfriends were always welcome at our cosy flat, a luxury Mum herself had never enjoyed, and our house rules were fairness, manners and kindness. I was loved and encouraged but never driven or pushed, and my childhood was an idyllic one.

* * *

MISCHLINGE

As I was growing up in London, events were about to take a dramatic turn in Berlin. As the 1960s dawned, Berlin was grabbing the headlines for being a 'loophole in the Iron Curtain', a magnet for those wanting to escape the grim regime of East Germany for the freedoms and monetary rewards of the West. By 1961 the figures had grown from thousands to more than three million people fleeing through Berlin checkpoints, many of them young professionals. Their loss was having a major impact on the economy and politics of the country, as were the 60,000 Berliners commuting across the border every day for better pay.

East German and Soviet politicians now met in secret to find a way to halt this exodus of talent and revenue, and rumours about what was going to happen were soon rife. Walter Ulbricht, chairman of the State Council of the GDR, said, 'No one has any intention of building a wall.' But then just two months later they did exactly that – starting in the middle of the night.

In the early hours of 13 August 1961, while most Berliners were still asleep, construction workers shocked the world by stringing barbed-wire fences across routes going from East Berlin to West Berlin, blocking railway lines and cutting phone lines. On whichever side of the almost hundred-mile-long perimeter you awoke that morning in August, you were stuck there.

Was Heini the luckiest or the unluckiest man in the world? At the age of 38 he now found himself trapped behind the Berlin Wall, confined to the Soviet sector. He'd counted himself lucky at having survived a labour camp, a concentration camp, a death march and illegal journeys to and from Israel, and now he was on the wrong side of history once

THE BERLIN WALL

again. He wouldn't be able to visit his ageing parents who lived only a few miles away in the same city. What had once been an open border, with checkpoints between the eastern and western parts of the city, was now closed, and no one could any longer leave East Berlin to work or just see family and friends in the British-, American- or French-controlled sectors.

Within days the barbed-wire fence was replaced by a concrete wall, then hundreds of imposing look-out posts with roaming searchlights were installed, manned by guards armed with machine guns. To Heini it looked just like the labour and concentration camps where he'd been kept prisoner. The Wall was strengthened over time, with the addition of another wall and a 300-foot-wide strip of no-man's land in between the two, electric fences, fiercely bright lights, guard dogs and even landmines.

For all the Bernsteins the erection of '*die Mauer*' (the Wall), as Berliners called it, was a devastating blow that divided them once again. Erna, now in her 60s, was utterly bereft at the thought of never seeing or hugging her son again. They'd spent years apart and now, completely unexpectedly, for no logical reason that she could understand, they were separated once again.

In the early days of the Wall some underground U-Bahn trains still ran between East and West, progressing slowly through each other's stations, neither stopping nor opening the doors. After months of separation, Erna and Heini were so desperate to see each other for a few moments that she arranged to stand in a particular spot on the Western platform while Heini told her which train carriage he was in and what he'd be wearing so she could glimpse him as the Eastern

MISCHLINGE

tube train passed slowly through her station. Even that small pleasure didn't last long, as the authorities blocked the station platforms from view to prevent families from doing just that.

The Berlin Wall became perhaps the greatest symbol of the Cold War between the free democracies of Western Europe and America and the oppressive regimes of the communist Soviet Union and its satellite countries in Eastern Europe, including Czechoslovakia, Poland and Hungary, where people's lives were heavily restricted. In the first year after its erection, 12 people were killed trying to escape over the Berlin Wall. In 1962 two 18-year-old boys tried to scale the Wall – one escaped, the other was shot by a border guard and left to bleed to death in no-man's land. The guards neither went to his aid nor shot him again, and he could be heard screaming in agony for an hour. Many others died in that desolate spot, later named the *'Todesstreifen'* ('death strip'). In total 100,000 men, women and children tried to escape from East to West Berlin, but less than 5 per cent succeeded and many died trying.

The brutal policing of the Wall was designed to keep East Berliners frightened and obedient to the state, and it largely succeeded in doing so, despite condemnation from around the world. Global attention was focused on it briefly on 26 June 1963 when US President John F. Kennedy visited West Berlin and declared solidarity with Berliners, saying *'Ich bin ein Berliner'*. His words, seen as a challenge to the Soviets and a confidence booster to Berliners, had little long-term effect, and he was assassinated in Dallas just five months later.

Heini believed he might have escaped across the Berlin Wall if he went alone, but taking Gerda or seven-year-old

THE BERLIN WALL

Angela with him presented too great a risk, so he never tried. He bitterly resented what he'd lost – not just seeing his parents but his close friend Gerhard and his family, along with many other friends and the places where he'd grown up. He'd never been political, but now he hated the regime, although cautious as ever he kept his criticism of the state to himself. It was well known that there were many informants who, for money or personal advancement, would willingly tell the government which citizens broke the rules. Neither Heini nor Gerda trusted the governing Socialist Party and they resisted joining, even though they were always being approached to do so. All they could do was get on with their lives – there was no alternative.

Heini and my mum never lost touch but could only write letters to each other. My grandparents came over by 'boat train' to stay with us in London, bringing Mum a little taste of Berlin: salami, marzipan and Christmassy things that I remember well. I found Grandpa Sigi quiet and a little grumpy, Granny Erna full of smiles and delighting in everything I did. I asked Mum to teach me a little German so I could talk to them, and I was thrilled when Dad announced that as soon as we bought our first car we'd all drive to Berlin, meaning that I'd get to meet my Uncle Heini for the first time.

It was the summer of 1964, a year after JFK's famous speech and three years after the Berlin Wall was put up, that Mum, Dad and I set off on the 1,200-mile journey to Berlin in the family's newly purchased Vauxhall Viva.

After many nights of planning around the kitchen table we were all very excited, and we enjoyed the drive through

MISCHLINGE

Erna and Sharon (on a rare grandparent's visit to London).

France all the way to Austria. In West Germany the atmosphere changed considerably when we stopped at the Helmstedt/Marienborn checkpoint – Checkpoint Alpha – queueing up with other cars to pay the road toll to drive along 'the Corridor', the access road run by the Soviets through West Germany to Berlin. (Heini had crossed here on his return from Israel years earlier).

THE BERLIN WALL

As we started along this bumpy and badly maintained road that extended for 100 miles, it was daunting to see the scary-looking fences on either side, topped with barbed wire and punctuated here and there by armed soldiers looking down from watchtowers. Every so often we'd hear a helicopter patrolling overhead. Dad said these measures were all designed to deter the many people who wanted to escape.

When we arrived in Berlin and Mum got a chance to look around, she said the city was largely unrecognisable from the place she'd left shortly after the war. Modern buildings now vastly outnumbered old, and very little seemed familiar. We drove straight to my grandparents Erna and Sigi's little flat in Wedding, where we were going to stay with neighbours who had a spare room. The following morning we headed for Checkpoint Charlie, and as we drove up to the Wall itself we saw several memorials to people who'd died trying to escape, a sobering reminder that we were entering a dangerous area

Jimmy and Edie pose, right outside Heini's flat, by their Vauxhall Viva, the car they drove to Berlin, 1964.

MISCHLINGE

where numerous rules applied and the border troops really did shoot to kill. The domineering watchtowers with their harsh searchlights and armed soldiers made us feel slightly threatened.

The entry barrier went up, and as we drove into Checkpoint Charlie we saw numerous uniformed men with guns, as well as patrolling guards restraining big dogs. You could feel the fear among those of us entering East Berlin for the first time. I could see Mum was uncomfortable, and Dad was watching over us like a hawk. We were directed where to park, then we had to enter a shabby wooden hut to fill in our application for a 24-hour visa. The lengthy form demanded the address of who we were visiting, the reason for our visit and what gifts we'd brought. There was a long list of things we couldn't bring, including – for no obvious reason – many everyday household items. Next we had to list every single penny of any foreign currency we might be carrying, as well as itemise all our valuables and the serial numbers of our cameras. We had lots of notes and coins as we'd travelled through several other countries to get here and it took an age to complete the form.

The whole idea was that you couldn't give or exchange any Western currency or valuables with those you visited in the East. The East German currency – the so-called *Ostmark* – wasn't recognised outside of the country, meaning that if you escaped you did so with nothing and had no way of supporting yourself. Ironically, this was an identical restriction to the one the Nazis imposed on Jews wanting to leave Germany in the 1930s – if you escape, it will be with nothing.

Mum handed in our form and all our passports through a slot in the wall and then we sat there in this austere waiting

THE BERLIN WALL

room awaiting their return with our access visa. A guard appeared after a while, mumbled our names and read out our passport numbers in German, which the non-German speaking visitors who were also waiting found challenging. When they returned our visa-stamped passports, Dad was keen to drive straight out, but there was something else to attend to first.

Every visitor had to exchange some cash for East German currency, a specified amount (3 Deutschmarks in 1964, rising to 25 Deutschmarks in 1989) per person, per day's visit. This meant queueing at another window. We were told we had to spend all the money we'd exchanged in East Berlin or put it in a donation box for the East German government on our return. The official said we might also be asked to produce receipts for our spending to show we hadn't given money away, and there could be checks to ensure that we still had our foreign currency too.

Back in the car park we found two armed guards waiting for us, one with a large dog on a leash. They asked Dad to unlock the car, then proceeded to inspect every nook and cranny with special tools we'd never seen before. The dog sniffed around, while the men poked about in the boot, inside the car, then under the bonnet. Finally, one of them rolled a long stick with a mirror on the end beneath the chassis, before poking something inside the petrol tank. Apparently East Berliners had previously escaped by hiding in a pocket under the bonnet of a redesigned car, so desperate were they to leave.

The whole lengthy process was tense and scary, even though we had nothing to hide. It was a relief when they lifted the exit barrier and we drove out of Checkpoint

MISCHLINGE

Charlie. The place had an air of menace, on top of the unsmiling bureaucracy of it all.

As we drove through the centre of East Berlin I thought it looked even bleaker than West Berlin. Mum said this had once been old Berlin, the heart of the city, and had suffered some of the worst damage in the war. What the Russians had rebuilt was modern and brutalist in style. We rode along wide and empty streets with very few cars and very little greenery or trees of any size – they hadn't had time to grow since the devastation of war.

We passed many huge housing estates, tall blocks of similar-looking flats poking up in identical rows, before stopping in front of the one where Heini lived.

Edie photographs Jimmy taking a cinefilm of newly rebuilt East Berlin, 1964.

THE BERLIN WALL

Heini was waiting downstairs for us and rushed over to hug my mum, then me, followed by Dad. Mum cried and railed at how mad it was that their parents couldn't be there with them. Upstairs in their modern flat, Heini introduced us to his wife Gerda and daughter Angela, who was just two years older than me. Angela showed me her room, but there were many more hand signals than words as I only had a few words of German and the one foreign language she learnt at school was Russian. Jimmy tried out his Cockney-accented German, while Edie struggled at times to remember hers, as she'd hardly spoken it since her arrival in England. The grown-ups sat around the dining table talking over the famous Berlin breakfast, with its endless Kaffee, crispy Kaiser bread rolls and a huge selection of salamis and cheeses. Chats ranged from swimming at Lake Wannsee to Berlin cuisine and the health of their parents, but never included the worst experiences they suffered the last time they were all in the same city almost 20 years earlier. Neither Heini nor Mum ever spoke a single word about those times, either then or on any other occasion during their time together in the years ahead.

Our trips to Berlin became a family pilgrimage every other year, because Mum's ageing parents were reluctant to travel, and Heini and his family were trapped inside the Berlin Wall. It was an expensive trip for the Rings – the petrol, the ferries and, most resented of all, the daily visa cost at Checkpoint Charlie. But this was unavoidable if we were to visit Mum's much-loved brother and his family, who were barred from leaving the city to visit or holiday anywhere other than to other communist countries.

One summer, driving along the Soviet-controlled Corridor to Berlin, the Vauxhall Viva got a puncture on the rickety

MISCHLINGE

toll-road surface. While Dad struggled to change the tyre in a lay-by, wishing he'd brought along a better jack, Mum and I stood by the busy roadside. A passing lorry pulled in and gave Dad a hand with a monster jack. Before long a police helicopter hovered overhead, peered down at us and then flew off again. We thought no more of it. Dad thanked the lorry driver, giving him a packet of cigarettes as a thank you, and we continued the drive to Berlin.

When we finally reached the other end of the Corridor at the Berlin checkpoint, the three of us were separated from the usual visa queue and ushered into a room by two guards. One started questioning Dad in broken English about what exactly it was we'd been seen 'passing' to the lorry driver on the Corridor. Mum swung into German, explaining about the puncture and the better jack. They told her the helicopter had taken our car registration number because they thought our behaviour looked suspicious.

The guard asked Jimmy a second time – what had he given the lorry driver? Jimmy stayed calm and explained politely that he'd done what any man would have done – he'd thanked a comrade who'd come to his assistance and the 'passing' was just a thank you in the form of a pack of cigarettes. Both guards went back to their office before emerging again and telling us that we were free to go. But we were left quite shocked and a little shaken by the whole incident. Mum was more upset than Dad, as I think for her it brought back memories of growing up there, although at that time I knew little about her childhood.

Even as a youngster I could sense that Berlin was neither a safe nor a relaxing place. One dark, rainy night, Dad got lost in a diversion as we drove back to Checkpoint Charlie and

THE BERLIN WALL

Young Sha and cousin Angela (Heini's daughter) stand on the balcony of his East Berlin flat.

we stopped on an empty street. He spotted a policeman, so, leaning out of the car window, Dad asked where we were in his best German. The unsmiling policeman told him he shouldn't have stopped to ask and issued an on-the-spot fine, before giving us directions. It was surreal and farcical, and Dad said, 'Let's just get out of here.'

Ever-cautious Heini would sometimes discuss 'the regime' at his flat, with Jimmy following some of it with his limited German, but he'd never say anything when we were out in public. Heini said the Stasi – the East German secret police – had a wide network of informants who were paid for information and it was always unwise to speak out in any way publicly. He also said that antisemitism was still rife in Berlin – and in East Germany in general – but elaborated no further.

MISCHLINGE

Visiting Berlin every other year as a child, a teenager and then as a young woman, it was obvious to me that East Berliners had a worse quality of life than both West Berliners and my working-class family in London. It wasn't just the architecture that was sterile and grey; the shops were dreary and their shelves frequently empty. Out food shopping with Gerda I saw she often couldn't find fresh fruit – bananas were seen as a rarity – and other items like fabrics and everyday household items were in short supply. Heini said there was widespread corruption, with the powerful and well-connected getting around the system and having access to special shops – stocked like high-end department stores – where they could buy both essential and luxury goods unavailable elsewhere. Ordinary families like his, however, could never access these places. As a result, we'd try to bring things that were scarce for them, sometimes bought new and other times items we no longer used or needed. Gerda amazed everyone by restyling fabric or clothes very cleverly into beautiful clothes or cushions.

One year Heini was bemoaning the fact he couldn't buy a reasonably priced hearth rug for the little bungalow they were renting in the countryside and asked if we might bring one with us. Mum bought a small rug from British Home Stores on our high street, nothing oriental or fancy. It was only when we reached Berlin that Dad discovered that rugs were on the list of banned gifts to bring into the East, so he placed the little rug in the boot of the car with our suitcases on top. Surely no one would notice it, would they?

We didn't declare it as a gift on our visa form and were pleased when Heini and Gerda both liked it. After a lovely long day together in the country, walking, eating and relaxing,

THE BERLIN WALL

Heini's bungalow on the outskirts of Berlin.

the three of us headed back to Checkpoint Charlie before the midnight deadline.

When the guards came to check over the car, one turned to Dad and asked, 'Where's the rug?' He must have noticed it when we came in.

'Oh, that old bit of old carpet in the bottom of the boot,' Dad said. 'I used that to lie on at the side of the road when I had to change my tyre. I just left it on the roadside.'

'Well, you better go back and get it then', said the guard.

Mum couldn't believe they could be so petty and tried to argue with the guard that it was a 20-minute drive back and senseless for a small, cheap rug. What did it matter? But the guard was immovable.

Looking at her passport again, the guard said, 'Ah, Edie Ring. I see your maiden name was Bernstein – a Jew. We're

MISCHLINGE

good to Jews in the GDR, you know. In the West, many Nazis went unpunished.'

The remark enraged Mum. 'I don't know about that,' she answered back. 'The way you lot behave, I can't see much difference between you and the Nazis.'

The guard looked angry. He just turned to Dad and said, 'Go back and get the rug.'

Dad looked concerned at Mum's effect on the guard. So he took Mum's hand and said calmly, 'Don't argue with these people, Edie, they hold all the cards. I want you to take Sharon and cross to the West and wait for me there in that corner café. I'll find the rug and be with you in two hours tops. If not, you'd better raise the alarm.'

Mum refused at first, insisting we should all stick together, but Dad convinced her she wouldn't be able to raise the alarm if she came with him or waited at the checkpoint – we'd all then be in the Soviet sector, so she'd help him most if she

Edie, cousin Gillian, Sha, Sigi and Jimmy pose with a fake Berlin bear, a symbol of the city.

crossed to the West and waited. She saw the sense in what he said and reluctantly we split up.

Heini was surprised to see Dad turn up at the bungalow in the early hours, but thankfully when he drove back to Checkpoint Charlie they checked the carpet and waved him through. And no one was happier than Mum and me when Dad turned up all smiles at the café. I'd been scared, but always felt confident with Mum and Dad by my side.

Experiences like that left Mum with very mixed feelings about our return trips to Berlin, although she always thanked Dad for taking her to see her family, since it was always a stressful and expensive experience, and they couldn't come to visit us in England. On our drive back home she'd often say, 'I could never live in Berlin again. I love England and I feel more English than German.'

By the end of the 1960s Heini's back pains had become both chronic and acute. He was diagnosed with 'a curvature of the spine' and medically retired. His work as a plumber – bending, carrying, crawling into awkward places – was no longer possible. Thankfully, his many years of regular employment had guaranteed him a government pension for his family to live on, and the East German health service was free and readily available. Becoming a pensioner brought with it a new freedom. Heini was now permitted to cross the Wall for a few visits every year to visit the parents he'd not seen for six years. Erna was thrilled to be reunited with her son once again, and father and son made the best of their uneasy relationship.

Heini – not yet 50 – vowed to learn to cook properly and became quite an accomplished chef, which we enjoyed on our visits. 'When you've starved,' he told his family, 'you really appreciate good food.' Now he was at home he became closer and closer to Gerda, the wife to whom he'd been divorced but never stopped caring for. His daughter Angela said, 'They never stopped loving each other. In their way they complemented each other and were quite devoted. Like the actors Elizabeth Taylor and Richard Burton, they found it hard to live with each other, and hard to live without each other.'

In retirement, just like Taylor and Burton, they married for a second time, on 19 November 1971. They decided it was time to officially change their surname to Gerda's maiden name of Wolter. Heini felt strongly that antisemitism would never disappear in his lifetime as it was simply handed down in families. He hoped the name change would give his little family some protection. He saw evidence of anti-Jewish feeling on both sides of the Wall in both East and West Berlin, not to mention what he read in the news of the situation around Europe. Heini spoke to his parents about it and they raised no objection, as they understood the prejudice against Jews only too well.

The international news wasn't always bad, however. In the late 1960s the West German government passed a series of laws that established a legal right to compensation for those who had been imprisoned in concentration camps, used as slave labour or deprived of their right to an education due to Nazi discrimination against their faith or ethnicity.

Sigi initiated a claim, told his son and daughter about it, and encouraged them to do the same and instruct a solicitor. It would be a long process, involving making statements and providing evidence that they had experienced persecution, lack of education, loss of work, slave labour and – in Heini and Sigi's case – imprisonment. After some time Sigi and Heini received notification that they'd been awarded the highest level of compensation, on account of the severity of what they'd suffered. For Heini, this regular pension enabled the Wolter family to raise their standard of living and live in more comfort.

The day the official decision letter from Germany dropped through the letterbox of our council flat in Hackney, Mum had to read it several times before she trusted herself to translate it to my dad in English. It said she'd receive a regular monthly sum from the German government in compensation for being a child slave labourer and for being deprived of an education for most of her school years. They accepted responsibility for limiting her life choices, enclosing a cheque for £6,786 in back pay.

There was shock, squeals, and hugs and kisses all round, and as neither of my parents drank alcohol, celebrations took the form of several cups of strong tea and rounds of cake. The back pay meant they could now afford to put down a deposit and arrange a mortgage to buy their own home. They found a pretty little three-bedroom semi-detached house in a quiet street in leafy Enfield, north London.

Now I was out of junior school, Mum was working full-time in the accounts office, where most people assumed she was South African because of her dark skin and slight accent. I'm not sure when I first noticed it, but other people mentioned there was always something special about my mum – charisma, warmth, whatever you call it, she drew people to her but on her own terms, and the past was always a closed door, never discussed.

MISCHLINGE

In the 1970s we heard that great-grandmother Emma Kosse had passed away at a grand old age, but not before her much-loved charge – Eva – surprised everyone by marrying a local young man late in life, and the pair seemed to take good care of each other.

Granny Erna, who'd fought so hard to keep her whole family safe and away from her murdering countrymen, lived quietly in her flat in Wedding, Berlin, to the age of 76. She died from a massive stroke just before Christmas in 1978.

It seemed fateful that Erna Bernstein – matriarch extraordinaire – should die near Christmas, as it had always been a special time for her and the Bernstein family. Her insistence on always putting up a Christmas tree in her homes from Berlin to Israel and back again seemed to offer continuity, familiarity and hope in their darkest of times. The fact she had to sometimes hide it seemed to mirror her *Mischlinge* family – half-Christian, half-Jewish. Sometimes they had to hide too, but they came through.

Only two more Christmases passed before my grandfather Sigi – emotionally crippled by the experiences he never shared in his lifetime, and lost without his wife of 56 years – followed Erna and died at the age of 80 in 1980.

As the 1980s dawned, their children – Heini and Edie – were set to witness another major historical event, and the past would also begin to give up its secrets.

16
THE LAST CHAPTER

Heini was in his 60s but still haunted by what he'd seen and how he'd suffered in his youth. Awful recurring images still disturbed his nights, and even in the day something as ordinary as seeing a bucket with a flannel draped over it could invoke flashbacks to his captivity and torture. His wife Gerda wondered if never talking about the past was itself the problem. Locking his memories away in his head was clearly not giving him peace. She wondered if telling her his story might just free him from his demons, and she argued that it was important for him to write down and record the unknown and untold story of *Mischlinge*.

Gerda had tried many times before to persuade Heini to just talk to her about his experiences, but he'd always brushed off her requests. This time the idea of writing it down seemed to appeal, and they began with the title *Quite an Adventure*. Gerda was a good listener but asked questions too, taking notes as he talked that she'd type up later in their native German.

MISCHLINGE

Heini asked her to record his reason for writing on the very first page:

Time and time again, young people with their safe lives have asked me about this period of hatred under the Nazis, during which any sense of realism was lost. Many years had to pass before my scars began to heal enough for me to be able to talk about the harrowing events I witnessed.

Now I will put my experiences down in words. My greatest wishes are to lead a free and dignified life, and enable others to do the same. I want to make it absolutely clear that terror contravenes every human right and ultimately doesn't solve problems. Empathy and understanding are the keys to living side by side in peace, even if sacrifices cannot always be avoided. This process is like a work of art, requiring constant, careful attention.

In the calm private space of their home Heini unburdened himself to the woman he'd married twice. Even then it was a long, slow process. He halted the narrative sometimes when the remembering and the telling of it gave him nightmares. There were tricky moments too; Heini hadn't met Gerda until he was in his 40s, and naturally there had been several relationships in his youth. He didn't want to be ungentlemanly, but these women were part of his story and had to be mentioned, albeit never in less than chivalrous terms ... Heini was committed now to tell his story, but it was still a deeply painful process.

Living in communist East Germany presented its own dangers. The Stasi secret police network were thought to

THE LAST CHAPTER

constitute 1 per cent of the population, and Heini wasn't inclined to share the details of his life with them. Caution had always served Heini well, so he decided to keep his memoir secret, to change the names of those mentioned and avoid any contemporary political comment or criticism, just in case.

With Gerda's encouragement and persistence his painful memoir was eventually completed after two years, although he wasn't ready to let anyone read it. In fact, this eyewitness account was placed in a brown envelope and not read by anyone for more than 20 years. Heini only allowed his daughter Angela to read it when she was 34 years old, quite some time after he'd written it. Incredibly, it was the first she knew that her father had even had an 'interesting' war, let alone the extent and awfulness of his persecution, imprisonment and torture. She'd known he'd been in a concentration camp, but little more than that. Reading her father's memoir, which her mum had to cajole and prise out of him, shed light on how he'd become such a damaged soul and why he took occasional refuge in alcohol.

Heini's newly rekindled memories took time to fade, but he felt better for telling his story for the first time and having it recorded on paper. It had been some kind of release.

As a medically retired pensioner he could now apply for a visa to leave the country and visit his sister in London. Because it was not an automatic right, he had to fill in forms, follow protocols and await permission, and he wasn't allowed to bring Gerda or Angela with him. He was delighted when his visa application was approved, and he phoned Edie to arrange the trip and finally leave Berlin after more than 25 years of being trapped behind the Iron Curtain.

MISCHLINGE

Heini booked a return ticket to London on Aeroflot in May 1986, and his journey began with an argument with airline staff when they refused to let him check in a large rectangular package with his suitcase. Heini told the staff he wasn't going to stay with his sister in London for a fortnight and not bring any kind of gift. They examined the two garden chairs and after some argument allowed him to check them in.

For Mum, Dad and me, Heini's arrival at Heathrow airport is an image we'll never forget. He was beaming from ear to ear, and carrying one small suitcase and a large, somewhat battered package. It was a highly charged emotional moment. As we drove through the suburbs to our home in Enfield, the journey felt poignant for so many reasons. Brother and sister were so happy to be together, on English soil and outside of

Heini and Jimmy at Tower Bridge with Scamp the Staffie, London, 1986.

THE LAST CHAPTER

Berlin, a place about which they both now had very mixed feelings.

Heini couldn't wait to give Mum his gift. They sat on those garden chairs on the lawn and put the world to rights while Dad and I kept them fuelled with *Kaffee und Kuchen* – coffee and cakes. They talked about the present and the future, never the past. Dad drove the pair of them around the major historical sights in the city and much thought had gone into what he was offered to eat at home. Mum cooked him steak and kidney pie, roast beef with all the trimmings and other English delights. Heini enjoyed it all. Only the range of food and household goods available in England overwhelmed him, the shops seeming like vast, glittering palaces compared with those in dour East Berlin.

When Heini saw the beautiful cut-glass wine glasses he'd bought Edie many years ago in Berlin with the promise that when he visited her in London one day they'd drink from them together, he became emotional. They gave him a sense of the many wasted years because he'd been stuck in Berlin, their parents were now dead, and – because of pointless restrictions – his wife and daughter still couldn't be there with him to make this long-awaited moment a complete family reunion. And he avoided the pleasures of wine nowadays in case he drank too deeply.

One evening Heini declared he was pleased to have confirmed with his own eyes what he'd always suspected: Edie and Jimmy had moved on from love at first sight, were devoted to each other, enjoyed an extremely happy marriage and had made a success of their life in London. As their mother always said, between them it was *'treue Liebe'*. All thanks to him, he joked, for introducing them.

MISCHLINGE

I was a busy freelance journalist then, working on several national newspapers on Fleet Street. I relished the chance to get to know my Uncle Heini, whom I found warm and fun, but politely unresponsive to any questions I asked him about the rise of Nazism or his own experiences.

Heini loved England, and as soon as he was able to bring his daughter Angela he visited, in time for Jimmy and Edie's ruby wedding anniversary – 40 years married. This time Heini had a surprise up his sleeve. He handed Mum the brown envelope containing his memoir and said, 'Do with it whatever you want.' Edie hugged him and said she'd read it after he'd gone. But the truth was she didn't want to. It was too painful for her. Like him, she'd never revisited her own past and wasn't ready to start now. She'd put it in her safe document box – as she had her own memories, not ready for

Phil (Sharon's husband), Jimmy, Edie and Sharon at Edie's 60th birthday, 15 July 1987.

THE LAST CHAPTER

Edie and Jimmy.

the light of day. She didn't tell her curious daughter the journalist anything about it. So Heini's memoir that had taken 40 years to write lay unread and untranslated at his sister Edie's home for almost another 30 years.

In spring the next year, Heini came to England for the third and last time, bringing his wife Gerda. She fell in love with the country, and both families had fun together on jaunts to city and countryside. A year later Heini phoned to tell us that Gerda, his wife of 16 years, had died quite unexpectedly of cancer at just 64.

The following year – 1989 – Berlin was once again at the centre of world events, when on 9 November came the dramatic and unexpected fall of the Berlin Wall. Iconic images of this historic symbol of the Cold War flashed across the world. *'Die Mauer'*, which had gone up almost overnight in 1961, came down just as suddenly.

Günter Schabowski, an East German official, in response to a question that day by an American journalist, had announced in his broken English that travel restrictions were going to be eased across the Berlin Wall with immediate effect. This saw people turn up in large numbers at the six checkpoints on the Wall. In the ensuing confusion and uncertainty, border guards were vastly outnumbered at the checkpoints, and they eventually just let East Berliners through, as many started to dismantle the Wall itself. In what seemed more fluke than decision, sparked by an unclear statement a politician had made at a news conference, the repercussions of a 'semi-comical, bureaucratic mistake' dominated the news for weeks.

Mum and Dad watched the history-making moment on television, as did millions of others. Dad was riveted to the footage, as he'd been one of the first British soldiers into Berlin in the final days of the war, taken part in the subsequent Allied victory parade and had come to know the city well over many decades. He only just lived to see its demise – having been diagnosed with lung cancer, he was in the middle of a course of chemotherapy.

The fall of the Wall brought a smile to his face; it had caused such unhappiness to his family and so many others, he said, and how great it was to see the end of it. He died just ten weeks later, at 67 years old. Typically, Dad had fought for his life until the end, and just three weeks before his death he managed to drive a hundred miles to and from East Anglia to

THE LAST CHAPTER

spend one last special family Christmas at my home in Norfolk.

My husband Phil made a touching funeral oration at the Catholic funeral mass, detailing his rescue of Mum at the end of the war and their great romantic love story. I was described as 'not just the apple of her father's eye but the whole fruit salad and the cream too'. Dad's last request was, 'Sharon, don't visit my grave when I'm gone – always visit your Mum instead.' A practical man, he'd left Mum well looked after, and he knew she and I would both be OK.

Mum, however, was heartbroken and utterly devastated. She was just 62 years old when she lost 'her Jimmy'. She was in a dark place for a while, but her backbone had been forged

Sharon's wedding – with her parents Jimmy and Edie.

in fear and fire, and she fought back from the sadness and near madness of bereavement.

She planned to spend some quality time with her brother now they were both widowed but sadly Heini died 16 months later, in 1991. Mercifully it was a quick death after a short illness. Heini died in the city where he was born, perhaps lucky to have lived 67 years, considering the traumas of his early life. Like the film character Forrest Gump, Heini's life always seemed to link with a major world event, and shortly after his death the Soviet Union and its satellite states disintegrated. By Christmas that year it was the end of the communist era in Europe.

Edie Ring lived on to have almost as remarkable an old age as she had the first part of her life. She learnt to drive within 18 months of losing Jimmy, passing her driving test first time at 64, and she bought herself a little car. She was lonely without him, but so very happy to always have me nearby. She'd often smile and tell friends, 'For me the world got brighter after Sharon was born on 21 December, the shortest day of the year – and of course it does!'

She had no trouble making new female friends with whom she travelled abroad and played bridge. She retained her prettiness as she aged, always smart, always made up and smartly turned out, with a youthful attitude to life and an interest in the world and trying new things. It was a different kind of resilience from that of her childhood, but she managed this well too.

When Mum was in her late 60s I persuaded her to return to Berlin one last time, to see the city since the Wall came down. We stayed with Heini's daughter Angela and her husband Werner on the woody outskirts of Berlin near

THE LAST CHAPTER

Edie ventures out on a cruise after losing her Jimmy.

Heini's old bungalow, where we heard nightingales sing. Mum enjoyed seeing the family, visiting the sights and, always a lover of good food, our meals out eating Berlin specialities. But she told me she could summon up little affection for Berlin, now a paeon to modernist architecture and riotous nightlife – a place for the young, she said – and she made it clear she never wanted to return. From now on, Angela and Werner would have to visit her, which they did.

Mum never lost her sound judgement, and after her 70th birthday she announced, 'I think I'll go ahead and retire to Norfolk, before you and Phil do – while I'm still young enough to make the move.' She'd grown to know and love our corner of North Norfolk. She found a home with a walled garden overlooking a village pond, just one village away from me, and she enjoyed 16 years there. She lived independently until the day she died, driving around in her little car, cooking and enjoying her food, and keeping a welcoming and stylish home.

At first she could walk her little dog to the beach and enjoyed gardening, but her years of poor diet, hard physical work and deprivation began to tell on her health in her 80s. She had trouble walking any distance and standing for any length of time, and her breathing deteriorated on account of her years of smoking. Despite large doses of painkillers and morphine patches, she was never pain-free. But life, she said, was too precious to give up on, even if it was painful.

Her pain was increasing, walking and standing was difficult, and she needed pumped oxygen around her home and while sleeping, just to be able to breathe. There were occasions, she sometimes admitted, when she wanted to be with her beloved Jimmy. Her faith, although of no particular denomination, made her certain that she'd be reunited with him in death.

As she became increasingly frail, she wanted to check that all her affairs were in order, and one rainy afternoon in Norfolk she asked me to help sort through her strong box of important documents, including her will. That's when I found the fat brown envelope Heini had given her so many years before, containing his neatly typed memoir, in German. She'd forgotten all about it, she said.

I was fascinated by the first few pages, even though I knew my German wasn't really good enough to read it properly. My mum's grasp of her mother tongue was no longer that

THE LAST CHAPTER

good either, as she'd barely spoken the language for years, so I asked her whether we should have it translated.

She paused a moment, then said, 'Yes, perhaps now is the time. It would be wrong to leave it unread. Heini told me it had cost him to revisit it, and he did entrust it to me.'

The discovery of Heini's memoir – hidden away and unread for years – proved a catalyst, a signal for Mum that it was time she should tell her story too. 'I'm old now,' she said, 'and who knows how much longer I have. People should know what happened. I will tell you about those awful times.'

How proud of her decision I was, because I knew it would cost her to tell even me, her daughter. So in the following weeks, Mum and I sat at her dining table with my tape recorder and notebook, and, a few hours at a time, she told her story for the first time. She didn't enjoy the process, she said, but thought it worth doing. At points in the story she sounded vulnerable and frail, but she'd pause, compose herself and say she was determined to finish it.

At points I felt I was more upset than her. Most of her story was new to me and I felt so sad she had to go through all of the things she told me about when she was just a child. When she described the scene where she was nearly raped and the Soviet soldier took the woman next to her instead, I got very upset, and she consoled me.

'Darling,' she said, 'I haven't had a bad life. That was then. I met your dad. He rescued me, I got you and the world was brighter, as I keep telling you. I've been very lucky, and only had some bad years early on.'

That was Mum – the optimist who hadn't let her past dominate her present or her future. How I admired her, how I loved her.

MISCHLINGE

Talking done, I wrote up our interviews and we awaited the translation of Heini's memoir with some apprehension. When the translator finished Heini's memoir, he admitted the process had made him fond of this resourceful young man, whom he'd never met.

It was certainly an emotional read for Mum and me. For me it was a revelation, a tremendous and moving story about my own family, of which I knew nothing. Mum said there were things in it she'd either completely forgotten or chosen not to remember. I was pleased Mum had told me her story before reading Heini's. Like an eyewitness statement, her memory was hers alone, although I realise that all memoirs, all recollections, are what the person chooses to remember and what they choose to omit. Now it was my task to pull the two together, research the wider family and set it all in its place in history.

The next step would be to find an agent and a publisher, but there was no thought of that when Mum and I went on holiday together in the summer of 2014, staying at a beautiful inn on the Chatsworth Estate in the Derbyshire Peak District. Mum thought the views beautiful, like the Austrian Alps that had been so much part of our trips to Berlin and our family holidays, as well as being the scene of Heini's great escape and his encounter with the milk maid.

After a splendid supper I kissed Mum good night and tucked her into bed. She didn't feel well, she said, so we held hands across the twin bed divide until she fell asleep. I woke to hear her thrashing in her sleep, I held her hand for only a couple of minutes before she died peacefully in her sleep, just weeks short of her 87th birthday. It was such a privilege to be with her.

THE LAST CHAPTER

She'd endured much pain and suffering, not just in her childhood but in her last few years, with spinal and breathing issues, surely a result of all the hardships she'd suffered. Her smoking certainly was a crutch for the anxiety that never left her.

Yet her demons never stopped her being a wonderful wife, the best of mums and a caring sister, a thoroughly decent woman who led a good life and made the best of everything right up until the day she died. Loving, warm, fair and fun, she was an exemplar.

Her funeral took place on her 87th birthday in a beautiful round-towered church in her beloved Norfolk, with a nod to her Jewish roots; the Menorah – the Jewish candelabra – was placed on the altar, and the Mourner's Kaddish – the Hebrew prayer in memory of the dead – was read.

Always one foot in each camp to the end.

The eulogy outlining her story surprised many friends who knew nothing of her history, and marvelled at how such a childhood could have seen her live a life with no trace of enmity or hatred.

She was buried, as she wanted, with her rescuer and *treue Liebe*, her beloved Jimmy, in Enfield, near the home where they'd lived so happily for more than 40 years.

Their gravestone reads:

Exceptional People
The Best of Parents
Loved by daughter Sharon

MISCHLINGE

She'd be pleased to know that her brother's memoir and her own account of their extraordinary *Mischlinge* existence live on – brother and sister having survived the barbarism of Adolf Hitler's Nazi regime – and are now published at last.

As Edie Ring told me: 'That man didn't dominate my life. I made it a happy one and gave you a happy life too, my daughter. That was my triumph.'

She never gave him the respect of naming him.

Acknowledgements

In the many years it has taken me to research, write and edit this very personal book, I have found it both challenging and lonely at times. I had never written a book before and I soon discovered that, unlike my journalistic career, writing a book is something you do for the most part alone. But this book would certainly not have been published had it not been for the professional skills and kind assistance of several others to whom I wish to pay tribute here.

I owe a large debt to my dear friend Sharon Sharpe, who used her considerable skills in archival research to help find the missing and murdered in my family, filling the gaps in Heini's memoir. Tragically, Sharon has not lived to see the book published.

For historical research I found Laurence Rees's book *The Holocaust* invaluable, Richard J. Evans's *The Third Reich in Power* and *The Third Reich at War*, and Anthony Beevor's *Berlin* immensely helpful in setting Heini and my mum's experiences in the wider context of the Holocaust and the Second World War.

Once the manuscript was completed, author Tom Bower gave me a valuable introduction, publisher Alan Samson went out of his way to guide me forward and novelist Rory Clements and screenwriter Stuart White gave me encouragement. Then editing guru Gillian Stern threw herself into making this first-time author refine her draft. And several drafts would not have progressed without the quick and calm response of my tech guru Dave Garnham. The original manuscript's translator was Gresham School's German master Francis Retter.

And – drum roll – huge thanks to my inestimable agent Tim Bates of Peters Fraser + Dunlop, who made this book happen by believing in it and quickly securing me a choice of major publishers.

Ajda Vucicevic's incisive editing at HarperCollins and Mark Bolland's informed copy-editing all helped to shape the important final stages of this long process.

Two unique women in my life have helped me keep the faith through the stumbling blocks along the way – my formidable sister-in-law Angie Walker and my grammar-school history teacher and longtime mentor Kate Reid – as well as Mel Taylor for just being there.

And, lastly, the ongoing inspiration of my mum Edie – inspiring in life and still inspiring through how she lived it.